C O U R T S
AS CATALYSTS

State Supreme Courts
and Public School Finance Equity

Matthew H. Bosworth

STATE UNIVERSITY OF NEW YORK PRESS

Published by
State University of New York Press, Albany

© 2001 State University of New York

All rights reserved

Printed in the United States of America

No part of this book may be used or reproduced in any manner whatsoever
without the written permission. No part of this book may be stored in a
retrieval system or transmitted in any form or by any means including
electronic, electrostatic, magnetic tape, mechanical, photocopying, recording,
or otherwise without the prior permission in writing of the publisher.

For information, address State University of New York Press,
90 State Street, Suite 700, Albany, NY 12207

Production by Diane Ganeles
Marketing by Anne Valentine

Library of Congress Cataloging-in-Publication Data

Bosworth, Matthew H.
    Courts as catalysts : state supreme courts and public school finance
equity / Matthew H. Bosworth.
      p. cm.
    Includes bibliographical references and index.
    ISBN 0-7914-5013-9 (HC : alk. paper)—ISBN 0-7914-5014-7 (PB : alk.
paper)
    1. Political questions and judicial power—United States—States.
2. Courts of last resort—United States.—States. 3. Law reform—United
States—States. 4. Education—Finance—Law and legislation—United
States—States. 5. Education—United States—Finance. I. Title.

    KF8775 .B67 2001
    344.73'076—dc21

                         00-061921

10 9 8 7 6 5 4 3 2 1

Contents

Acknowledgments

It is a truism to say that a project of this scope is necessarily a group product, but the statement is even more accurate in this case. At the heart of this work are the results of interviews with ninety-four necessarily anonymous policymakers and observers who gave quite generously of their time to a researcher who could offer them nothing but an attentive ear. Future academics could count themselves quite fortunate to study a group as genial and unselfish as these interviewees regardless of their positions in the school finance debates.

Also worthy of mention are certain individuals who made the stays of a traveling researcher much more pleasant than they could have been. Brian and Sonela Schlottmann, then of Austin, went far beyond the call of friendship in offering a place to live and work for three crucial weeks. Don Brown and Glenda Barron of the Texas Higher Education Coordinating Board (neither interviewees) provided both important background information and generous hospitality, as did one other individual who was useful enough that he unfortunately must remain anonymous. Professors Bradley Canon and Penny Miller of the University of Kentucky also were very giving of their time and assistance. Two individuals in particular were very friendly and helpful getting research started in North Dakota, but again must remain anonymous.

From a broader perspective, though, I must thank in particular my faculty advisor throughout my time in Madison, Professor Joel Grossman, whose encouragement, sharp eye, and wise advice improved this project immensely. I also must thank Professor Herbert Kritzer, who helped me focus on the big forest of this project when the trees were getting thick. Professors Dennis Dresang, Charles Jones, and Allan Odden of the University of Wisconsin-Madison also provided helpful suggestions from their own unique perspectives. Michael Gauger lent invaluable editing assistance, without which this book would not be publishable. Finally, I must thank my undergraduate senior thesis advisor at Johns Hopkins University, Professor J. Woodford Howard Jr., who not only suggested that I look into what these state supreme courts were doing on the school finance issue, but pushed me to take the necessary first steps in the execution of this larger project.

Of course, I would not have been able to start, much less finish, this work without the support and advice of numerous friends both here in Madison and scattered across the country. It is a debt I will always try to repay by doing the same for others. Lastly, an academic work is not the best place to give thanks to one's family, because it cannot contain the fullness of the connection. However, I should especially note my grandmother, Nigel Herrick, whose love both for her family and for the value of education opened doors for me and others that might not have opened otherwise. Her example sets a standard for us all.

CHAPTER 1

~

Courts and Social Reform

This book is about judicial policymaking. In it, I argue that the role of the courts in the American system of government cannot be understood without seeing them as actors in a complex and dynamic struggle over public policy. Courts cannot command their fellow political actors to obey "higher" constitutional rules, but they are not powerless to influence others. Courts do not merely reflect larger political and social forces: they help shape those forces. I examine closely the influence of state supreme courts on public school funding equity to demonstrate this conception of the judicial role in American government. I focus on three case studies—in Texas, Kentucky, and North Dakota—which each show in a different way how court decisions altered the political environment in each state concerning a central political issue. After analyzing my data, I developed the theory that informs this book, that of courts as active and relevant participants in ongoing dialogues over policy.

In this chapter, I show how this theory fits into contemporary scholarship concerning judicial policymaking and further explicate the design of this study. In chapter 2, I discuss the public school finance equity reform issue in more detail. Chapters 3, 4, and 5 present the case studies. I analyze the results from these case studies in chapter 6, and then discuss the implications of these findings for future research on questions of court power.

The Place of Courts in American Government

The role for the judicial branch in the American system of "separated institutions sharing powers" (Neustadt 1960:29) has always been problematic. On the one hand, the judiciary is entrusted in the public mind to guard the most sacred symbol of political life, the

1

U.S. Constitution (and state constitutions by extension). The Constitution embodies the strong American faith in the rule of laws, not men. The function of the judiciary in the standard civic model, therefore, is to hold the Constitution above mere politics. The judiciary's role as protector of the Constitution is the major source of the judiciary's legitimacy.

On the other hand, this insulation (at least in theory) from the political process, the judiciary's greatest strength, is also its greatest weakness. The courts cannot claim the legitimacy that stems from popular election or the American principle of representative democracy, at least not as legislators or chief executives can. Even where judges are elected, this popular selection is not usually seen as a source of their power (that is, state judges do not usually argue, for example, that "I received a ninety percent retention vote in the last election, and therefore my interpretation of the law is the correct one"). Thus, courts that void legislative acts are always vulnerable to the charge of illegitimate usurpation of popular sovereignty. The seemingly endless debate over the propriety of judicial review encapsulates this tension between judicial authority to interpret law and the majoritarian will as embodied in legislative acts.

Furthermore, the division of power constructed by the U.S. and state constitutions provides the judiciary with few powerful weapons that could force coordinate political branches to comply with a court decision. The classic expression of this reality is Alexander Hamilton's observation in Federalist No. 78 that the judiciary "has no influence over either the sword or the purse" and therefore will be the "least dangerous branch" (Hamilton et al. 1961:465). The judicial branch must rely heavily on mere persuasion to ensure acquiescence with its rulings. The next logical question for judges and judicial scholars, therefore, is how courts can persuade most successfully.

Courts often must balance fundamental values to define their role in the American system of government. More specifically, they must reconcile the principle of the rule of law with that of popular sovereignty. And they weigh their view of what the law requires against what is politically possible to achieve, given the judiciary's near-sole reliance on the powers of persuasion. These balances are fundamental to the system of separated powers.

Scholarship on Judicial Power

Given these fundamental tensions concerning the judiciary's role in American government, it is unsurprising that academic work on the courts has focused on these conflicts. To generalize, this work can be divided into two groups. The first concerns the normative question, "What *should* the courts do?" and the second regards the empirical question, "What *can* the courts do?" Of course, these questions are interdependent, and nearly every academic study of the courts takes some position, either explicit or implicit, regarding both of them. This division, however, at least helps to frame the particular contribution of my study to these debates.

The Normative Question: What Should *Courts Do?*

I argue that in the three school finance case studies, state supreme courts acted as policymakers. Some would argue, however, that these courts had no right to behave in this manner, and that their actions were inconsistent with their proper "role." The concept of judicial "role" often has been operationalized by drawing a distinction between "judicial activists" and "judicial restraintists" (Glick 1971). "Judicial activists" see their function as that of promoting the common good (however defined) through law. Often they justify this goal-oriented behavior by stressing the impossibility of interpreting the laws in any other way than as a modern observer would (Brennan 1985). "Judicial activists" do not necessarily confine their activism to the discovery of constitutional wrongs, either; these judges are more likely to devise expansive remedies for these violations. The rise of "public law" litigation (discussed below in more detail) was spurred by activist judges using their equitable remedy powers to address significant social problems thought to be solely under legislative and executive control. Judges supervised prisons, schools, and mental health facilities, ordered large sums of money raised and spent, and dictated policy when they perceived any deviation from constitutional standards that the judges themselves set. In other words, judicial activism of interpretation and judicial activism of remedy are part and parcel of the same view of the judicial role.

"Judicial restraintists," on the other hand, view the judicial function as interpreting the law and applying it as closely as possible to the case at hand. According to this philosophy, finding the "plain meaning" or "original intent" of laws is not as impossible as judicial activists would like to believe. Judicial restraintists further fault judicial activists for substituting their own policy judgments for those of the democratically elected officials whom the courts second-guess. Judicial restraintists do not see the courts as qualified or legitimate to make independent policy choices (Berger 1977; Bork 1990). This view extends to questions of appropriate remedies for constitutional violations. "Judicial restraintists" have been much more critical of "public law" litigation as breaching the separation of powers, among other faults. Judges are not competent or empowered to manage state institutions normally left under the care of executive authorities. The proper judicial role for restraintists is to hear a case, issue a final judgment, and move on to the next case. Extended supervision of compliance with the court order should not be necessary and can easily lead to difficulty.

Until recently, the judicial activism/restraint debate contained a strong ideological element as well. Political liberals tended to favor greater activism, as in the Warren Court decisions of the 1960s. Political conservatives decried these "public law" decisions and trumpeted the virtues of judicial restraint. As the U.S. Supreme Court has become more politically conservative, however, these conservative justices have discovered the advantages of judicial activism as well, muddying the waters of the debate considerably. For example, in the 1997 term, despite the relatively small number of decisions issued, the Court voided four Acts of Congress, including parts of such major legislation as the Brady gun control bill and the Communications Decency Act on Internet pornography (Lewis 1997).

Furthermore, in some of these decisions, conservative justices began to sound activist themselves. For example, in the Brady decision (*Printz* 1997), Justice Antonin Scalia, even though he cited historic practice as justification for voiding federal commandeering of state and local law enforcement agents, did not rely on any one constitutional provision to support this view. Instead, he asserted that the act was "fundamentally incompatible with our constitutional system of dual sovereignty (ibid.)." This reasoning drew sharp criticism from the bench from Justice John Paul Stevens, who asked whether the conservatives were now embracing the method of constitutional interpretation that produced the "penumbras" of rights leading to the right of privacy in *Griswold v. Connecticut* (1965) (Greenhouse 1997). The recent decisions on state sovereign immunity (for example, *Alden v. Maine* (1999) continue this debate, with a conservative majority finding in favor of this immunity even though it is never explicitly mentioned in the Constitution.

It is true that Supreme Court conservatives have not yet issued comprehensive orders concerning state institutions in the spirit of "public law" litigation, but perhaps one only needs to wait a while. In any event, it seems clear that politics has a great deal to do with the identities of judicial "activists" and "restraintists." The roles themselves, I would argue, are still distinct in the view judges have of their capabilities and legitimacy as policymakers, and their view of the capabilities and legitimacy of their coordinate constitutional branches.

This debate over the nature of the judicial role is seemingly eternal. In the second chapter, I will present an alternative typology of judicial roles from a more empirical perspective, specifically tied to the experience of state supreme courts with school funding equity litigation. For now, though, I will discuss the question of "judicial role" in normative terms.

The three case studies display courts engaging in behaviors which, depending upon one's view, could be characterized as "activist" or "restraintist." In general, I define "activism" as a court giving orders to the legislature and executive with which the political branches must comply, and "restraint" as the absence of such orders.

For example, in Texas the state supreme court repeatedly voided the state's public school funding system on constitutional grounds. On each occasion, the court refused to specify fully what a constitutionally legitimate system would look like, but offered suggestions as to what policy solutions would pass constitutional muster. The court could argue that its unwillingness to mandate its own plan demonstrates its commitment to "judicial restraint." The back-and-forth negotiation between the legislature and the court over constitutional principles also could be viewed as quite "activist," however. In Kentucky, the supreme court not only declared the state school financing mechanism to be unconstitutional under the state constitution, but found the entire state school system to be invalid. The court promulgated a list of goals for the new system and a set of ability standards that a graduate of the new public school system must meet. This court ruling seems clearly activist. On the other hand, the Chief Justice justified his opinion with the language of judicial restraint, arguing that "we (do not) intend to substitute our judicial authority for the authority and discretion of the General Assembly. We are, rather, exercising our constitutional duty" (Cases Cited: Kentucky 1989:189). And the Kentucky court issued only one strong opinion and did not negotiate and compromise with the political branches, as the Texas court was forced to do. In these ways, the Kentucky decision was more "judicially restrained."

The North Dakota study also shows a court acting with a mixture of judicial activism and restraint. It narrowly upheld the state's school financing system from constitutional challenge. But the Chief Justice none too subtly threatened in his decisive opinion to change sides and declare the funding system unconstitutional if the legislature did not correct its problems. One could argue that the court exhibited "judicial restraint" by declining to overtly enter the battles over school funding that the court clearly felt were better fought in the popularly elected legislature. On the other hand, threatening to change a vote if action is not taken is hardly within the usual dictates of judicial restraint. Thus, the Chief Justice was also "judicially activist."

As these examples suggest, the normative question of the proper role of courts in American government is difficult to answer in practice. But ambiguity, intended or otherwise, does not foreclose normative judgments. Nearly everyone I interviewed for this project had some view as to whether his or her state supreme court was acting legitimately in dealing with the political branches on the school finance issue, and this normative outlook helped to shape responses to the court rulings. Conservatives in Texas, for example, did not just oppose redistribution of district wealth, but felt it was illegitimate for the court to reinterpret the state constitution to require it. On the other hand, supporters of the low-wealth districts in all three states saw the court's proper function as that of intervening when the political branches were not living up to a constitutional mandate of school finance equity, which these activists viewed as quite clear.

Even though the normative outlook of the participants in the school finance debates helped shape their responses, many other factors contributed. Political calculation of benefits and costs, public opinion, interest group response, leadership vs. followership, and the like, all played roles in the decision-making. It is difficult to say what the outcome in each state would have been if legislators voted only upon their normative beliefs. What one can attempt to measure, though, is the multitude of considerations that affected these participants in the debates as they happened. Therefore, this study, although mindful of normative considerations, will focus primarily on empirically ascertaining the factors that led or did not lead to court effectiveness in producing public school finance reform. Readers are invited to make their own judgments concerning the normative questions. In all likelihood, both "judicial activists" and "judicial restraintists" will find ample support for their arguments.

What Can Courts Do? The Empirical Question

As the social activism of the 1960s recedes in the public consciousness, "hard-headed realists" skeptical of government effectiveness in improving society challenge its tenets. One of the most recent core 1960's beliefs to come under attack is the notion that courts can produce social change through far-reaching declarations of rights and strict orders to enforce those rights. Using *Brown v. Board of Education* (1954) as the model, scholars have championed this type of "public law" decision (Chayes 1976) or scoffed at courts futilely trying to make the rest of society listen to them. The latter group claims that society and, more specifically, popularly elected officials generally ignore courts, acting only when political self-interest requires (Horowitz 1977; Rosenberg 1991). This debate between defenders and skeptics of judicial effectiveness and capacity can be divided into two closely related but conceptually distinct arguments. The first of these contests, begun in the 1960s, concerns the question of court capacity. How effective are courts and legal processes at producing sound implementation policies, as compared with legislatures and executives? The second and more recent debate over judicial power deals with the utility of legal action for activists in producing social change, as the goals of judges and reformers might differ. Is use of the courts just a "hollow hope," or does it produce unique and worthwhile benefits to political entrepreneurs?

"JUDICIAL IMPACT" STUDIES

Studies of the impact of judicial decisions on other political institutions and society as a whole began in earnest in the 1950s and 1960s, mostly as a result of the Warren Court's increasing activism concerning civil rights and liberties issues. The U.S. Supreme Court in this period challenged long-established societal practices, such as racial segregation, school prayers, and often harsh treatment of criminal suspects. The Court's new position as would-be leader of public opinion rather than follower intrigued many judicial scholars who questioned how effective the Court could be in that role. Therefore, numerous studies focused on implementation of the Court's rulings. These works are often referred to as "gap" studies because their usual finding was that there was a large "gap" between court decision and implementation (Sorauf 1959; Peltason 1961; Muir 1967; Becker and Feeley 1969; Dolbeare and Hammond 1971). This gap stemmed from a number of reasons, including lower-court resistance to the Court's readings of the Constitution, political unpopularity of the rulings with the general public and local elites, the complexity of devising appropriate and effective remedies, and lack of clarity in the Court's rulings themselves.

As the Warren Court and then the Burger Court of the 1970s progressed, federal courts, concomitant with the trend toward judicial leadership in social change, increasingly became involved in a variety of so-called "public law" or institutional reform cases. Courts issued orders concerning school desegregation, mental health facility conditions, prison overcrowding, and welfare administration, just to name a few. Federal courts cast aside traditional boundaries of federalism and separation of powers to supervise a wide range of state institutions (Feeley and Rubin 1998). The judicial presence in American life was extensive and ongoing, to a greater extent than ever.

This increased role of courts represented a departure from the traditional view of the courts as passive dispensers of law. Under the more traditional model, judges were neutral arbiters in a litigant-driven adversary system (Fuller 1978). A case involved just one plaintiff and one defendant. The issue was relatively simple and discrete, such as the enforcement of a contract or a property boundary dispute. The judge's role was to allow each side to present its case fully, and then to make a ruling on the claim of right. If the plaintiff was upheld, a money judgment against the defendant was the most likely outcome, with the judgment paid summarily. There was no ongoing judicial supervision of either side or of the disputed issue. With the advent of the "public law" litigation of the 1960s and 1970s, however, nearly every element in this formula changed (Chayes 1976). First, cases were no longer confined to a single plaintiff versus a single defendant. Courts increasingly allowed so-called "class actions," in which all persons similarly situated regarding a claimed injury by a defendant could be lumped together for purposes of a lawsuit. Furthermore, courts were increasingly willing to let multiple parties join cases to represent their own interests, as in Lon Fuller's "polycentric" case (Fuller 1978).[1]

For example, in the Texas school finance case, responsibility for arguing that the state's school funding system was unconstitutional was divided between the original plaintiffs, mostly from predominantly Hispanic urban school districts, and a group of "plaintiff-intervenors" representing mostly low-wealth white rural districts. Similarly, on the defense, it was often difficult to tell who was the real respondent: the state whose school financing system was being challenged or the wealthy suburban and oil districts that benefited most from that system. Often the interests of these parties diverged, especially because the putative state defendant, the Texas Education Agency, also had a natural interest in securing more funding for the state school system. The wealthy districts, however, were mostly concerned with protecting their tax base.

Courts became increasingly willing to accept these complex multiparty arrangements because the issues that the judiciary now was attempting to resolve were much more complicated than the traditional bipolar disputes. The federal courts in particular used such flexible terms as "due process" and "equal protection" to find previously undiscovered constitutional violations in state institutions. The traditional model of adjudication would shy away from these types of cases on the grounds that they were "political questions" better left to the legislative and executive branches, but the newer theories of adjudication were not willing to accept court incapacity to change conditions in these state institutions (Horowitz 1977). The theme in this expansion of judicial role was that of basic "fairness." Judges began to view their function as that of guaranteeing a minimum level of protection, or a "safety net," for the clients of these institutions, whether these were schoolchildren, prisoners, welfare recipients, or the mentally disabled. Often the assumption was that these people could not adequately protect themselves through the normal political process, building upon the theory that the courts should be particularly solicitous of the claims of so-called "discrete and insular minorities" that would never exercise real political power for one reason or another (*Carolene Products* 1938:152). Courts attempted to right that balance by requiring institutions to follow fixed procedures before taking action that would harm these "clients," such as hearings and rights of response before termination of welfare benefits (*Goldberg* 1970). As we shall see, much the same impulse motivated school funding equity decisions by state supreme courts. These courts did not necessarily mandate absolute equality between rich and poor public school districts, but wanted to ensure that the poorest districts were adequately protected from the vagaries of politics. Poor districts populated by racial minorities (Texas) or economic underdogs (Texas and Kentucky) could not take care of themselves politically, so the courts were obligated to intervene.

Another judicial tactic was to create minimum standards of decent treatment for institutionalized persons, like prisoners and mental health patients, and declare these living conditions to be constitutionally required (*Wyatt* 1971). One might criticize judges for willfully taking the Constitution into their own hands. However, the conditions that the courts were asked to remedy often were so execrable, with little possibility of self-improvement, that many judges could not close their eyes to the failures of these institutions to insure humane treatment of the populations that state officials were charged with serving (Johnson 1976). Again, there are parallels in school finance litigation, with many courts allowing some funding variation as long as an "adequate" education is provided to all schoolchildren.

Another consequence of this quiet revolution of public law cases was the widening and lengthening of the remedial process. No longer were remedies confined to merely a monetary judgment. As noted above, courts that found violations of constitutional rights in state institutions often required broad equitable remedies, such as rules, procedures, and standards implemented to cure these legal defects. Consequently, compliance with court orders became more problematic. Legally required reforms often cost money that was not always under the defendant's control (*Missouri* 1990). For example, corrections officials charged with reducing inmate overcrowding had to persuade the state legislature, which was not necessarily a party to the litigation, to appropriate the funds to build more prisons (*Estelle* 1976). Other court-ordered changes met obstacles such as union rules over working conditions or general bureaucratic inertia (Diver 1979). Furthermore, in many instances opposition to the court orders could become a source of political capital, as in school desegregation (Peltason 1961).

For these reasons and others, the implementation necessarily would have to be lengthened in time, exemplified by the U.S. Supreme Court's phrase in *Brown v. Board of Education* requiring compliance "with all deliberate speed" (*Brown* II 1955). Judges would have to play an ongoing role in supervision of their orders. Courts would have to issue multiple orders, often repetitive, on a range of issues to ensure that their constitutional dictates were met (*Clements* 1989). Again, school finance fits this model, as many state high courts, including the Texas Supreme Court, were forced to adjudicate the issues involved again and again.

This alteration of the legal landscape in the "public law" cases could not help but affect the role of the judge. Far from the traditional position as passive arbiter, judges were now required to take an active role in all facets of litigation. At the outset, judges had to determine which of many parties had sufficient interests at stake in the case to be allowed to intervene, unlike in the traditional bipolar cases in which the parties and interests were easily discernible. As litigation proceeded, the discovery process became more complex, as the "facts" found increasingly turned on interpretations of dense and sometimes speculative social science evidence.

Most important, though, the question of compliance with the court order, as noted above, became problematic. Judges now were forced to make increasingly political judgments as to how much reform of these state institutions was practically possible to achieve. Fashioning a remedy and determining its extent became a "complex and contingent exercise in prediction" (Diver 1979:62). Instead of the traditional source of judicial authority, coercion of private individual parties backed by state force, courts were forced to rely upon negotiation and bargaining, in no small part because the targets of the negotiations were the state authorities themselves. Colin Diver referred to this new role of the judge as that of "political powerbroker" (Diver 1979).

As the name "powerbroker" suggests, judges had certainly expanded their scope of influence beyond the constraints of the traditional passive arbiter conception of judging. Courts were making important policy decisions concerning the direction of key elements of the new welfare state institutions of the twentieth century. Arguably, judicial protection of individual rights significantly aided the people that the courts attempted to protect, such as prisoners, mental health patients, and juveniles. At a minimum, judges curtailed most of the worst institutional abuses. Such success, however, might have come at the price of a degree of judicial legitimacy. As noted in this chapter, courts derive a great deal of their power from the social perception that judges are neutrally and fairly applying law, not just imposing their own personal political opinions. To the extent that the new "public law" litigation moved judges away from their role as passive impartial arbiters and toward the position of "political powerbrokers," court legitimacy was potentially endangered. In this way, the very source of the judge's political power was ultimately its limitation (Diver 1979:104).

There is some evidence that judges themselves, even when deciding these institutional reform cases, were quite aware of this constraint on their authority. While requiring state bureaucracies to make significant changes in their operating procedures, many judges referred to their role as mere interpreters of law and not as legislators. Courts remained quite conscious of the principle of separated powers even when pushing its boundaries. This built-in constraint often limited judges in the reforms they were willing to require. For example, judges were usually quite reluctant to issue contempt citations to foot-dragging officials. For this reason, Colin Diver argued, "instititutional reform litigation almost invariably must fall far short of its goal" (Diver 1979:105). One sees this hesitance in the U.S. Supreme Court's more recent pullback from far-reaching remedies for desegregation violations (*Freeman* 1992; *Missouri* 1995).

As time passed, this pessimistic note regarding judicial capacity sounded in the academic community with increasing volume. Perhaps the single most influential work in this regard was Donald Horowitz's 1977 book *The Courts and Social Policy*. Horowitz summarized the new trends toward institutional reform litigation and then attempted to measure court efficacy in producing successful policy in these cases. He focused on four case studies of federal court decisions regarding citizen participation in the Model Cities program, school finance equity in Washington, D.C., juvenile court procedures, and law enforcement requirements concerning evidence seized without warrants. In all these case studies, Horowitz found serious defects in the judicial response. Courts were ill-equipped to handle these complex social policy cases, and their involvement, when not just irrelevant and time-consuming, often exacerbated the existing problems. Underlying these claims was the argument that institutional reform was better left to legislative and executive action.

The problems with judicial involvement in these cases, Horowitz argued, began at the top, with the judge him/herself. Judges are trained to be generalists, not policy specialists. Instead of finding "legal" facts, they were forced to ascertain "social" facts turning on questions of interpretation of social science statistical data. Few judges had any experience with this kind of evidence. The more complex the litigation, the more judges would be asked to make decisions with very little knowledge of the possible consequences of their rulings. Problems with court involvement in social policy cases went far beyond issues of judicial training, though. According to Horowitz, the very nature of the legal process severely handicapped the courts in formulating good public policy. The nature of law, Horowitz argued, centrally concerned questions of rights and obligations. These rights and duties, once found, were supposed to be distinct and absolute within their sphere. There was no room for compromise and balancing; right was present or it was not. The process of institutional reform litigation, however, forced courts to negotiate and compromise, as noted above. This dualism created an inevitable tension and often led to courts using a blunt rights-oriented approach when compromise would have led to a much more effective policy.

Furthermore, according to Horowitz, the legal process of finding rights and duties was most effective when dealing with questions of past conduct. The discovery process was ideally suited for ascertaining facts after they occurred. But in social policy cases, past conduct was less important, especially in the remedial phase, than future conduct in implementation of a solution. The adjudicative process possessed few tools to aid judges in formulating a prospective plan of action. One of the primary reasons why judges were handicapped in constructing a remedy was that they could not control all the parties that would have to take action in response to a court order. The more complex the litigation, the greater number of interests that would be affected. It would be impractical and legally questionable to order testimony from all possible targets of the litigation on the defendants' side. On the plaintiff's side, the nature of the judicial process raised the question of whether the litigants were truly representative of the persons adversely affected by institutional conditions. If these plaintiffs were atypical, a solution devised in response to their claims could backfire when applied to the "normal" case.

The inability to control the litigants also pointed to the final serious defect in court involvement in social policy cases noted by Horowitz. The judicial process, unlike the legislative process, is not self-starting. Courts have to wait for a case to be brought before taking action, and cannot ensure that the case before them was truly the most all-encompassing example of the policy problem. Furthermore, if plaintiffs want to drop the litigation and pursue relief by other means, there is nothing courts can do to stop them, no matter the stage of the remedial process. More likely, though, even if plaintiffs wanted to keep the case alive, judicial monitoring would have to be haphazard. Aside from the issue of overflowing dockets, structural legal constraints made it quite difficult for courts to hold hearings whenever problems emerged in the implementation. The length of time necessary for full discovery also limited the efficacy of legal action in remedying complex and quickly changing social conditions. For all these reasons and others, Horowitz claimed, the trend toward judicial involvement in institutional reform litigation was potentially destructive, not only to good public policy, but to judicial legitimacy itself. The appropriate response for the courts was to remove themselves from these types of cases and direct the parties to the legislative and executive policy-making processes, which were better equipped to deal with their concerns.[2]

As might be expected, not everyone in the judicial politics academic community shared Horowitz's views. A number of smaller studies followed soon after *The Courts and Social Policy* was published. They attempted to cast doubt upon its pessimistic conclusions (Fair 1981; Reedy 1982; Youngblood and Folse 1981). Specifically, some scholars highlighted the use of "special masters" or "monitoring commissions" to avoid some of the problems with judicial fact-finding and ongoing supervision that Horowitz identified (Fiss 1979; Aronow 1980; Sarat and Cavanagh 1980). Others pointed to the benefits that legal action still possessed for the litigants themselves even if courts were ineffective in constructing solutions, but that debate will be dealt with in the next section of this chapter.

One of the most direct and comprehensive responses to Horowitz's work was Michael Rebell and Arthur Block's 1982 book *Educational Policy Making and the Courts*. Rebell and Block decided to test Horowitz's thesis that the courts were incapable of handing complex institutional reform litigation in two ways. First, they gathered a database of sixty-five cases concerning a range of education policy issues, excluding school desegregation. For each of these "caselets," they contacted the attorneys involved and used publicly available information in order to get thumbnail sketches concerning the capacity issues Horowitz discussed. They found that Horowitz's concerns were generally overstated, at least regarding the vast majority of cases. The discovery process, for example, tended to be effective and uncontested. There was no pattern of social fact distortion, usually because judges found ways to avoid having to decide these complex issues of interpretation. Furthermore, concerning implementation, the defendants often participated in constructing the remedies, and the courts emphasized the least intrusive means of monitoring. Contempt citations were extremely rare. One may ask whether this harmony was useful for realization of the plaintiffs' goals, but at least Rebell and Block did not observe the horror stories that Horowitz cited in support of his arguments.

Second, Rebell and Block specifically compared judicial effectiveness with legislative effectiveness concerning similar education policy issues in two states, New York and Colorado. Somewhat surprisingly, they found little difference between the legislative branch and the judiciary in terms of the availability of information, the outside participants involved, and the construction of a solution. In both the legislature and the courts, the authors argued, "the structure and details of far-reaching education policy reforms are likely to be formulated largely by negotiations among interested parties" (Rebell and Block 1982:195). The only difference was that courts tended to negotiate over what Rebell and Block call "principle," while legislatures negotiated over political concerns. Rebell and Block concluded, therefore, that Horowitz's concerns over judicial capacity, at least regarding education policy issues, were somewhat overstated. The authors specifically exempted school desegregation, though, arguing that the issues were so uniquely confrontational that courts would likely struggle in devising appropriate remedies.

Jennifer Hochschild reached a somewhat different conclusion in her 1984 book *The New American Dilemma*, an analysis of school desegregation policy, and at least implicitly, a response to Horowitz. In her survey of twenty years of school desegregation, Hochschild noted a strong tendency toward incremental, or slow, small, piecemeal solutions to this vexing social problem. Incrementalism is the most common American method of problem-solving, as it fits best with the system of separated institutions sharing powers noted earlier in this chapter. Incrementalism also possesses the advantages of adaptability and, usually, popular input into construction of remedies for problems.

In the case of school desegregation, however, Hochschild argued that incrementalism had failed on a grand scale. First, letting desegregation policy develop slowly allowed time for resistance to develop on a massive scale. Second, the usual incremental bias toward implementation over a small area meant that "white flight" could completely foil any effective race-mixing. In addition, to the extent that desegregation was still possible, the white areas bearing the "burden" of busing, and so forth, were disproportionately working-class, not wealthy suburbs, again maximizing resistance from those who felt they were lab rats in someone else's social experiment. Third, the incrementalist value of popular input before action tended to slow effective reform, because the majority of the community were placed in the position of defending their power and privilege against its potential dilution. Popular input in this case could do little good in devising solutions that would effect real change.

Hochschild argued that policymakers were faced with three options in their attempts to produce racial equity in the schools. First, one could give up on the goal of desegregation and allocate resources to other issues, such as finance equity, housing policy, or affirmative action, which might prove more effective in achieving reform. Second, one could continue along the same slow, incremental path to school desegregation, although with little hope of success. Third, one could implement more far-reaching desegregation through the courts.

Hochschild cited a number of studies to support her claim that although incremental school desegregation had largely failed, "full desegregation" might succeed. Full desegregation would involve a large-scale busing plan involving cities, suburbs, and whatever other areas are needed to involve both rich and poor. Change would be rapid, would involve all grade levels, and would be carried out with little/no popular input. However counter-intuitive this plan might be from the standpoint of liberal democracy, Hochschild argued that it had the greatest chance of success in moving toward a desegregated society.

The courts would have to be the primary implementers of full desegregation, according to this plan, because they would be the least likely swayed by incrementalist arguments and popular pressure. Hochschild acknowledged the criticisms of judicial capacity made by Horowitz and others, but asserted that if it were not for courts, virtually no desegregation at all would have occurred. In addition, with greater experience, judges were becoming more skilled at handling school desegregation cases. Therefore, the courts represented the best hope for the achievement of the near-universally supported goal of racially mixed schools. One can compare Hochschild's prescription of "full desegregation" to the Kentucky Supreme Court's decision declaring the entire Kentucky public school system to be unconstitutional—a rejection of incrementalism.

But, the U.S. Supreme Court did not share Hochschild's expansive view of its power to effect school desegregation. In a series of 1990s cases, the Court limited lower federal court authority in constructing desegregation remedies and maintaining judicial supervision over school districts (*Missouri* 1995; *Freeman* 1992; but see *U.S. v. Fordice* 1992). For example, in *Board of Education of Oklahoma City v. Dowell* (1991), the Court ruled that a school district that had been following judicial orders for over a decade could be removed from supervision, even though the district itself was still highly segregated. It is likely that concerns over judicial capacity to effect more far-reaching remedies for these complex social problems played a role in these decisions limiting judicial power.

Since the work of Horowitz, Rebell and Block, Hochschild, and others, judicial impact scholarship per se (leaving aside the Rosenberg/McCann debate on utility of legal action) generally has blunted its ideological edge. Charles Johnson and Bradley Canon's *Judicial Policies: Implementation and Impact* was a good example of this trend. Johnson and Canon were less interested in making a normative argument for or against judicial involvement in social policy cases than about constructing a comprehensive model of judicial impact. In this model, they distinguished five different implementing "populations" for court decisions and sketched out various psychological and social theories to explain how impact might occur on each of these groups. Their conclusion, rather unsurprisingly, was that court impact was complex, variable, and difficult to measure.

Joel Grossman's article "Beyond the Willowbrook Wars: The Courts and Institutional Reform" also presented a more balanced perspective regarding judicial involvement in public law litigation (Grossman 1987). Grossman argued that neither the judicial activist stereotype of courts swiftly and surely avenging social wrongs nor Horowitz's picture of court ineptitude and disaster was correct. Instead, "a more accurate picture is of a loose policymaking partnership held together by the threat of judicial sanction and various political forces mobilized by the litigation, from which judges can remain relatively insulated" (Grossman 1987:256). A "semicyclical pattern of crisis and equilibrium" characterized judicial involvement in these complex cases (ibid.:258).

Most recently, Malcolm Feeley and Edward Rubin's (1998) study of prison reform litigation built on Grossman's notion of a "policymaking partnership" to argue that modern courts can be likened to policy-making administrators in "public law" cases. Courts identify a problem, look for a theory to apply to the problem, try a solution, and, if the solution is ineffective, give up or implement another solution, just as an administrator would. Regarding the prison cases, Feeley and Rubin argued that courts were neither more nor less capable than legislators and executives in remedying the terrible conditions in many prisons across the country. Feeley and Rubin's conception of courts as players, although not dictators, in policy-making is very similar to the argument I will make in subsequent chapters concerning school funding equity.

The debate between those who believe that courts can effectively make social policy, even in "public law" cases, and those who are skeptical of the wisdom and efficacy of court intervention in these areas, continues to the present day. Another concern is whether the litigation was useful for the plaintiffs themselves.

THE UTILITY OF LEGAL ACTION

The use of litigation by organized interest groups battling for social change is a relatively recent phenomenon in American history. In earlier times, most notably in the nineteenth century and the early twentieth century, going to court was the preferred option for interests that wanted to slow or halt social reform, such as large industrial concerns, with only limited exceptions. The role of courts in the progress of social movements began to change after World War II, however.

The use of courts to advance social reform was sparked by Thurgood Marshall and the National Association for the Advancement of Colored People (NAACP). Marshall and fellow NAACP lawyers filed case after case against all aspects of segregation, fitting their arguments to the issues at hand and to the federal courts' increasing willingness to hear such cases (Tushnet 1994). The eventual result of this strategy was the decision in *Brown v. Board of Education of Topeka* (1954, 1955), which invalidated racial segregation in public schools across the nation. On paper and as a symbol, the *Brown* decision was a great victory for Marshall and his allies. The reality was more complex, however. Full implementation of *Brown* did not take place in the South until well over a decade after the decision, at least partly because of Supreme Court reluctance to order swifter change. Furthermore, even today, many schools are de facto racially segregated, although no longer de jure segregated. This potential gap between legal victory and political change leads one to ask whether litigation is a useful strategy for movement activists.

Stuart Scheingold's *The Politics of Rights* (1974) provided the first comprehensive treatment of this question. Earlier studies had focused on single issues (Wirt 1970; Sax 1970), but Scheingold set forth a synthesis and extension of that previous work. *The Politics of Rights* centered on two main concepts, the "myth of rights" and the "politics of rights."

The "myth of rights," according to Scheingold, is the American idea that all citizens possess a set of basic fundamental rights. These rights encompass all that is truly important, such as life, liberty, and property. They are inalienable—neither government nor any other actor can deny them to anyone—and the law is designed to protect these rights. Little further monitoring, supervision, or input by citizens is needed because the legal system will "go of itself." People believe in this idea of rational ordering and structure, even if the reality is much different.

This "myth" fed into the "politics of rights" for Scheingold. The American conception of rights and legal order in fact is a myth because it conceals the underlying politics involved in seemingly neutral processes. First, according to Scheingold, the framework of government and rights under the U.S. Constitution clearly envisioned a limited government devoted to the protection of free-market entrepreneurial capitalism and a general individualistic ethos. Therefore, arguments based on rights found in this document are unlikely to provide the basis for fundamental social change toward a more socialistic or community-based society in which greater attention is paid to needs than rights.

Second, legal forms often divide and conquer social movements by encouraging small incremental change and differentiation of the movement. Incremental change is often accomplished through legal reliance on precedent or stare decisis. In effect, attorneys have to argue for change by claiming that there is no change in the status quo, merely a new application of traditional principles to modern facts. Differentiation of cases occurs because some legal arguments that benefit certain members of the social movement are more likely to succeed in court than others. Therefore, certain elements of the coalition are excluded from the fruits of success, likely fracturing the alliance if litigation persists.

Third, and perhaps most important, powerful actors often can block implementation of the few and limited victories that social movement attorneys win in court through their control of the levers of power in the "political" branches—namely, the legislature and executive. The momentum of the movement stops once the court decision is issued, leaving plenty of time for forces resistant to change to regroup and attack implementation of the ruling. Moreover, as noted in the previous section, courts are often limited in their resources and willingness to force compliance with their decisions, especially in the types of "public law" cases about which social movements are likely to care the most.

There is a glimmer of hope in Scheingold's work: he argued that legal action can be effective if coupled with a strategy of political mobilization. The "myth of rights" might actually help in this regard, because if the activists can successfully tie their claim to some preexisting fundamental American value, the target population might well respond to the perceived denial or unfairness that they had assumed the legal system would remedy by taking political action. In addition, rights can be useful in lobbying policymakers because activists can threaten to take legal action if change does not occur. Policymakers sometimes take such threats seriously because of the time, effort, and cost of litigation; furthermore, they might even believe the "myth of rights", and wish to avoid a judgment that they had violated those rights. But, this strategy is not sufficient in and of itself; it needs to be coupled with serious grassroots mobilization. In this way, rights are less like a trump card than a bargaining chip (my terms.) Scheingold was not optimistic about the frequency of this occurrence, however, because of the training of lawyers to believe in the "myth of rights" (although this may be changing), the structure of the legal profession, which discourages such work, and the difficulties of implementation noted earlier.

If Scheingold was skeptical about the general utility of legal action for social movement leaders, Gerald Rosenberg was positively despairing. In *The Hollow Hope: Can Courts Bring About Social Change?* (1991), Rosenberg compared two views of courts, labeling them the "Dynamic Court" model and the "Constrained Court" model. The "Dynamic Court" model posits courts as powerful leaders of social change and avengers of injustice. By contrast, the "Constrained Court" model sees courts, in Hamilton's phrase, as the "least dangerous branch" (Hamilton et al. 1961:465). Constrained courts rarely push for radical social reform, and when they do, the political branches and other implementers are likely to ignore them. Rosenberg tested these models by examining landmark the U.S. Supreme Court decisions, such as *Brown v. Board of Education, Roe v. Wade,* and *Baker v. Carr,* on the assumption that if any decisions support the Dynamic Court model, it should be these. In all these cases, Rosenberg comes to the somewhat surprising conclusion that the decision had little impact on policy, so the Constrained Court view fits better with the reality of Supreme Court policymaking.

In the case of *Brown,* for example, Rosenberg argued that compliance with the court decision was not achieved until Congress and the executive branch, particularly the Justice and Health, Education, and Welfare departments, decided to make school desegregation a priority nearly ten years after *Brown* and used aggressive strategies to induce school districts to comply. Also, Rosenberg claimed that *Brown* had little impact, even indirect, on public opinion or movement-building.

Regarding *Roe,* movement activists received scant benefit from legal action as well, according to Rosenberg. First, the number of legal abortions was increasing even before the Court decided *Roe* in 1973. The court's action, in Rosenberg's view, merely ratified a movement toward liberalized abortion laws. Second, the consequence of the Court's intervention, paradoxically, was to reduce the momentum of the pro-choice forces, who believed that the fight was over, and to galvanize the anti-abortion movement into active opposition. The effect of *Roe,* Rosenberg argued, was to decrease the number of hospitals and doctors providing abortions because of the renewed anti-abortion backlash, regardless of the expanded legal right. The other case studies similarly showed the Supreme Court's ineffectiveness in producing significant social change in the direction desired by movement activists, he argued. Therefore, the promise of the Court was a "hollow hope," not only useless to activists, but actually damaging to their movements, in as much as time, money, and other resources are wasted on legal action when they could have been better utilized in grassroots mobilization.

Some scholars faulted Rosenberg for what they found to be his unrealistic measures of "significant social change" and lack of discussion of the relative capacity of *any* branch, including the courts, to move a system of separated institutions sharing powers (Feeley 1992). Others criticized his specific measures of shifts of public opinion after the court rulings, as in *Brown* (Bohte, Flemming, and Wood 1995). One could also argue that Rosenberg left out or significantly underplayed important effects of these decisions, such as making all early-term abortions legal in the U.S., which was arguably a real benefit to the women involved. Also, the resurgence of professionalized and efficient state government, especially state legislatures, has been traced in no small part to *Baker v. Carr* (Sabato 1983:78-82), but is an effect that Rosenberg never mentioned. Lastly, Rosenberg did not fully discuss the possibility that the Court itself might have weakened its rulings through excessive caution.

The response to *The Hollow Hope* did not just center on the execution of Rosenberg's study, but also its approach. Michael McCann was perhaps the most prominent critic of the top-down, positivist methodology of the book. He argued that it was misleading to look for court-led social change in the circumscribed way Rosenberg did. It would be much more useful, according to McCann, if one were going to try to give advice to movement activists, to examine *their* perspectives on the courts rather than to focus exclusively on the court decisions themselves and their immediate impact. McCann employed this approach in his book *Rights at Work: Pay Equity Reform and the Politics of Legal Mobilization* (1994). McCann focused on the issue of "comparable worth," or gender pay equity reform, and the effects that legal tactics had on the movement for change. He gathered data from twenty-eight different sites of struggle, from state governments to city governments to private companies. These data came from in-depth semistructured interviews with the activists involved, documentation from the files of the organizations, newspaper coverage, and other scholarly work.

McCann concluded that even though the movement achieved relatively few favorable court decisions, legal tactics were quite useful. Two benefits of litigation stood out. First, as Scheingold had speculated, the legal claim of "rights" served as a powerful tool for movement leaders in mobilizing women who had never thought about the pay equity issue or who believed that nothing could be done about the perceived disparity between men's and women's wages. Once movement goals could be phrased in terms of a natural, even constitutional, right to equal treatment that was being unfairly denied, the women involved could feel that they had a stake in the pay equity fight. This legal construction of the claim was quite useful in mobilization.

Second, going to court affected the response of some defendants, the institutions or companies charged with violating their female employees' rights. McCann argued that the mere threat of legal action would often persuade defendants to take steps to remedy the perceived greivances to avoid a protracted court battle. The time, cost, and effort spent defending a lawsuit might outstrip the value of any concessions made to the workers, a dynamic that has been referred to as politics "in the shadow of the law" (Jacob 1992). Furthermore, an unfavorable court decision might mean a loss of institutional control by the defendants if the court decided to issue a comprehensive order designed to correct the problem. For some defendants, virtually any concession was worth avoiding that outcome.

McCann concluded that both "neorealists" such as Rosenberg and "structuralists" such as many critical legal scholars[3] were mistaken concerning the effectiveness of law in the struggle for social change. Both camps would argue that going to court was a waste of time and effort, either because courts themselves are not powerful or because legal discourse traps the activists in an illusion of rights. McCann claimed that in his interviews he found that legal tactics could be useful *and* that the activists themselves viewed law quite "realistically." They realized that victories on paper had to be translated into real people's lives with continued mobilization and political pressure. Going to court was only one strategy among many, useful at certain times and not others. Therefore, according to McCann, there was reason after all for cautious optimism concerning the utility of legal action in the production of social change.

Implications for this Study

This work borrows some elements of all the literature cited in this chapter, such as the judicial impact studies of Horowitz; the concern with the utility of legal action of Scheingold; the court-centered approach of Rosenberg; and some of the methodological tools of McCann. Regarding judicial impact, one has to be quite clear as to what this study does and does not do. It does contribute to the judicial impact literature by assessing the efficacy of courts in persuading the legislatures and governors to pass legislation that, at least on paper, is more equitable than previous funding distribution systems. I will discuss the significance of the funding formula changes that the legislatures made in response to the courts, at least on a general level.

Of course, school funding issues are highly complex and variable; changes on paper might look quite different when applied in the real world. Ultimately, of course, the question is what effect the court decisions requiring greater funding equity had on student achievement. Unfortunately, at the present time there is no good way to answer that question. One would first have to measure the effects of the court on the legislature and governor (the purpose of this book), then examine the significance of the legal changes for alterations in funding district by district, and finally assess the consequences of increased (or decreased in some cases) funding for student learning, likely measured by standardized test scores—a project that is beyond the scope of this book. Still, one can at least take the first step of examining the court's impact on the political branches, as this ought to give some clues as to the strength of any causal chain down to the schoolrooms.

Despite my criticism of Rosenberg's approach and findings, I share some methodological assumptions with him. Specifically, I borrow from his positivist approach (Rosenberg 1996). Positivism, to generalize, is the theory that actions can be explained by looking for the causal chain of events that led to those actions, whether in the natural or social world. These causal chains are always present, if the researcher looks hard enough. This approach has often been labeled "mechanistic," for better or worse. It requires many simplifying assumptions about human motivations and causality that many researchers are not willing to make. The benefit, however, is a relatively coherent theory that can yield testable propositions much more easily than the interpretivist approach discussed below. Rosenberg employed positivist methodology to look for a causal connection between court decisions and significant social reform. He found little to no causal relationship (although again, his results are much disputed, even from a positivist perspective). This work shares with Rosenberg's work and the literature on judicial impact a top-down court-centered perspective, although not to the complete exclusion of other approaches. The role of the state supreme court in each case study is the key independent variable, so to speak, with the legislative and executive response the dependent variable.

The single most important question I asked in the interviews borrowed heavily from this perspective. "Without the court intervention, do you think these changes (to the funding formulas) would have happened anyway?" This is the qualitative equivalent of regression analysis controlling for all the variables except the court.

This work also borrows from McCann's interpretivist approach (McCann 1996). Interpretivism, again to generalize, rejects the positivist emphasis on causal connections, because, according to interpretivists, such "discoveries" are misleading and overstated; everything influences everything else in one way or another. Social relations are much too rich and complex to be reduced to a chalkboard model. What is more important, according to the interpretivists, is "the social construction of reality" (McCann 1996, citing Berger and Luckman 1966). To quote McCann, "People reason as they act, but they do so as creatures whose reflexive capacity is facilitated by the constructed conventions and discursive formations that inhere in institutionalized social life. . . . Human relations are viewed as ongoing, dialectical processes rather than as aggregations of isolated causal connections" (McCann 1996:462–63). The complex and contingent character of social relations requires researchers to interact closely with their subjects, as in ethnography, to fully comprehend the subject's interpretive framework, instead of the positivist approach of assuming motivations from actions. This is why the interviews of movement activists were crucial to McCann's project.

This project followed McCann's lead in that I have concentrated on three specific case studies concerning one issue, instead of attempting to measure judicial impact in every state on the school finance issue. I believe that this choice can be justified partly by the range of states selected, but also because of the increased depth of knowledge gained in each case-study state. Additionally, the data collection techniques I used were, following McCann, designed to understand why policymakers believed it was necessary (or unnecessary) to comply with court decisions in this area. This is an especially interesting question, given the political drawbacks to making changes in the funding formulas, and the like, including the strong possibility of tax increases. Would elected officials decide to take the political risk to support such changes just because a court said so, and if so, why? Such questions could be answered only by talking with the officials themselves and other close observers of the policy process. Like McCann, I conducted semistructured interviews with a range of participants in each case-study state.

McCann "triangulated" his data by combining the interviews with archival research into newspaper articles, documents used by the activists, and academic research. I also undertook this triangulation by examining a wealth of newspaper articles in each state, documents that the interviewees provided to me, and previous academic work as well (see chapter 2.) This triangulation was especially necessary to check any self-serving comments by the interviewees. McCann's synthesis of his data revealed a complex and contingent process of policymaking partly through legal means. My study reaches many of the same conclusions, albeit concerning a different issue area and from a more court-centered perspective. I do examine the question of the utility of legal action from the perspectives of the participants, as per Scheingold and McCann, but this aspect is not the major emphasis of this work.

The positivist/interpretivist debate between Rosenberg and McCann raises the question of whether one can say that the courts involved in this study "caused" change in a positivist sense or merely "influenced" change from an interpretivist perspective (Rosenberg 1996; McCann 1996). It is difficult to devote oneself completely to one approach or another, because both possess clear advantages and disadvantages, as noted. Perhaps the best solution to this quandary is to borrow from each perspective. Rather than seeking causality, I will assess whether the courts exerted "independent influence," for example, whether the courts made an independent contribution to policymaking by convincing legislators and executives to make decisions that they would not have otherwise made.

The term "causality" seems too strong to apply in this case. Multiple forces internal and external to the policymaking institutions converged, of which the courts were only one, to produce the policy results in each case-study state. Also, when one examines human motivations, "cause" seems to me to apply less and less the deeper one goes. The term implies a deterministic process, whereas the interviewees with whom I talked made conscious choices whether to comply with the court decision, and to what degree. This study will test to see whether the courts made a unique contribution to the process. Were the courts exercisers of power, rather than mere participants?

To summarize, the term "independent influence" as the measure of court effectiveness does not necessarily mean that the courts
were disengaged in some way from the policy process. I will argue
below that they were an integral part of policymaking. I will also
claim, however, that the process would have been different in each
state without court involvement. This result shows a degree of
court effectiveness that varied depending upon the actions of the
court and upon the conditions in the larger political environment,
but which was universally present.

⌇

CHAPTER 2

Funding American Public Schools

Why study public school finance? The best reason is that education finance is one of the most important policy areas in which state courts have intervened, and one of the most significant functions left principally to state and local governments even after the rise of Great Society government and "cooperative federalism." One can see this in the percentage of state resources that go to education, by some measures the single largest item in state budgets (Augenblick 1998). Discussions of education, taxes and spending, and budgets have to go hand in hand in state governments merely because of the size of the state commitment to public education.

The second reason to study public school funding is that in many ways, the debate over equalization of school resources is the continuation of *Brown v. Board of Education* (1954) by other means. In both instances, the courts are trying to intervene in issues that contain a strong racial and class element. Although the issues are much more complex in school finance, at the core is a struggle between the haves and have-nots in society. Wealthy suburbs are pitted against poor rural and urban areas. Feelings are deeply ingrained in the participants, making a solution much more difficult. If the courts can step in and have an impact on this kind of issue, they might succeed where the battle lines are not as clearly drawn and the stakes are not as high.

This chapter is divided into three sections. First, I trace the history of litigation concerning school funding disparities from district to district. Second, I explore the scholarship specifically devoted to judicial intervention in school funding to establish a framework for my approach to the research problem. Third, I describe the methodology of this study and its relation to the scholarship on judicial involvement in public school finance debates.

History of Education Finance Litigation

The fundamental problem underlying public school funding in America is the tension between two strongly held values: equality of opportunity and local control of education (Coleman 1970). Traditionally, schools have been financed at the local level through property taxes, with only varying state support. Such a system is beneficial for districts with large local tax bases, such as wealthy suburbs. However, poorer rural or urban districts are disadvantaged due to their smaller tax bases. Even if tax rates are high in these poorer districts, often they cannot raise as much money as their wealthier suburban counterparts.

These inequalities between rich and poor public school districts eventually led in the late 1960s to two concurrent developments that would help to shape education finance for thirty years and likely beyond. First, a national reform network of various school finance activists, policy professionals, academics, and sympathetic politicians developed (Fuhrman 1982). In some ways, this network was an outgrowth of the civil rights movement. For these activists, a crusade against inequalities in public school finance was in the same tradition of battles against racial and gender discrimination, fights for access for the disabled, and contests over the right to welfare benefits (Enrich 1995). In fact, school finance was second only to racial discrimination in importance because of the central role early education plays in the lives of children and adults. The reform network could share information about developments in each state and supply data to use in persuading recalcitrant state legislatures of the breadth and depth of the funding inequalities (Fuhrman 1982).

The network still needed a focus to rally behind, however, leading to the second development. In the case of civil rights, litigation culminating in *Brown* provided a catalyst. Court cases also served that function in the case of school finance.

The "First Wave"[1]: Establishing a
Fundamental Right to an Education

Courts became school finance battlefields in the late 1960s, soon after Arthur Wise published a book titled *Rich Schools, Poor Schools: The Promise of Equal Educational Opportunity* (1967). Wise outlined the inequalities inherent in the current system of financing public schools. He then summarized the legal issues, both state and federal, and noted a number of justifications for a U.S.

Supreme Court decision finding a violation of the Fourteenth Amendment right to "equal protection of the laws" in all state systems that did not provide equal educational opportunity. Advocates for the poor and disadvantaged saw in Wise's book a new opportunity for litigation to help remedy the conditions of their clients. It is no coincidence that the first notable decision over equalizing school funds was handed down in 1969, two years after the publication of Wise's book.

McInnis v. Shapiro (Cases Cited: Illinois 1969) involved a federal court challenge to Illinois's public school finance system on the grounds that children in poor districts were denied the Fourteenth Amendment guarantee of equal protection. The reasons for using federal courts instead of relying on state courts were clear. Not only had the Supreme Court handed down a number of decisions favorable to the poor in the mid to late 1960s, but state courts were often more conservative. The major reason, though, was that a federal court decision under the Fourteenth Amendment would affect all states, not just Illinois. The district court rejected the plaintiffs' claim, however. The plaintiffs had argued that only a finance system that allocated funds on the basis of each pupil's "educational need" would be constitutional. The district court noted the complexity of the issues involved, both in "equality" of finance and "equality" of need. The presiding judge declined to overturn the system, citing the lack of "judicially manageable standards" for mandating a different system. Illinois had a "reasonable basis" for legislating the current system under the principles of local control and local choice. The court of appeals upheld the judgment, and the Supreme Court declined to hear the case (Illinois 1969).

After *McInnis*, advocates for poor districts turned to both federal *and* state courts for a ruling on the federal issues. Even though the Supreme Court refused to hear *McInnis*, advocates were hopeful that state litigation could provide the basis for a landmark opinion that might help persuade the Supreme Court to look more closely at the issue. Also, the work of Coons et al. (1970) provided a stronger legal claim than "educational need." The professors argued that provision of education conditioned on property wealth was invidious discrimination in violation of the Fourteenth Amendment, the so-called "fiscal neutrality" standard.[2] The advocates (although not the professors) also claimed that there was a fundamental right to an education.

Both legal issues were important because of the way the Supreme Court interprets the equal protection clause. The Court has constructed a three-tier system for judging equal protection claims against legislation. At the top is judicial "strict scrutiny": to pass strict scrutiny, legislation must have a "compelling interest or purpose" and the legislature must use the "least restrictive means" to achieve its objective. Almost no laws pass this test. Successful claims that trigger strict scrutiny involve a fundamental right or an invidious classification. Fundamental rights are explicit (free speech, right to criminal counsel) or are implicit in the Constitution (right to travel or right to privacy). The advocates attempted to add "education" to this list. An "invidious classification" is discrimination based on suspect factors such as race, nationality or alien status. In the early 1970s, a history of oppression and political powerlessness because of these characteristics also was needed. The poor districts wanted to add wealth, or the lack thereof, to these suspect classes. If no claim that would trigger "strict scrutiny" is raised, then the challenged legislation is tested for a "rational basis." If the legislation has a "rational relationship" to a "legitimate state objective," the legislation is constitutional. Because there is almost always some reason for passing a law, legislation is very rarely struck down on these grounds.

The California Supreme Court was a favorable haven for the advocates' equal protection claims: the court was known to be liberal, and the size of California created many opportunities for pockets of extreme wealth and extreme poverty, sometimes side by side. Litigation commenced under the name of *Serrano v. Priest* (1971). A nearly unanimous Court accepted all the important arguments of the *Serrano* plaintiffs, declaring that the U.S. Constitution guaranteed all children a right to a public education. The state therefore had a responsibility to provide this education equally. Justices justified their classification of education as a fundamental right by emphasizing the social importance of education in the lives of citizens. "Education is the lifeline of both the individual and society" (*Serrano* 1971:1256.) The Court noted the importance of education in improving an individual's chances for economic success, and its "unique influence on a child's development as a citizen and his participation in political and community life" (ibid.).

The current system of public school finance was unconstitutional because it discriminated on the basis of wealth of the district. Local control was not a "compelling state interest" that could justify the system. This ruling was supported by U.S. Supreme Court cases outlawing the poll tax (*Harper* 1966), requiring that a free trial transcript be provided for a criminal appeal (*Griffin* 1956), and requiring a court-appointed lawyer on appeal for the indigent (*Douglas* 1963). The California court's decision stated that education may not be conditioned on wealth, essentially the "fiscal neutrality" standard. This is a negative definition, not specifying what justifications *would* produce a constitutional system. The court remanded the case to a lower state court to adjudicate the issue of remedy, but noted that it would defer to the California legislature if that body passed a new equalizing plan.

Serrano created widespread interest in public school finance issues; much legal and political commentary and action resulted. In the next legislative year, eleven states reformed their public school financing systems (Grubb 1974). Federal district courts struck down financing methods in Texas (1971)[3] and Minnesota (1971). The Michigan Supreme Court (1972), and lower state courts in Kansas (1972) and New Jersey (1972), also found constitutional violations. Thirty-one states had litigation pending. Academic publications were buzzing with viewpoints on the issues raised.

The interest in the subject and the urgency for a U.S. Supreme Court ruling led the Court to take the Texas case, *San Antonio I.S.D. v. Rodriguez* (1973), directly from a three-judge panel. The choice was unfortunate from the perspective of the national school finance reform network because the facts were not as convincing as those in other states, and not fully available to the plaintiffs (Cortez 1998). Furthermore, the lead attorney was not part of the reform network; but the coalition members could not persuade the lawyer to drop his suit. A closely divided Court ruled 5-4 to uphold the Texas public school financing system. In the majority opinion, Justice Lewis Powell began by examining the question of whether the finance plan "invidiously discriminated" against a "suspect class"—the poor. He could not find a "suspect class" for two reasons. First, he cited a student Note in the *Yale Law Journal* that studied income relative to geographic distribution in Connecticut (Note 1972). The article found that poor people often do not live in poor districts, because of large industrial properties located in otherwise low-income areas. This study was later criticized for its incompleteness and unrepresentativeness of the nation, but it was the only one extant at the time. The point is that if poor people do not usually live in poor districts, there can be no discrimination against them under this system.

Powell's second reason for denying that poor people were victims of unconstitutional discrimination was the difference between a *relative* deprivation and an *absolute* deprivation of a benefit. After all, children in poor districts were still receiving an education, if not as complete an education as that offered in rich districts. "Where wealth is involved," Powell argued, "the Equal Protection Clause does not require absolute equality or precisely equal advantages" (*Rodriguez* 1973:24). As long as the children got an "adequate" education, there was no violation. Inconsistent with the rest of his opinion, in which he declined to judge issues of educational quality, Powell asserted that Texas schoolchildren were all receiving an "adequate" education.

A second way to define the "suspect class" was to treat as discriminees all children residing in *districts* with a tax base smaller than the richest one. Poor people were not the issue, poor districts were. The majority rejected this argument as well because of the power of the state to draw school district boundaries. The Court was reluctant to mandate to each state a specific school district map that would ensure equality, although it did so for voting districts in *Baker v. Carr* (1962). Also, the Court said, poor school districts did not have the "traditional indices of suspectness" such as a history of discrimination or obvious political powerlessness. Strict scrutiny still could be triggered if the Court found a fundamental "right to an education."

Powell noted that education was the most important function of state and local governments, but denied that importance was the issue. After all, benefits such as food, clothing, and shelter were at least as important as education, but the Court had declined to find "fundamental rights" to those. Powell then elaborated the most important overall federal legacy of the *Rodriguez* case. He declared that a right is "fundamental" only if it is explicitly or implicitly guaranteed in the U.S. Constitution. Because education fit neither category, there was no federal right to it.

The plaintiffs had argued that education was implicit in the Constitution because of its connection with the right of free speech and the right to vote. The plaintiffs asked how there could be truly free speech and how a citizen could make an informed choice at the ballot box without an education. Powell responded that the Constitution does not require that speech be *effective*, only that it be free (just as the right to a lawyer in a criminal trial does not imply a right to the *best* lawyer). Similarly, the right to vote is protected, not the right to an informed vote. There would be no means to judge how informed a vote or a speech truly was. Finally, the claim of a right to an education suffered because it was a claim of positive right, a right to a benefit, as opposed to the usual constitutional claim of negative right, a right against government intrusion.

As the Court declined to find either of the bases present for triggering "strict scrutiny," the Texas school finance system was analyzed on the level of "rational basis." Unsurprisingly, the Court found a rationale for the system on grounds of "local control." It' was rational for the legislature to let each school district keep what it taxed. "Local control means . . . the freedom to devote more money to the education of one's children," Powell wrote. "Equally important, however, is the opportunity it offers for participation in the decisionmaking process that determines how those local tax dollars can be spent" (*Rodriguez* 1973:50).

The Court cited other reasons for its decision; among them were the complexity of education matters, in which experts had reached no conclusion on any of the fundamental issues; a desire for local experimentation; and principles of federalism. The Court was reluctant to overturn the financing systems of nearly every state before the issues were much clearer. Still, the Court hinted that the Texas system had significant problems, and that states were free to experiment with their own standards.

Justice Thurgood Marshall wrote the major dissenting opinion in *Rodriguez*. He stated "The Court today decides, in effect, that a State may constitutionally vary the quality of education which it offers its children in accordance with the amount of taxable wealth located in the school districts within which they reside" (*Rodriguez* 1973:70). Marshall, repeating the arguments of the California Supreme Court in *Serrano* and adding a few of his own, asserted that education was a fundamental right because of its central importance to a start in life, claiming that as the interest becomes more fundamental, the level of judicial scrutiny should rise, whether or not the right is specifically mentioned in the Constitution. He cited examples of "rights" that do not appear to have any textual backing, such as the right to procreate (*Skinner* 1944), the right to vote in state elections (*Reynolds* 1964), and the right to a criminal appeal (*Griffin* 1956).

Discrimination on the basis of wealth was invidious and irrational, Marshall claimed, because the amount of property wealth in a school district had no more relevance to education than the number of telephone poles in the district. Either one of Marshall's conclusions would trigger strict scrutiny, under which Texas would surely fail. He even disputed the majority's reasoning under the "rational basis" test. The majority cited "local control" as a justification for the system, to which he responded by asking how much local control a poor district taxing at its breaking point and still only receiving half, or worse, of the funds of the richer districts truly possessed. Marshall ended his dissent with an appendix of figures showing the extent of the disparities in Texas and pleaded for political action to remedy the situation.

Rodriguez closed off the federal equal protection argument for advocates of equality. Poor districts were forced to seek a new constitutional avenue, litigation under provisions of state constitutions. Of course, state court rulings under state constitutions were protected from federal review as long as no federal constitutional or statutory standard was violated. In fact, in *Rodriguez*, the U.S. Supreme Court had tacitly encouraged the state-by-state approach.

The "Second Wave": State Litigation 1971–1989

All fifty states mention education in their constitutions, in recognition of the primary state role in providing for education of its citizens. Most of these clauses date from the period immediately after the Civil War, when many states were writing new constitutions and constructing statewide free public school systems for the first time. Later, for the sixteen newest states, an education clause was a requirement for admission into the Union (*Pauley* 1979:864). A few southern states repealed their clauses after *Brown* for fear that the provisions would be used against them, but they eventually reinstated the sections. Even though the wording of most education provisions is unique, the clauses fall into three general patterns. Some merely provide for "a system of free public schools." Others require that the school system be "general and uniform." Most important for litigation, several states are mandated to create and support a "thorough and efficient" public school system (Hubsch 1992). As we shall see, the wording of the provision is not always crucial to judicial decision-making, but it often plays a role.

Ironically, the clauses that courts now employ against state legislatures initially boosted legislative power. When states first created full public school systems in the nineteenth century, many localities resisted the move, principally because they did not want to pay the taxes needed to support the systems. This issue took on added significance in the 1930s when the Depression caused local tax systems to break down. States attempted to ameliorate some of the most extreme disparities by instituting "foundation plans," which established a minimum state-supported funding level. Many of the wealthier districts complained because they believed it to be unconstitutional for property taxes raised from one district to be used to support the children of another. State courts nearly always rejected these arguments (Wise 1967). The Tennessee Supreme Court spoke for most in 1927 when it said:

> The public school system is a matter of state, and not local concern, and the establishment, maintenance, and control of the public schools is a legislative function . . . The exercise of the taxing power to promote a system of public schools for all the counties does not infringe upon the right of local self-government, because a public school system, like a highway system, a penal system, or a matter of public health is not purely local, but of state, concern. The state is a unit, and the Legislature is the state's source of legislative power, from which flows the mandate of the state. (*State v. Meador* 1926:891)

The education clauses provided strong support for such decisions. These clauses were nearly forgotten, however, in the intervening years until the early 1970s. After *Rodriguez*, the advocates for poor districts decided to employ these clauses, coupled with state equal protection clauses, as strong evidence of the importance of education in each state and as evidence that each state was obligated to provide education equally. The first successful use of a state education clause argument came only two weeks after *Rodriguez*, in *Robinson v. Cahill* (1973) in New Jersey.

Article VIII, Section 4 of the New Jersey constitution begins: "The legislature shall provide for the maintenance and support of a thorough and efficient system of free public schools for the instruction of all the children in the State between the ages of five and eighteen years." The Supreme Court of New Jersey, at the time an activist court, ruled unanimously that this clause required the legislature to provide education on an equal basis to all schoolchildren in the state. For lack of better standards, this meant that dollar input per child must be equalized. This did not mean that the legislature could not rely on local school districts and the property tax. Nevertheless, "The obligation being the State's to maintain and support a thorough and efficient system of free public schools, the State must meet that obligation itself or if it chooses to enlist local government it must do so in terms which will fulfill that obligation" (*Robinson* 1973:292).

Unfortunately, the state legislature did not act. After two intervening legal actions, *Robinson v. Cahill* (IV:1975) returned to the New Jersey Supreme Court on the question of remedy. The Court refused to delineate systemwide changes, but in the interests of equity ordered a slight redistribution of state appropriations for education in the next school year from richer districts to poorer districts. Defending its action from the claim of the dissent that it was invading legislative taxing and spending power, the Court reasoned that the money was already appropriated for education, and that the Court was not requiring more money be spent. Besides, the people of New Jersey had an interest in maintaining a constitutional system over an unconstitutional one. The court's remedy got the legislature's attention: the next legislative session produced an act providing relief from the worst disparities, a law that the Supreme Court pronounced constitutional in *Robinson v. Cahill* (V:1976). The consensus of the majority was that the bill was as good as the Court would get from the legislature.

Even though the New Jersey court declared the school funding system unconstitutional on the basis of the state education clause, this was not the most common constitutional grounds for a pro-plaintiff ruling. Reformers and judges were still more familiar with equal protection jurisprudence than any independent reading of the state education clause. Therefore, in the early period of litigation from 1971 to 1989, when supreme courts in California (1977), Arkansas (1983), Connecticut (1977), and Wyoming (1980) all voided their state's school funding systems, their rulings were based on equal protection grounds. Only the New Jersey (1973) and Washington (1978) supreme courts used the education clauses; the West Virginia Supreme Court (1979) relied on both clauses. This history should not give the impression that all state courts accepted the arguments of the forces of equality, for local control was compelling for a majority of state courts. From the early 1970s to 1989, supreme courts in Arizona (1973), Colorado (1982), Georgia (1981), Idaho (1975), Illinois (1973), Maryland (1983), New York (1982), North Carolina (1987), Ohio (1979), Oklahoma (1987), Oregon (1976), Pennsylvania (1979), South Carolina (1988), and Wisconsin (1989) all upheld the legality of the challenged systems. It should be noted that legislatures and courts across the nation did (and do) pay close attention to one another. Most state courts deciding a school finance case cited decisions from other states justifying their own reasoning.

Two of these cases deserve special mention. In *Hornbeck v. Somerset County Board of Education*, the dissent pointed out a reason why other state courts, unlike the Court of Appeals, the highest Maryland court, might be reluctant to declare education a "fundamental right," even on the state level. Many state constitutions contain references to more trivial matters that could have been left up to statutes. A decision for the fundamentality of education could have led to the argument that these other provisions were fundamental also. For example, the New York Constitution provides that "the lands of the state, now owned or hereafter acquired, constituting the forest preserve as now fixed by law, shall be forever kept as wild forest lands." No one but the most extreme environmentalists would claim that that creates a "right to forestation" in New York. Similarly, the Colorado Constitution requires that the legislature provide for the proper ventilation of mines, and the Oregon Constitution charges the legislature with allowing the sale of liquor by the drink. Few would consider these provisions "fundamental."

The other notable pro-local control decision came from Oklahoma. The Oklahoma Supreme Court ruling in *Fair School Finance Council v. State* was not surprising, considering the conservative politics of the state and that the Oklahoma Constitution provides only for "a system of public schools." What was unusual was the court's deference to the state legislature. The decision observed the above-mentioned fact that many state constitutions contain matters of a statutory nature. Accordingly, it rejected the *Rodriguez* formulation of "explicit or implicit" fundamental rights, because the document itself gave no clue as to what is fundamental. This is in contrast to the U.S. Constitution, in which all provisions are supposedly important and the government is limited to the powers granted in the document. The Oklahoma legislature (like all other state legislatures), on the other hand, is not so limited: it may do whatever the state constitution does not *prohibit* it from doing. The Court thus declined to question the wisdom of the legislature.

The "Third Wave": 1989 to the Present: Equity, Adequacy, Thoroughness, and Efficiency

These strongly worded decisions in favor of judicial restraint could have led one to believe that the issue of equality in school finance had subsided. But the supreme courts of Kentucky (1989), Texas (1989), Montana (1989), and New Jersey (1990) proved this theory wrong. Factors such as large disparities, fairly activist courts, and favorable constitutional provisions spurred the highest courts in all four states to strike down the systems. The decisions, however, represented shifts from the previous rulings declaring funding systems unconstitutional in two related ways.

First, all four courts cited the state education clause, not the equal protection clause, as the reason behind their verdicts. The

Texas (see chapter 3) and Montana rulings were the most notable
in this regard, because even though both courts focused on per-pupil
funding disparities, these inequities were used to justify findings of
constitutional "inefficiency" (Texas) or denial of "equal educational
opportunity" (Montana), not violations of the state equal protection
clauses. State education clauses are often more popular with state
courts as grounds for decision in public school finance cases for two
reasons. First, employing the education clause clarifies the issue of
"adequate and independent state grounds" necessary to insulate the
decision from U.S. Supreme Court review (*Michigan v. Long* 1983).

Relying on the state equal protection clause raises the question of why the state court's finding would be different from that of
the U.S. Supreme Court in *Rodriguez*. The state court would have
to contradict the federal court or devise some completely new way
of interpreting the state equal protection clause. Neither option
sounds appealing. Second, reliance on the state education clause
limits the potential scope of the ruling (although see the Maryland
court's reasoning above). A finding of unconstitutionality in a school
finance case applies only to education, not any other area. If the ruling were based on the equal protection clause, by contrast, the
state court would have to justify why education has to be provided
equally statewide and not other important government services,
such as police and fire protection. The court likely would have to
declare education to be a fundamental right or wealth to be a suspect classification, either of which could lead to unanticipated negative consequences (McUsic 1991).

The second notable development in the 1989 and 1990 cases,
related to the first, was that arguments shifted from a sole focus
on fiscal equity between districts to a discussion of "adequacy," or
educational quality, regardless of the level of funding (Minorini and
Sugarman 1999b). The Kentucky Supreme Court in particular
employed this line of reasoning, although the New Jersey Supreme
Court (in its second round of litigation) took significant steps in
this direction as well. To quote the New Jersey court, "(The) clear
import is not of a constitutional mandate governing expenditures
per pupil, equal or otherwise, but a requirement of a specific substantive level of education" (*Abbott* 1990:368). The court's educational quality approach echoes the first concept mentioned in this
chapter, the plaintiffs' claim in *McInnis* that funding and schooling
generally must be based on "educational need." "The inadequacy of
poorer urban students' present education measured against their
needs is glaring. . . . They are getting the least education for the

greatest need," the New Jersey tribunal declared (*Abbott* 1990:366). "We find that under the present system the evidence compels but one conclusion: the poorer the district and the greater its need, the less the money available, and the worse the education" (*Abbott* 1990:363). The concept of "educational need" thus had come full circle. It started out under the equal protection clause of the Fourteenth Amendment, was rejected and discredited for over twenty years, and now reappeared under a state education clause.

The Kentucky court voided not just the school financing system, but the entire state educational structure (see chapter 4), ruling that the state constitutional mandate in the education clause of "efficiency" required both equity and adequacy standards. The court then promulgated a long list of these constitutional demands, including goals for all graduates of the Kentucky public school system. The shift in focus from equity to adequacy in part stemmed from reliance on the state education clauses, which can be much more easily read to set minimum educational standards than to require a specific level of district-to-district equity. Perhaps more important, the debates in the wider education policy arena had changed by 1989. Unlike in the 1970s, policymakers had reduced faith that rapid infusions of money alone would solve the problems of underperforming school districts. The problems in these schools began to be attributed to a combination of factors, of which money was only one. Publication in 1983 of the federal report *A Nation At Risk* highlighted the mediocre to poor education that many children were receiving even with adequate funding (National Commission . . . 1983). As the debates changed, the court decisions followed.

Since the "third wave" began, results from litigation vary substantially. In Massachusetts (1993), the state supreme court issued a comprehensive ruling similar to those in Kentucky and New Jersey, although it applied only to the school funding system before a sweeping reform law passed days before the ruling. The New Jersey Supreme Court in 1994 voided its state's financing mechanism for a third time, yet granted the legislature three more years to come up with an acceptable solution. When Governor Christine Todd Whitman persuaded the legislature to enact a bill setting statewide education goals but without funding, the court voided that plan as well (1997). However, the Supreme Court remanded the case to the trial court for development of a remedy. The state commissioner of education, a special master, and the plaintiff parties all made suggestions, many of which were adopted by the trial judge, who attempted to define a set of programs that would bring the state into constitutional compliance. On appeal, the Supreme Court (1998) basically accepted this set of reforms as constituting constitutionality. It then relinquished jurisdiction over the case, trusting in the good faith of the education commissioner and the state legislature.

Supreme courts in Tennessee (1993), Arizona (1994, 1997, 1998), Wyoming (1995), New Hampshire (1997, 1998, 1999), Vermont (1997), and Ohio (1997, 2000) also declared their state's funding systems unconstitutional. Generally, these decisions were not as far-reaching as in Kentucky or New Jersey. These courts left the promulgation of a solution to the legislative and executive branches, although the Arizona court was willing to make suggestions to the politicians. Results of this strategy have varied. The typical legislative response has been moderate, including a funding increase, but not fundamental change. In Tennessee, for example, the legislature appropriated over one billion dollars through a state sales tax increase to plaintiff rural districts. However, teacher pay differences are still present, and overall spending is still low by national standards (*Commercial Appeal* 1998).

The Kansas Supreme Court (1994) rejected a constitutional challenge by wealthier districts to a law redistributing funds, although the court itself did not require the law. In Wyoming (1995), the legislature appropriated some new money for the larger plaintiff school districts, but also redistributed some funds from wealthy and rural districts, leading to a countersuit yet to be resolved (Associated Press 1999). In Alabama (1997), the Supreme Court did not itself void the state's school funding system, but it upheld a far-reaching trial court declaration of unconstitutionality that the state's political leadership failed to appeal in a timely fashion.

The Arizona Supreme Court's ruling only applied to facilities funding, not operating expenses. The legislature and governor, after much wrangling, appropriated $400 million to bring the poorer districts' buildings up to par, an amount that initially satisfied these districts, although now a plaintiff lawyer alleges the legislature has fallen a bit short of its promise (Mattern 1999). In Ohio, the legislature also appropriated more money to poorer districts, but did not significantly restructure the tax system to lessen reliance on local property taxes. This reluctance to reduce the role of local property taxes led the state supreme court to void the funding system a second time. Consistent with the increased focus on adequacy, the Court also noted the lack of clear statewide standards regarding student learning expectations. It is unclear as yet how the legislature and governor will respond to the court decision. In New Hampshire, the legislature created a new statewide property tax designed to equalize school funding. However, both poor and wealthy districts are now suing the state due to perceived unfairness (DiStaso 1999).

The state that arguably did the most to comply with a court declaration of unconstitutionality was Vermont. Act 60 set a minimum foundation of spending for each district, but allowed districts to tax themselves to spend more than the minimum. However, any district that wanted to spend extra money through additional taxation, whether rich or poor, will receive the same yield per additional mill of tax. Rich districts could tax beyond the minimum, but any "excess" yield beyond the state-set yield will be redistributed to boost the lower yield/mill of poor districts who choose to levy additional taxes. In other words, every district was treated as having an identically valuable tax base for purposes of choosing the local property tax rate.

Poor district plaintiffs were not successful everywhere. State supreme courts in Alaska (1997), Florida (1996), Idaho (1993), Illinois (1996), Minnesota (1993), Nebraska (1993), New York (1995), North Carolina (1997), North Dakota (1994, although see chapter 5), Oregon (1991), Rhode Island (1995), Virginia (1994), and Wisconsin (2000) turned down plaintiff claims of unconstitutionality, arguing that the state was meeting its legal obligations. Virtually no regional patterns appear in these or the earlier decisions, although the core states of the old Confederacy have yet to see a supreme court declaration of unconstitutionality (Maryland, Virginia, the Carolinas, Florida, Georgia, Alabama [but see above], Mississippi, Louisiana).

Therefore, it is difficult to say what the future holds for education finance litigation. The shift from equity issues to adequacy questions likely will continue as research and debate progress concerning appropriate educational goals for children.[4] One should not expect too many unifying themes, however; litigation results have varied considerably from state to state, with varied consequences for the funding systems involved. It is thus appropriate to shift to a discussion of more in-depth research into the fruits of going to court on school finance inequity, and any role the judiciary might play in its reform.

Research on Judicial Involvement in School Funding Issues: The State of the Discipline

The complex nature of school finance equity battles and their importance for state government provide fertile material for academic studies of state politics. In addition, the intervention of the judicial branch into many of these disputes has drawn in many scholars of judicial politics who would like to see whether courts are more or less effective on the state level than on the federal level concerning an issue of this complexity and highly political nature. I shall now attempt to summarize much of the work that has been done in the last twenty years or so, most of it postdating the *Rodriguez* decision in 1973. Academic research on court involvement in school funding equity issues tends to fall into one of three groups: a nationwide overview, a single case study, or a multiple case study, often involving three states. As with many other areas of political science scholarship, the methodological approach tends to affect the results, although there is a wide variation of findings even within each of the three groups noted above.

National Overviews

Presenting national overviews of judicial involvement in school funding issues is at once simple and difficult. It is simple in that the limited number of units of analysis (that is, the fifty states) allows for ease of presentation. One can fairly quickly classify states for purposes of one's argument or calculate a fifty-state table regarding specific issues, such as state share of spending or total state plus local revenue for the average district in each state—for example (Anthony and Hickrod 1993). On the other hand, if one wants to make comparisons that are scientifically valid between groups of states, such as states where the supreme court has voided the school funding system and states where an unfavorable ruling or no decision has been rendered—the methodological issues become much more difficult. The limited number of states then becomes a real problem, as it is nearly impossible to meet the usual ninety-five percent confidence test for statistical significance using any kind of comparison. Furthermore, full data on the extent of funding disparities in each state are often hard to come by, especially if one wants to analyze over an extended period. Other methodological problems arise, as noted below, depending upon the question one asks.

Scholars have dealt with these issues in two ways. One set of research does not attempt to test hypotheses and run regressions; rather, the more impressionistic approach suffices, at least for a journal article. This is not to say that these articles do not provide useful information: they often do present plausible arguments and good syntheses of experience across the fifty states. However, the limitations of this approach are fairly clear. These types of qualitative national overviews are often sanguine about the effects of judicial involvement in public school funding issues, although this is not always the case (e.g., Note 1991). On the pessimistic side, Verstegen (1994) argued that the education reform movement of the 1980s produced more money in some states, but that there were no gains in equity between districts and that disparities among states themselves were exacerbated. Similarly, Ward (1990) claimed that the elite-driven nature of school finance reform had led to a gap between legal reform goals of "fiscal neutrality" between districts and substantive goals of improved educational outcomes for children, which he argued were not being met despite the reform movement.

On a more optimistic note for legal reformers, Susan Fuhrman (1982) argued that even though the school finance litigation of the 1970s did not always produce legal victories, it greatly aided the cause of equity reform by putting the funding issue on the legislative agenda in most states and persuading legislatures to take preemptive action in twenty-eight states to avoid a lawsuit. The national reform network aided in this regard by disseminating information in each state. Similarly, Camp and Thompson claimed that "courts exercise a powerful force in stimulating change" not least because of anticipatory action by legislatures (Camp and Thompson 1988: 237). More recently, Odden and Clune (1998) assert that over the last twenty years, even though change has been slow, "the most substantial progress was made when courts insisted on greater equalization" (Odden and Clune 1998:159). Specifically regarding states whose supreme court declared the funding systems unconstitutional, Salmon and Alexander (1990) found that in all these states, major structural changes to the funding formulas occurred. Total spending on education did not necessarily rise, yet its distribution, not only among districts but between state aid and local taxes, changed significantly. On the other hand, in the states where the funding system was upheld by the supreme court, few structural changes were made, although funding increased in some of those states.

The most in-depth of these national overviews is perhaps Charles Smith's (1994) work on state supreme court influence on legislative policymaking. Smith discussed three policy issue areas: school finance, right to die, and right of counsel for indigent criminal defendants. He employed some quantitative analysis, but nothing more complicated than a chi-square test, and usually relied on simple comparisons of raw percentages of states falling into one category or another. He supplemented this data by interviewing on the record sixteen policymakers across four states: Arkansas, Texas, Kentucky, and West Virginia. Smith concluded that of the three issue areas, legislators were much more likely to respond to a state supreme court decision on school finance than right to die or provision of counsel.

Smith argued that the two major reasons for the effectiveness of courts in school finance were, first, the overall importance of the issue for state government in terms of education, budgeting, and taxation, and second, the higher visibility of school finance. Smith supported this conclusion through analysis of newspaper coverage in each state. A court order concerning school finance was much more likely to get prominent newspaper coverage than rulings concerning the other two issues. This coverage in turn might lead legislators to take more notice of the issue and to feel more pressure to solve the problem.

If the qualitative national overviews were often positive in their assessments of the effectiveness of courts in producing school finance reform, quantitative national studies were more ambiguous in their conclusions. Of course, these studies had to cope with the problems noted above of small sample size and limited data. For example, Bundt (1995) regressed a number of variables, including the presence of a court decision voiding the school funding system, on the coefficient of variation of district expenditures in each state and found that the presence of a pro-plaintiff court decision did not have a significant effect on the extent of disparities. The presence or absence of divided government in the state had a much greater effect on the disparities.

These findings, however, are significantly limited in at least two ways. First, Bundt examined these states only at one point in time (apparently 1982), even though several court decisions occurred well before and after that time. Second, in a related vein, there is no measure of the disparities before the lawsuit in each state. It could be that courts are more willing to void school funding systems in states where disparities are initially greater, and less likely to void where disparities are smaller, yet the work does not account for that possibility (but see Van Geel 1982).

But quantitative studies that support judicial effectiveness in producing finance reform also are limited. For example, Hickrod et al. (1992) divided states into eight categories depending upon the presence and outcome of litigation. The authors then calculated both the change in total state plus local revenue for each state in 1970 and 1990, and the change in the state share of total school spending from 1970 to 1990, assuming that an increased state share will signify greater equity, a generally plausible hypothesis. Finally, they then compared the states in each of the litigation groups with the 1970 and 1990 data. They concluded that the presence of a court case, regardless of the outcome, significantly increased both the total spending in each state and the state share as well. Winning the court case did not seem to affect total revenue; it did slightly increase the relative state share, though. In other words, going to court was the big decision and winning was just the icing on the cake. Although these findings are quite interesting, they are suspect. Like Bundt, Hickrod et al. are using very blunt instruments for their dependent and independent variables. Only examining total revenue and state share in two somewhat arbitrary years, 1970 and 1990, and not accounting for the timing of litigation in each state, might well lead to skewed results. Moreover, they have not really isolated the effects of litigation from any other factors in these states, as a more comprehensive regression equation might have done (Heise 1995).

Probably the most sophisticated quantitative study of judicial effectiveness on school funding equity issues was done by Evans, Murray, and Schwab (1997, 1999). These authors examined school finance data over the entire period from 1972 to 1992 from more than ten thousand school districts. Unlike many other studies, the Evans et al. work controlled for the timing of the court decision in each state in order to measure temporal causality, comparing equity both before and after the decision. They argued that court declarations of unconstitutionality had improved equity more than legislative reforms not spurred by a court ruling. As the authors admitted, however, reform in one state is quite different than reform in another. Even though these national overview data are useful, they cannot capture the dynamics within each state to explain not just what happened, but why.

Single Case-Studies

Many scholars have attempted to avoid the problems of national overviews by focusing in-depth on single case-study states to track the effect of courts on school funding. Researchers of single-case studies have found widely varying results over time, depending in large part upon the state chosen, but also on the methods employed, even when focusing on the same state. Single-case studies are more likely to be booklength than national overviews, although there are exceptions noted below. I shall summarize the work done in each state in the rough chronological order of the state supreme court decisions issued.

As noted in this chapter, the California Supreme Court in *Serrano v. Priest* (1971) became the first high court in the nation to declare a state school finance system unconstitutionally unequal. After the U.S. Supreme Court decided *Rodriguez*, the case was remanded to the state court, which voided the finance system again, this time on state equal protection grounds. The legislature was then forced to take action to meet the court's demands. The California battles are the subject of Richard Elmore and Milbrey MacLaughlin's book *Reform and Retrenchment* (1982). The authors argue in a richly detailed study of not only the legal battles, but also the intricate political maneuvering between the legislature, the governor, the executive bureaucracy, and education interest groups that the supreme court played an important role in the reform process by firmly placing the school finance issue on the policy agenda. Policymakers felt that after the court decision, they could not ignore the issue any longer. Still, the California court was remarkably unhelpful, according to the authors, in aiding legislators in constructing a solution. The court required a constitutional standard of "fiscal neutrality," meaning that property wealth should not play a role in the amount of money available for a child's education. This was a relatively simple legal standard, but devilishly difficult as a practical matter, especially given the complex politics of school finance. In fact, some of the original plaintiffs, mostly minority-majority large urban districts, left the suit when it became clear that the "fiscal neutrality" standard would actually *decrease* their revenues from the state. This fracturing of the reform coalition meant that the court had no natural constituency for its opinion, which limited its effectiveness in guiding a solution. Faced with a choice of politically unpalatable options, legislators decided to make some progress toward equity and hope that the court would accept it as enough, which the court eventually did.

In California we see a court that can set the policy agenda, but cannot follow through to a solution, in part because of the opinion itself. Nonetheless, one should not underestimate the effects of the *Serrano* case on California school finance. Work done after Elmore and MacLaughlin's book found that California's funding system was one of the most equal in the nation, but at a low level for all districts ("equalized mediocrity"), owing to a combination of *Serrano*'s equity mandates and the Proposition 13 property tax cap, which severely limited local revenues (Silva and Sonstelie 1995, but see Minorini and Sugarman 1999a).

Richard Lehne, in his book *The Quest for Justice* (1978), justifiably the single most commonly cited case study in this area, examined the other early ground-breaking school finance court decision, the New Jersey Supreme Court's voiding of the funding system in *Robinson v. Cahill* (1973). As noted, the Court and the legislature then began a dialogue that ended only after the Court threatened to enjoin funds to public schools, effectively closing them. The legislature finally acquiesced, passing a reform package, although not a far-reaching restructuring by any means. Like Elmore and MacLaughlin, Lehne argued that the Court was much more effective at setting the agenda of the political branches than it was in crafting solutions to the school finance problems. Turnover and inexperience in all three branches were impediments. The Court's intervention made debates more ambiguous, as the Court did not want to construct a solution itself. On the other hand, Lehne argued, judicial participation gave the funding equity issues much more persistence, immediacy, legitimacy, and visibility than they would have had otherwise. Groups that had never been part of the legislative process had a voice in deliberations.

Regarding the funding issue itself, school aid increased substantially, but it was on an upward trend before the Court ruling. Lehne assessed that the Court decision produced slightly more equity than would have otherwise occurred, perhaps as much as seven percent, which may not seem like a lot but could make a difference for the poorest districts. Later studies, however, were not that optimistic regarding the extent of New Jersey's funding reforms in the 1970s (Mintrom 1993; Harrison and Tarr 1995). In addition, though, Lehne maintained that if one wanted to assess the effects of judicial participation, one had to go beyond the confines of the specific policy issue to examine the broader institutional effects of court intervention. For example, he argued that the Court decision decreased public support for the New Jersey legislature, which was seen as incompetent and backward during the school finance battles, but increased the legislature's real capacity by giving responsibility to lawmakers to solve a problem traditionally handled by the governor. Regarding the Court itself, according to Lehne, it gained greater appreciation of its limits in setting policy and made it warier of accepting "public law" cases. These institutional effects might be "good" or "bad" depending upon one's perspective, but certainly should be noted.

The experience of Washington state with court-ordered school finance reform also showed mixed results. The state supreme court upheld the funding system as constitutional in 1974, only to reverse itself four years later. Legislators had already been working on the finance issue in response to the trial court decision voiding the system and passed a reform law before the supreme court ruled on the validity of the previous system. One study concluded that legislators responded to the courts because the courts were telling them what they knew already, but did not have the political will to carry out without the impetus of a court decision (Gale 1981). Therefore, the state supreme court was effective in persuading the legislature (also see Darling 1998). But another study found that the Washington reform law passed in response to the court produced California-like equalized mediocrity, with large urban plaintiff districts benefiting little from the lawsuit (Theobald and Hanna 1991).

The West Virginia experience with court-ordered school finance reform was also mixed at best. The state supreme court declared the funding system unconstitutionally unequal and "inefficient" in 1979, then remanded the case to the trial judge, who appointed a three-hundred member advisory commission representing a broad range of perspectives to construct a solution. As might be expected, the commission's recommendations were delayed, overlong, and somewhat contradictory, not giving legislators much guidance. Inertia largely prevailed, as the supreme court did not retake authority in this area. The legislature made some changes partly in response to the Court, but certainly nothing close to far-reaching reform (Shank 1995; Sites and Salmon 1992).

Single case-studies of the "second wave" of school finance litigation after *Rodriguez* and before the "third wave" of 1989 presented a mixed picture for court effectiveness. Courts in these cases were able to put school finance reform on the policy agenda, except perhaps in West Virginia. In some of these states, the reforms passed produced some equalization, as in California and Washington, although with unforeseen drawbacks ("equalized mediocrity"). Full compliance was not uniform, as in New Jersey and West Virginia. On the other hand, the courts themselves could shoulder some of the blame for their ineffectiveness because of their inability to give the legislatures adequate guidance and political backing to make the necessary changes.

Regarding single case-studies of "third wave" decisions, New Jersey has been studied the most. Numerous academic works focused on the Quality Education Act (QEA) initiated by then-Governor James Florio and passed by the legislature in response to *Abbott v. Burke* (1989). The QEA raised taxes substantially in order to increase funding in the twenty-eight poorest urban districts that were the subject of the court's ruling. However, due to strong public opposition to the tax increases, the QEA was amended to decrease costs by abolishing a minimum spending level for each district, and a system of counting students in special needs districts more often for state aid purposes. Some authors have argued that the QEA made little progress toward equity (Harrison and Tarr 1995; Gernant 1992; Skolnick 1993; Goertz 1998). However, this opinion is not unanimous (Jaffe and Kersch 1991). There have been fewer studies done on the effectiveness of the more recent CEIFA act passed by the legislature, and so it is more difficult to judge court success in advancing equity.

Another "third wave" state is Alabama. As Hershkoff (1998) outlined, poor district plaintiffs, backed by a business-led reform movement, succeeded at the trial court level. The trial judge issued a comprehensive order similar to the one promulgated by the Kentucky Supreme Court. In a strange twist of events, however, the state missed the deadline for appeal, therefore finalizing the decision. Due to opposition from the state teachers' union, a no-new-taxes governor, and a recalcitrant legislature, though, very little has changed in response to the court order (Augenblick 1999). Ironically, the lack of an authoritative ruling from the state supreme court may have weakened the legitimacy of the court's ruling, especially since its author, the trial judge, later used his opinion in support of an unsuccessful campaign for higher office, and subsequently was forced to recuse himself from further proceedings due to this politicking.

The only other major single-case "third wave" study came from Kansas. By contrast, this experience with judicially led school finance reform has been more positive, at least for supporters of equalization. After low-wealth districts filed a suit, the trial judge convened a meeting of the state's top political leaders, including the governor and key legislators. At the meeting the judge outlined the principles he was going to use in deciding the case, strongly hinting to the politicians that if changes were not made, he would declare the system unconstitutional. After much wrangling, the legislature passed and the governor signed an extremely strong equalization law that effectively capped the wealth of the richest districts in the state (Tallman 1993). Subsequently, the state supreme court turned aside a suit from wealthy districts that would lose under the law (*Unified School District ... 1994*).

It appears that policymakers pay attention to courts, but the strength and direction of their response is hardly uniform (also see the "third wave" litigation history earlier in this chapter). What factors contribute to judicial success or failure in this area? Are there commonalities among cases? Single-case studies can suggest answers, yet often cannot transcend their particular circumstances. Generalizability would be increased by incorporating more cases, and avoiding the traps of the nationwide surveys. Multiple case studies offer a solution (Ragin 1987).

Multiple Case Studies

Perhaps surprisingly, given the potential utility in examining theories of judicial effectiveness in school finance intervention, there has not been a flood of multiple case studies in this area. There have been some, however.

Regarding the time before the "third wave" in 1989, two studies stand out. First, Peggy Siegel (1976) examined four upper midwestern states that enacted school funding reforms soon after *Serrano*, although none were under a court order. She found certain similarities in the reform process across these states, including the perceived threat of litigation as a means of publicizing the issue and getting it on the legislative agenda (also see Fuhrman 1979). Beyond threatened lawsuits, the rise in the costs of education and concomitant increases in local property taxes demanded attention. In all four states, governors and key legislators took the lead in constructing a solution, with relatively little input from educational interests (as in Kentucky in 1990—see chapter 4). Therefore, a combination of actors and circumstances, including the courts, led to reform. Michael Heise's study (1995) of the long-term effects of judicial intervention was not quite as sanguine in its conclusions concerning court effectiveness. Heise looked at the two states, Wyoming and Connecticut, that met his selection criteria, including the presence of a supreme court declaration of unconstitutionality, the absence of further litigation modifying the order, and the accumulation of at least ten years of postdecision data to assess compliance. He found that the court orders did not seem to have appreciably increased total state spending on education in either state in any consistent way, although he did not measure distribution.

Once more, we see mixed results. Issues of case selection, time period, and measures of court effectiveness all come into play. The final studies this section will examine come closest to my particular method of resolving these issues. First, John Dinan (1996) examined the experience of courts in Texas, Kentucky, and New Jersey in interacting with the political branches. Dinan tested the model of court intervention that hypothesized that courts can be effective when they strongly articulate a clear remedy to constitutional violations, closely monitor the political response, and aggressively enforce their rulings (Dinan 1996:431) (Unfortunately, he did not as fully address the alternative hypothesis from Horowitz, Rosenberg, and others, that courts cannot be effective *no matter* their role [to generalize]). Combining analysis of the decisions, newspaper coverage, and academic articles, he concluded that courts can be effective in producing change, but only when the general public and at least one of the political branches already support the goals of the decision and when the court gives the legislature enough flexibility to construct an acceptable method of achieving the court's aims. In other words, Dinan was more optimistic than Rosenberg concerning court effectiveness, but not by a large amount.

Douglas Reed (1995) presented a stronger case for court success in his study of judicial intervention into school finance policy in Texas, New Jersey, and Connecticut. Using in-depth case studies relying on extensive policy data and newspaper articles, he found that courts can make a difference in pushing for reform. Although Reed noted that the wording of the constitutional clauses at issue did not seem to make a difference to the legislative responses, he claimed:

> But does this mean that the decisions judges write do not matter to the policy-making process? . . . Two factors seem to argue against this view of the significance of jurisprudence. First, newspapers and legislative debates record numerous occasions on which legislators refer directly to specific passages of court decisions. . . . Second, and in a related fashion, we can see within the programmatic elements of a school finance reform bill concepts developed and advanced by either trial court judges or state supreme court justices. That is, we see judicial priorities expressed in the legislative product.
>
> . . . From my examination of the stages of school finance reform, it becomes clear that state supreme courts do more than strike down an existing system; they sketch outlines of major policy

features of the new systems. That is, state supreme courts can set policy parameters that will be, most likely, very closely followed. Courts have tremendous agenda-setting powers, powers that result in their own judicial priorities finding their way into legislative enactments. Within these priorities, however, different reforms create different political and economic winners and losers. My findings do not indicate that state supreme courts are in any position to dictate these outcomes, but they do provide legislatures with blueprints for the construction of new school finance plans. . . .

Rosenberg and others have argued that the courts cannot effect meaningful social and political change unless they have substantial backing and support of other branches of government. My study indicates that is not true—at least not within the realm of school finance equalization. Although it certainly helps, institutional cooperation is not necessary for the courts to alter the distribution of educational resources. The judiciary—when it wishes to be—is an effective agenda-setter that can structure political conflicts in order to maximize its institutional strengths. By forcing legislatures to directly confront the problems of equity in school finance, state supreme courts have delivered significant resources to students who would not have otherwise had them. That is significant social change. (Reed 1995:340–42, 352)

In a more recent work, Reed (1998) again found significant social change due to court intervention. He examined the distribution of education funds in eight states, five of which had experienced court orders and three which had not, and concluded that the presence of the court ruling led to a more equal allocation. In his concluding section, he sketched out a model of judicial capacity to effect change, featuring three factors: voter sentiment, interest group pressures, and judicial scope or effectiveness. Reed's model is useful, and I test for the presence of each of these factors, along with several others, in the case study chapters.

Research Approach and Methodology

Like Dinan and Reed, I will attempt to assess court effectiveness in contributing to school finance reform in the states. Also like these authors, I will employ a multiple case-study approach.

The multiple case-study possesses its own advantages and drawbacks, both of which can be inferred from what it is not, a national overview or a single case-study. Regarding the benefits, the multiple case study is more generalizable than the single case-study, as the researcher is more free to explore alternative ways in which the process at issue unfolds. The multiple case-study can also be more useful than the national overview or comprehensive quantitative study in that it provides more depth and insight into highly complex and variable processes that raw aggregate data might not capture, which is especially true in the case of school finance reform. Those who employ this approach will always be vulnerable to the charges of qualitative and quantitative scholars that they have sacrificed the advantages of the single case-study and the national overview without corresponding benefits. It is true that the multiple case-study cannot provide the depth of insight of a single case-study or the generalizability of a national overview. Therefore, one must have a specific rationale for choosing this particular approach that is closely linked to one's research question.

I attempted to answer this question: How successful can courts be in persuading policymakers to take action concerning public school finance reform? To answer it, the multiple case-study approach seems best. It now makes sense to continue the process that Dinan and Reed, among others, have started of generalizing the specific lessons from each state. Like Dinan and Reed, I examined the experience of three states with court-ordered school finance reform. This number of case studies was impelled partly because of practical limitations of time and resources, but I believe that if chosen carefully, it provides enough breadth of data to be instructive.

In selecting the three states, I had four main criteria. First, the supreme court decision had to have been issued in the "third wave" of cases in 1989 or later. This limitation made sense because I wanted to test whether the experience of the first two "waves" of cases had informed succeeding courts in devising their persuasive strategies. Also, choosing a case decided in 1989 or later allowed me to conduct a wide range of in-depth interviews with participants whose memories were still relatively fresh concerning the roles that each set of actors played in the school finance debates.

Second, the school finance litigation had to have concluded, at least on paper, although school finance debates in state legislatures, of course, are never-ending. This limitation was necessary because interviewees would be much less candid if they thought there was any possibility their statements could be used against them in ongoing litigation. Also, as in the Texas case (see chapter 3), one should not assess the effectiveness of litigation until the court is actually finished prodding the legislature to act, as the final result might be larger than the sum of its parts. (Note: at the time of selection, the New Jersey case was not finished.)

Third, I wanted to select states where there was not already a lot of scholarship concerning judicial intervention. This is not to downgrade the fine work done in Texas by Rocha and Webking (1993), Hobby and Walker (1991), and others, and in Kentucky by Ronald Dove (1991), and others. But I felt that I could add more depth and breadth of research to the stories there than I could to the work on a state such as New Jersey, which has been the subject of at least one book (Lehne 1978), three dissertations (Gernant 1992; Skolnick 1993; Lane 1994), and numerous journal articles, book chapters (Corcoran and Scovronick 1998; Goertz 1998) and conference papers. Readers are invited to compare my results with the conclusions drawn by these and other authors concerning other states, such as New Jersey, for a more complete picture of judicial intervention in this area, although I will make some comparisons in the concluding chapter.

Fourth, and most important, I wanted to select states where supreme courts had assumed a wide range of "roles" vis-à-vis the legislative and executive branches to test whether the positions and tactics that the courts used in their opinions made a difference in the political response to these decisions. If so, that would be powerful evidence that the courts do exert independent influence over the policy process and are not isolated, as some scholars would suggest (for example, Rosenberg 1991). Furthermore, I did not want to duplicate work by choosing case studies in which the courts had taken the same roles as earlier courts in different states. To be more specific, the California Supreme Court that Elmore and MacLaughlin examined and the New Jersey Supreme Court that Lehne analyzed issued decisions that negated the school finance system, but gave no guidance as to how to construct a new one. The conclusions that these authors reached were persuasive regarding the pros and cons of this particular judicial approach, and I did not want to replicate them with a more recent case in which a supreme court employed the same strategy (for example, Tennessee in 1993).

Given these criteria, there were only a few states among which to choose, but fortunately, they did provide a wide spectrum of judicial roles, ranging from strong judicial activism to clear judicial restraint (although see chapter 1). For an example of a state supreme court that assumed a prominent role in leading school finance reform, I chose the Kentucky Supreme Court, which in *Rose* voided not only the state school funding formula but the entire Kentucky public education system (see chapter 4).

Another state supreme court that played a major part in school finance debates was the Texas Supreme Court, although in a different manner. Instead of issuing one comprehensive order, the court handed down a series of rulings, "negotiating" with the political branches as to how much equality was required and by what means a constitutional funding system could be constructed (see chapter 3).

On the other end of the spectrum, I chose the North Dakota Supreme Court. This court failed to gain the super-majority of justices needed to void the state's school funding system, but the Chief Justice threatened a different outcome if legislature and governor did not act on their own to ameliorate the disparities (see chapter 5).

This case-study, then, will test whether a more restrained judicial role was more or less effective than the more up-front parts played by the Texas and Kentucky courts. (Note: these judicial roles are not necessarily unique to the states selected, giving this work greater generalizability. After completing research, I noted parallels between the Texas "negotiations" and debates in Arizona and Ohio, and the North Dakota Supreme Court's "threatening" decision and the ruling by the Florida Supreme Court [1996]).

Even given my choice of a multiple case-study, I had a wide range of options for data sources. Reed, for example, relied on a combination of quantitative analysis of voting patterns and finance disparities with qualitative measures such as news articles, floor debates, and statutory language in order to arrive at his conclusions concerning judicial effectiveness. My data sources included district-to-district finance data, newspaper articles, primary documents, and personal interviews, among others. Such a wide range of sources is necessary for "triangulation" of data, or approaching an event from multiple angles to best assess the full story. This triangulation is especially important in such a complex area as school finance politics, in which either reading newspapers or analyzing numbers by themselves could give misleading results.

The major original contribution this study makes to scholarship on judicial involvement in school funding debates is the collection of semistructured interviews with policymakers in each of the three case-study states. For each state, I first drew up a long list of potential interviewees gleaned from newspaper articles, other primary sources, and personal contacts with knowledgeable observers.

I was looking for people who had some influence over the policy choices the legislature made in response to the court ruling or who had a close view of the process. I also attempted to represent a wide range of institutional positions and a full spectrum of ideological viewpoints in my sample. The range of institutional positions included legislators, both leadership and rank-and-file (although leaders and members of the education committees were overrepresented), legislative staffers, supreme court justices, executive branch officials (including governors when possible), lawyers, journalists, and interest group leaders. Overall, thirty-one interviewees were legislators or their staffers (mostly lawmakers), eighteen were executive branch officials, eleven were judicial sources, twenty-five represented either interest groups or the plaintiff districts, and nine were other policymakers and observers not neatly classifiable. Given the sample size, not all groups and viewpoints were proportionally represented. When that bias is significant, I note it in the text.

About half the people on my initial list in each state eventually consented to an interview, either in person or by telephone. In the fall of 1995 and the spring of 1996, I conducted ninety-four interviews with various policymakers and observers: thirty-seven interviews in Texas, thirty-two in Kentucky, and twenty-five in North Dakota. The totals at least partially reflect the length of each state's school finance battles, as a longer battle involved more participants. Interview duration ranged from a low of ten minutes to a high of nearly three hours, with the bulk of interviews lasting from fifty to ninety minutes. I promised interviewees confidentiality of response, including their identities when possible, and of their answers in all cases, meaning that I would quote from the interview, but would not identify the speaker. This choice had advantages and drawbacks, although in the end I believe that the tradeoff was worthwhile. Such a procedure is certainly not unknown in political science; a check of my bookshelves reveals its use in John Kingdon's *Agendas, Alternatives, and Public Policies* (1984), Mark Peterson's *Legislating Together* (1990), and, on the judicial side, Michael McCann's *Rights at Work* (1994, especially pp. 18–21 and appendix 1), all well-respected and award-winning books.

The principal advantage to this approach was that it eased fear of retribution for any comments respondents might make and so increased their candor. This factor was especially important considering that most, if not all, of these participants had ongoing relationships with other actors that they would not wish to damage. In all three states I found a relatively small group of actors that made most of the major decisions, and who all knew each other. Furthermore, the questions I asked attempted to reconstruct a series of events and actions that participants took. Such accounts are quite open to dispute, especially because I also asked about motives and attitudes. Therefore, I felt confidentiality was necessary to achieve a useful amount of candor.

The drawbacks to this approach, of course, are, first, difficulty of replication, and second, lack of accountability of response (that is, how do I know the interviewees weren't lying to me?). Concerning replication, I feel confident that if other researchers looked at the same research question and traveled to these three states, they would essentially arrive at the same large interview list that I did and likely would get the same acceptances/rejections. (As noted, a relatively small and identifiable group of people made the important decisions.) Of course, interview answers by the same person to the same question (see appendices 1–3 for the standard list of questions for each state) could vary from interviewer to interviewer, but there is no real way to control for this.

Second, regarding the authenticity of interviewee responses, this is an issue in that these respondents, mostly experienced politicians, have an incentive to shade their answers toward their own point of view. There are two mitigating factors, however. First, the sample size from each state has been expanded as much as possible to include all who participated or closely observed the school funding debates. A variety of perspectives should be the best check on political "spinning." Second, some of the most important questions I asked did not necessarily lead to a partisan or self-interested response, such as "Would the legislature have acted anyway even without the court?" or "Did previous court orders influence the legislative response here?"

Now that I have explained the place of this project in the larger school finance literature and provided justification for my research methodology, I shall turn to the three case studies that form the heart of this work.

CHAPTER 3

∽

Texas: "We Want To Surrender, We Just Don't Know Where to Turn Ourselves In"

The Texas experience with court-ordered school finance reform will begin the case-study chapters. In 1989, in *Edgewood Independent School District v. Kirby*, the Texas Supreme Court began a long and winding journey toward the goal of equality of resources for the one-thousand-plus school districts in the state. The Court encountered many obstacles, including reluctant legislators and governors, public opinion that eventually turned hostile, and the justices' own missteps and second thoughts. For better or worse, the journey was prolonged by the Court's evolving role as a "negotiator" with the political branches. The Court and the legislature began a dialogue in 1989 that encompassed five decisions and three reform laws over a five-year period. This dialogue was prolonged enough for one observer to comment: "School finance in Texas is beginning to resemble a 19th century Russian novel. The story line runs across generations, the plot is complex, the prose is tedious, and everybody dies in the end" (Mark Yudof in Hobby and Yudof 1991).

However lengthy and arduous the process was, though, the result was a school finance system which, according to one prominent observer, is one of the most equal in the nation (Picus 1995). How was the Court able to achieve this outcome, and how much responsibility can the Court take for the funding system today? Was "negotiation" with the political branches the optimal means to gaining this reform? How was the Court able to overcome the difficulties of lengthy and costly institutional reform litigation?

Texas Public Education: From Statehood to *Edgewood*[1]

The history of Texas public education funding resembles that of many other American states, only more exaggerated, in keeping with Texas tradition. Texas today has over one thousand school districts, the most of any state, is second only to California in the number of children educated, and is third nationwide in total dollars spent on education. Until recently, the school finance system, although fairly equal for the majority of students, suffered from one of the widest gaps in school spending equalization in America between the very richest and very poorest school districts. The history of public education in Texas is characterized by numerous fits and starts, retrenchments, and promises that outstrip reality, along with slow progress toward statewide equalization of opportunity. The current constitution was adopted in 1875, although it since has been amended frequently. Its education article reads in part: "A general diffusion of knowledge being essential to the preservation of the liberties and rights of the people, it shall be the duty of the Legislature of the State to establish and make suitable provision for the support and maintenance of an efficient system of public free schools (Art.VII, Section 1)"—the provision that the Court used in 1989 to invalidate the school financing system in *Edgewood v. Kirby*.

This "system of public free schools" did not take full shape until 1909, when the legislature finally divided the entire state into districts. These districts were financed through local property taxes, but over the next twenty to thirty years, the legislature began to give certain qualifying districts supplementary aid for various reasons, such as extra costs for rural districts, textbooks, transportation, and the like. Districts not receiving the aid resented their exclusion, and so sued the state in two companion cases heard by the Court in 1931. The Court handed down two rulings that had large implications for the future. In *Mumme v. Marrs* (1931) it ruled that granting aid to "financially weak" districts was a constitutionally "suitable provision" by the legislature; equalization could continue. In *Love v. City of Dallas* (1931), however, the Court ruled that districts could not be forced to spend their own tax money to educate children not residing in the taxing district. The interpretation of this decision was at the root of much of the later acrimony and confusion between the legislature and Court during *Edgewood*.

By the end of World War II, Texas districts were fighting for their lives against the combination of expanding enrollments, increasing costs, and minimal state aid. A solution had to be found. Political leaders appointed a select committee, known as Gilmer-Aikin, whose most important recommendation was for a "foundation plan," setting a floor of per-pupil spending, regardless of district wealth, but allowing richer districts to supplement the base up to their desired level of spending. This plan, although a significant step forward from previous school funding methods, also suffered from the weakness that seems to plague all foundation plans: there is not enough incentive in the legislature to raise the foundation level over time as costs and enrollments rise. Texas fell into this same "trap" soon after it was adopted.

Since San Antonio was the first Texas city to have a free public school system, it is perhaps appropriate that the push for statewide equalization of funding should originate there as well. A lawsuit was filed in 1968 by Demetrio Rodriguez, a parent of four children in the poor Edgewood area of west San Antonio. Rodriguez sued his home district, the San Antonio Independent School District, for violating the Equal Protection Clause of the Fourteenth Amendment.[2] Rodriguez claimed that the system of financing schools unconstitutionally discriminated by wealth against students living in property-poor areas. Texas leaders were relieved by the eventual 5–4 U.S. Supreme Court decision in 1973 upholding the constitutionality of the school funding system (see chapter 2), but the narrowness of their escape put the issue on the political agenda. In each of the next three legislative sessions (the legislature meets every two years), Senate Education Committee chair (and later Justice) Oscar Mauzy spurred the legislature to raise the minimum foundation level and to target some extra aid to poorer districts. The 1975 law also created a "second tier" of funding, a "guaranteed yield" beyond the foundation level, that guaranteed some of the poorest districts a higher return per extra penny of tax effort than they otherwise would receive with their low tax base.

The funding increases were not enough to produce much equalization, however, as enrollments and costs increased over time. The legislature's commitment to reform also waned after the crisis of the *Rodriguez* litigation. An economic downturn due to a sharp drop in the price of oil in the early 1980s led to retrenchment on state spending in all policy areas, including education (Cortez 1998). Therefore, by the early 1980s, the poorest districts were convinced that it would take more court pressure for the legislature to make significant progress toward equalization. James Vasquez, who was superintendent of Edgewood Independent School District at the time of the new lawsuit, was quoted later as saying "We realized we would never have anything" (Rugeley 1991a). This legal effort would have to be more sophisticated and inclusive than the *Rodriguez* litigation was, though, to be successful. In early 1984, the advocates were ready to begin. This was also an opportune time because a select commission, led by Texas billionaire H. Ross Perot, had been appointed a year earlier to look at education reform generally, not just school finance. It is unclear whether the preparations for the lawsuit influenced politicians to appoint the commission or vice versa, but the pressures for reform were mutually reinforcing.

The lawsuit was filed in the 250th District Court in Travis County, which contains Austin. Most cases against the state are heard in this court. There is some evidence that aside from convenience, the plaintiff groups were also "forum-shopping" to select Judge Harley Clark to hear the case, who they believed might be sympathetic. The lawsuit, named *Edgewood Independent School District v. Bynum*,[3] was nominally against the sitting state commissioner of education. The suit raised two main issues, both under the state constitution. First, the low-wealth districts argued that the school finance system was a violation of equal protection for students living in poor districts. Because of the participation of the Mexican-American Legal Defense and Education Fund (MALDEF), the plaintiffs made equal protection claims based both on wealth and on race. The second set of claims relied on the state education clause of 1875 requiring that the legislature construct a public school system that was "efficient."

At the time of the filing, the legislature was about to go into special session to deal with the recommendations of the Perot commission on education reform. The result was an act originally known as House Bill 72.[4] This law touched on nearly every aspect of public education. Nonfiscal issues, such as teacher testing, replacement of the elected state board of education with an appointed board, and the "no-pass, no-play" rule concerning extracurricular school activities dominated the bill (Hobby and Walker 1991). The school finance solutions contained in House Bill 72 put significantly more money into the same basic system. Partly due to the court suit, the Foundation School Program got a large boost of nearly a billion dollars in new money, and a promised five billion more over eight years.

Many of the state's leaders thought that with House Bill 72, they had "solved" the school finance problem, at least for a while, but the plaintiff groups were not so certain. They had put the lawsuit on hold while the legislature was working on the new law, and then waited to judge its effectiveness. However, House Bill 72 ultimately proved unacceptable to the low-wealth districts for a number of reasons. First, the act did not change the basic system of funding schools. Rich districts could still spend as much as they wanted, and poor districts were still far behind them with little hope of catching up. As one advocate said, "the tail would never catch the head." Second, the equalization gains made by in House Bill 72 were swallowed up quickly by mutually reinforcing state economic problems, including the oil bust, a huge drop in real estate values, and the savings-and-loan crisis (Hobby and Walker 1991). Poor districts were no better off than before the act, although without it, their situation would be even more desperate. Third, the legislature either could not or did not keep its promises to the low-wealth districts concerning continuing funding for House Bill 72 because of budget problems and resistance to tax increases (Cortez 1998).

The plaintiff groups decided to revive the lawsuit in 1985 to put pressure on the legislature in its regular session. When no further progress was made, the groups pushed ahead to trial on the claims of unconstitutionality. The trial before Clark did not officially begin until early 1987, though, when the lack of success of House Bill 72 in satisfying the poor school districts became fully apparent. Although the plaintiff districts were not surprised, many other Texans must have been when Clark ruled the state's school funding system unconstitutional, and gave the state until the end of the 1989 regular legislative session to fix the problem (*Edgewood* 1987). Because of scarcity of resources at the trial court level, Clark let the winning side write the opinion with his approval. The opinion invalidated the system both on equal protection grounds and efficiency grounds, although Clark denied the claim of racial discrimination.

Since the legislature had just finished its 1987 regular session, there was no immediate pressure to coalesce around any one plan. State leaders could afford to wait for the Austin court of appeals to hear the case; the Third Supreme Judicial Circuit further reduced the pressure by overruling the trial court decision on a 2–1 vote, arguing that the legislature's provision for public education was essentially a "political" question over which the courts had no authority (*Edgewood* 1988). The dissent, written by future Supreme Court Justice Bob Gammage, replied that the system was so inefficient that the courts had a duty to step in and right it.

The case was then appealed to the Supreme Court. Even considering sharp divisions in the Court noted below, the Justices were able to put aside their differences, at least concerning the first *Edgewood* case. On October 2, 1989, the Court declared the state's school funding system to be unconstitutional on a 9–0 vote (*Edgewood*

[I] 1989), ruling that the system was not "efficient" in violation of Article VII, Section 1 of the state constitution Rich districts could tax at a much lower rate than poor districts and still receive more money per pupil than low-wealth districts taxing at a high rate (one of the fundamental problems of school finance).

The Court used a number of examples at the extremes to make its point. For example, the poorest district in the state possessed a tax base of only $20,000 per student. The richest district, on the other hand, could tax from a base of $14,000,000 per student, which calculates to a 700:1 disparity. The state's foundation program had no hope of compensating for that gap. These two districts were not just freaks of nature and geography. The one hundred richest districts (out of over one thousand total) had an average tax base of twenty times that of the hundred poorest districts. Edgewood tax base was $38,854, while the neighboring district of Alamo Heights had $570,109 in base per student. Edgewood could tax to the limits of its capacity and never hope to catch up with Alamo Heights. To reinforce that point, the Court cited statistics showing that the one hundred poorest districts taxed at an average rate of seventy-four cents per one hundred dollars of property value, while the one hundred richest only taxed an average of forty-seven cents per one hundred dollars for a much larger return. The Court called these one hundred richest districts "tax havens" (*Edgewood* [I] 1989:393).

The Court was very careful not to specify what *would* be an acceptable system, a stance that gave policymakers more flexibility but also frustrated them to no end. This opinion began the process of "negotiation" between the court and the legislature. The best explanation of what the Court wanted is:

> Efficiency does not require a per capita distribution, but it also does not allow concentrations of resources in property-rich school districts that are taxing low when property-poor districts that are taxing high cannot generate sufficient revenues to meet even minimum standards. There must be a direct and close correlation between a district's tax effort and the educational resources available to it; in other words, districts must have substantially equal access to similar revenues per pupil at similar levels of tax effort. (*Edgewood* [I] 1989:397)

The Court noted, however:

> This does not mean that the state may not recognize differences in area costs or in costs associated with providing an equalized

educational opportunity to atypical students or disadvantaged students. Nor does it mean that local communities would be precluded from supplementing an efficient system established by the Legislature; however, any local enrichment must derive solely from local tax effort. (Edgewood [I] 1989:398)

The Court did not say how "direct and close" the correlation between tax effort and educational resources had to be, or what "substantially equal access" to revenues or "similar levels of tax effort" would mean. Because of the necessary compromises, the Court could state the desired goals but had to allow the legislature some flexibility in achieving them. The Court gave the legislature only seven months to construct a new and constitutionally satisfactory system. If the legislature did not meet the deadline, the Court would order the district court to enjoin all state aid payments to school districts, essentially closing most schools in the state.

When the special sessions on school finance reform convened in the spring of 1990, the leadership plans in both legislative chambers reflected the interests of moderates and liberals, such as Education Committee chairs Senator Carl Parker (D-Port Arthur) and Representative Ernestine Glossbrenner (D-Alice). Both plans put more money into the existing system—the preferred solution of most of the established education interest groups, such as those representing school boards, school administrators, and teacher's organizations. Since it was not clear what the Court would accept, it made sense to these groups and to many legislators to minimize the possible disruptions to the system. At least some interviewees said that after the *Edgewood* I decision, Senate Bill 1 was passed as a kind of "dare" to the Court, to see how far the Court was willing to go for equity. The legislature was playing "chicken" with the Court, in the words of one interviewee.

Compromise on the amount of money needed, though, was quite difficult because of pressure from opposite sides of the political spectrum. On one side, Republican Governor Bill Clements' pledge of "no new taxes" was a real obstacle. On the other, if the amount of equalization was reduced too far, the Hispanic caucuses would (and did) vote against the compromises. For example, when a plan costing $750 million over two years was turned down by a coalition of conservative Republicans and liberal Democrats, House Hispanic Caucus chair Eddie Cavazos (D-Corpus Christi) argued in justification: "If we did not have the court's leverage behind us, I'd be jumping at this money. But I think we have a once in a lifetime opportunity to really fund education like it should be funded because of the court order and I think we really ought to take advantage of it" (Clausing 1990a).

This position did not prevail, though, as both chambers finally agreed on a $555 million compromise funded by a half-cent increase in the sales tax (Clausing 1990b). As many legislative leaders must have anticipated, Clements decided to veto the measure as unnecessary and wasteful. Although no Texas governor had been overridden on a veto in over a decade (Clausing 1990e), the legislature came close, succeeding in the Senate and failing by only two votes in the House. The branches were still at an impasse as the May 1 Court deadline passed. The *Edgewood* case then fell into the hands of a new Austin district judge, F. Scott McCown, Clark's replacement. Since there were multiple district judges for this same court, the selection of McCown turned out to be very fortunate for the poor districts. He was relatively young for a judge, but he had experience with large institutional reform cases, such as the long-running *Ruiz* prison overcrowding case. McCown was described by his supporters as committed and fair, and by his opponents as ideological and ambitious. Either way, as one legal observer said about him, "If he agrees with you, he's the type of judge who will run your case for you."

McCown's first decision was to extend the Court's deadline by a month to give the legislature more time to act. Second, he appointed a special master, former Justice William Kilgarlin, who was known to be quite liberal by Texas standards, to devise a plan to implement if the legislature did not produce an acceptable solution. The threat of the special master sobered up both the legislature and the governor, by most accounts. House Speaker Gib Lewis (D-Fort Worth) was quoted as saying, "I don't think the governor's going to be happy with a court plan. The indications I've seen from the court and just the vibes I've received from the court, I don't think the governor's going to like the plan at all" (Langford 1990b). The legislature was worried as well; House Ways and Means Committee chair James Hury (D-Galveston) said "The master is going to have more BTUs than the rest of us combined" (Clausing 1990d). Kilgarlin helped feed these expectations, saying that the plan would involve redistribution from rich to poor, and that "I hope the Legislature and Governor get the message that if they're not up to the job, the judge (McCown) is" (Clausing 1990c).

Even with the threat of the master plan, the legislature and governor took the full month to pass a new bill. Eventually, though, after four special sessions on education finance, Clements accepted

Senate Bill 1.[5] This bill again raised $555 million, but with only a quarter-cent increase in the sales tax, plus hikes in "sin" taxes. The bill established the goal of equalization of tax base up to the ninety-fifth percentile in five years, or "95 in 95." The only other change from previous plans is that the legislature transferred the power to appoint the state education commissioner to the governor (Clausing 1990f).

There were a number of reasons why the poor districts and liberal legislators were not satisfied with Senate Bill 1. The richest five percent of districts, mostly wealthy Dallas and Houston suburbs plus "oil" districts, were exempted from the system. The system would move forward, but only to the level of the ninety-fifth percentile. It was not clear whether the legislature had the incentive to live up to the promise of Senate Bill 1. The legislature defined all the terms for calculating ninety-five percent equity, such as "adequate," "efficient," "sufficient," "basic program," and "discretionary budget," and so forth. As one interviewee said, "the state was holding all the cards." The poor districts feared that if the state got into a fiscal jam, it would just redefine equity to cover whatever system was in place. Also, there was no real means to enforce compliance with the standard other than a court order. The legislature set up a new commission that would issue a report each legislative session on the necessary resources to achieve system equity, but there was no mechanism in place if the state ignored the commission. As McCown later said, this commission was more of a "thermometer" than a "thermostat." Because of these reasons, the poor districts continued the suit.

These issues of "trust," and the like, were the focus of the second *Edgewood* trial before the district court. The state claimed that Senate Bill 1 should be given a chance to work, while the poor districts argued that the system was still "inefficient." McCown ruled in September 1990 that Senate Bill 1 was unconstitutional; it did not live up to the mandate of the Court in *Edgewood* I. Both sides sought immediate appeal to the Supreme Court, bypassing the Court of Appeals; the high court eventually granted this request on shaky legal grounds to expedite the case.

A slightly different Court heard the second *Edgewood* case in the fall of 1990. By January of the next year, however, the result was the same as that of *Edgewood* I—a short and unanimous opinion striking down the school funding system as unconstitutionally "inefficient" (*Edgewood* [II] 1991). *Edgewood* II was perceived as even more sweeping than the first decision for two main reasons.

First, the opinion was written by Chief Justice Tom Phillips, who had run for election as a judicial restraint Republican, instead of Mauzy, the author of the first opinion. Many observers were surprised that Phillips and the rest of the Republican members would sign on to another opinion striking down the system. Second, *Edgewood* II was seen as a large leap beyond *Edgewood* I because the Court made it very clear that it meant its statement in the first opinion that a "Band-Aid will not suffice; the system itself must be changed." According to one interviewee, Senate Bill 1 and the subsequent unanimous *Edgewood* II decision striking it down were a "necessary step" in the process so each side could see that the other was committed to its position. The key sentence in *Edgewood* II reads: "The fundamental flaw of Senate Bill 1 lies not in any particular provisions but in its overall failure to restructure the system" (*Edgewood* [II] 1991:496).

The Court's opinion again focused on the extreme districts, especially the wealthiest five percent of districts exempted from Senate Bill 1. The Court noted that the 170,000 students in these districts still possessed the same amount of tax base resources as 1,000,000 of the students in the poorest districts. That large base allowed the richest districts to tax at a low rate and still spend more than the districts covered under Senate Bill 1. This system did not provide a "direct and close correlation" between tax effort and school spending. The clear message of *Edgewood* II, therefore, was that *all* districts had to be incorporated into the new system; ninety-five percent was not good enough. The Court next had to decide whether to give guidance to the legislature in constructing the new system and if so, how much. The Court was worried about seeming too "Delphic," in the words of one Justice, in its pronouncements to the legislature. On the other hand, no one thought that writing a Court plan would be feasible or appropriate. The compromise was to give the legislature a list of permissible solutions, an action that at least some Justices later regretted.

The Court in its list repeated some of its suggestions from the first *Edgewood* opinion, such as tax restructuring or district consolidation, although neither option was truly politically feasible, as many of the Justices suspected. Another suggestion was possible "recapture" of wealth from the richest districts and redistribution to the poor districts. Here the question of Court expertise arises. Many interviewees outside the Court criticized the Justices for a lack of experience with the details of school finance. The Justice with the most familiarity with the issues was Mauzy, and his ideological nature made it difficult for some of the other Justices to trust his judgment. In any event, it is not clear whether the Court fully realized the redistributional consequences for the rich districts that they wanted to incorporate into an equalized system.

The last and eventually the most controversial suggestion also raised the question of Court inexperience and eventually fractured the Court consensus. Phillips stated that "The Constitution does not present a barrier to the general concept of tax base consolidation " (Edgewood [II] 1991:497). Under this option, the current district system would still remain, but taxes would be levied by a larger entity containing multiple districts, and then distributed in an "efficient" manner among those districts. McCown in the *Edgewood* II trial opinion had ruled that tax base consolidation was barred by *Love v. City of Dallas*, voiding forced transfer of funds from one district to another. Now, the Court said that McCown was incorrect, that the "general concept" of tax base consolidation was constitutionally acceptable, and that *Love* was no bar, without overruling *Love*. The problems with the Court's statement were: first, that the Texas Constitution barred a statewide property tax, and second, that the Constitution also required voter approval before consolidation. The Court never contradicted these caveats in its opinion, and even hinted at their existence, but never emphasized these potential constitutional problems, either.

The *Edgewood* II opinion was handed down on January 22, 1991. The Court gave the legislature only until April 1 of that year to produce a new law, to have the new system in place for the start of the next school year. Again, if the Court were not satisfied, the threat of an injunction against state aid to education (and therefore school closure) was in the background. The Court definitely had the legislature's attention. At least according to some interviewees, the legislative leadership was frustrated with the Court but also was angry with the educational interest groups that had touted Senate Bill 1 as the way to "buy" the state out of the problem. The leaders pursued two concurrent strategies to resolve the issue.

One track was taken by Senate Education Committee chair Carl Parker. Parker's attitude toward *Edgewood* II, according to some, was "Let's do exactly what the Court wants and see how they like it." He proposed a bill creating twenty "superdistricts" that would levy a uniform property tax. Local enrichment would be allowed, but only under limited circumstances and with a great deal of recapture in the wealthiest districts; it would be a radical step toward equity. This plan would be phased in over a four-year period and would require constitutional amendments to get around the redistribution problem. The Parker plan got the support of both newly elected Governor Ann Richards and Lieutenant Governor Bob Bullock as a means to remove the courts from the debates. Richards was quoted as saying "Faced with the dilemma of having the courts run your school system, I really believe that the people are going to take a long, hard look at the option" (Langford 1991a). The Parker plan passed the Senate easily on a mostly partisan vote on February 19. At this point, the second parallel track the leadership had taken intervened.

After reading *Edgewood* II, the plaintiff-intervenor groups were unsure of the meaning of the Court's language concerning recapture of funds and tax base consolidation. The Court appeared to sanction these two options, but explicitly declined to overrule *Love v. City of Dallas* on transfer of funds. Since the Parker plan would involve recapture on a statewide basis, *Love* was central to its constitutionality. Accordingly, they filed a motion for rehearing. Several legislative leaders took this opportunity to file a defendant *amicus* brief asking the Court to clarify whether local enrichment was still acceptable after *Edgewood* II's language ordering all districts to be incorporated into the system. The legislative leaders' *amicus* brief also asked the Court whether all local taxes should now be considered state taxes.

Normally, the Court would deny the motion for rehearing without comment. On February 25, though, as the Parker plan was heading for the House, the Court took the unexpected step of issuing an opinion concerning the *Love* issue, but also addressing the legislative concerns about local enrichment and local taxation for schools (*Edgewood* [IIA] 1991). This opinion permanently fractured the fragile school finance consensus on the Court that had held through two opinions, even given the deep divisions between the Justices on other civil law issues. Phillips again wrote the majority opinion for the Court, although he only spoke for a five-Justice coalition instead of all nine members. Phillips disposed of the *Love* issue raised by the plaintiffs in one paragraph, stating that *Love* was still good law and that the legislature must not unconstitutionally transfer property from one district to another. He then discussed the issues raised by the legislative defendants, stating that "The motion for rehearing and defendants' response suggest the need for greater clarity in our resolution of defendants' argument" (*Edgewood* [IIA] 1991:499).

On the question of local supplementation, the Court repeated its language of the first *Edgewood* opinion, which noted that once an "efficient" system was constructed, some local supplementation beyond efficiency was permissible. The Court did not explain how that "supplementation" was consistent with fiscal neutrality between districts. The opinion did hint, however, that an "adequate" level of funding might be acceptable, even if not completely fiscally neutral (*Edgewood* [IIA] 1991:500), a position which returned in the *Edgewood* IV opinion four years later. Furthermore, the Court ruled that local taxes were *not* all legally state taxes. The constitutional bar on a state property tax meant that "local tax revenue is not subject to statewide recapture" (*Edgewood* (IIA) 1991:499). Constitutional amendments would be necessary to implement the Parker plan, and it was not clear whether the Court would give the legislature time for this process, which would require a two-thirds vote in both chambers and popular approval in a statewide referendum. The majority opinion closed with a statement that the Court would not entertain any more motions for rehearing.

Edgewood IIA represented a real turning point in the Court's attitude toward the school finance issue. Equalization was no longer the paramount goal, merely one among a number of ends. The Court also could no longer count on its unanimity as a source of strength in convincing the legislature to act, as four Justices wrote dissenting opinions, including a particularly bitter attack from Justice Lloyd Doggett, joined by Mauzy, who accused the Court of "racing to publish" an "advisory opinion" before the House passed the Parker plan (*Edgewood* [IIA] 1991:502, 505). One legislator said that the fracturing of Court consensus led to a divergence of views in the legislature, as now every interest tried to promulgate a plan that satisfied its own constituency and might get a Court majority. The interview respondents generally agreed that the motion for rehearing opinion did not help the legislature resolve the issue. It did let the lawmakers know that the results did not have to be completely equal, but did not aid them in determining what finance structure would achieve an acceptable outcome. After *Edgewood* II, in the words of one legislator, "we thought they were giving us instructions." After *Edgewood* IIA, according to another lawmaker, "we were like rats in a maze."

Paradoxically, though, the two most redistributive solutions of the *Edgewood* process were yet to pass the legislature. Three days after the *Edgewood* IIA opinion, the House voted to pass a bill somewhat similar to the Parker plan, but creating two hundred taxing districts instead of twenty, consistent with the House's more local focus. Local enrichment was still possible, but was severely limited by an overall local property tax rate cap. Ten days before the latest Court deadline, a House-Senate conference committee agreed to the creation of one hundred eighty-three districts, most along county lines (Donahue 1991), which became known as CEDs, or "County Education Districts."[6] The CEDs were funded by a combination of new state money and increased local taxes for some districts. The bill increased funding by $1.2 billion in the first biennium, a significant amount. The source of funding the state contribution was unclear, but at the local level, the minimum tax rate necessary for participation in the state system increased, as it had under Senate Bill 1, for low-tax effort districts. The CED bill, Senate Bill 351, increased the first-tier foundation program for each CED, raised the second-tier guaranteed yield plan, but at the top imposed an overall tax rate cap of $1.50 per $100 property value. The first and second tiers increased in the out-years without a commensurate increase in the cap, which therefore eventually would lead to a very equalized system (Picus and Hertert 1993).

The conference committee held a series of hearings on *Edgewood,* and took testimony from various legal experts as to the Court's likely response to the CEDs, although no one could give an authoritative answer as to what the Court would accept. The problems of uncertainty and inexperience were exacerbated because no one had ever tried to create a structure like this before. Two of the central concerns of the committee involved: first, the issue of whether the CED structure constituted a statewide property tax, because the taxing rate was set statewide by the legislature, although levied in the CEDs themselves, and second, whether a popular vote of approval was constitutionally required before the CEDs could levy taxes. Neither answer was clear. Some experts thought that the Court might overlook these issues to end the *Edgewood* litigation, while others were more skeptical. Because of these concerns, the initial bill drafted by the conference committee contained a provision for an election in each CED to approve the tax rate. This section, however, was removed on the last day before the bill passed out of the joint body back to both chambers. At least one interviewee told me that the reason for the switch was that some legislative leaders, especially Parker, did not want to take the chance that voters in the richest districts would turn down the levy and rely solely on local funds; the tax had to be mandatory.

In essence, the legislature, led by Parker, decided to "gamble," in the words of some interviewees, that the Court would accept the CED structure as a way to exit the *Edgewood* mess. No other solution that had a chance of satisfying the Court was politically viable. The CED system, in the words of one interviewee, was "pretty much dictated by the Court." As it turned out, this was an overstatement, but it reflected the attitude of the leadership. A key legislator said of this period: "We were hanging on the edge of what the Court said." On April 14, the legislature finally reached agreement on the CED bill. Richards signed it thirty minutes before the scheduled hearing before McCown, claiming it would "definitely pass court muster" (United Press International 1991a).

Unfortunately, the governor and other state leaders would soon have to deal with a court challenge from a new source. It was around this time that the term "Robin Hood" appeared in news stories as the name for the CED legislation (Langford 1991d; Rugeley 1992b). In popular legend, Robin Hood was a hero who defended the hard-working poor from the greedy rich. In Texas, however, the label "Robin Hood" became derogatory, signifying unjustifiable expropriation of property. Middle-class Texans believed that their tax money would be sent to poor districts under Senate Bill 351, and they did not like that idea. If middle-class Texans were worried and skeptical, many residents of wealthy districts were angry. They reasoned that because they had worked hard for their money and tried to build up a first-class school system in their districts, why should their schools stagnate or retreat to pay for other people's problems? The general attitude in the richer districts was not in opposition to the needs of the poor districts, but was strongly against any hindrance to their schools to produce what they thought was a vacuous goal of "equalization."

These frustrations with Senate Bill 351 led one hundred sixty of the state's wealthiest districts to file a lawsuit against the CED plan (Langford 1991b;1991c). The rich districts, led by a father-and-son team of Dallas lawyers, Earl and Robert Luna, raised a long list of constitutional issues, but the three most serious involved the questions noted above of a statewide property tax, voter approval of the CEDs, and *Love v. City of Dallas*. The latest *Edgewood* hearing commenced in June 1991 before McCown. In contrast with earlier suits, in which the rich districts either wrote *amicus* briefs or were allowed to intervene on behalf of the state, and the plaintiff districts challenged the state's provision for education, the roles were now reversed. The high-wealth districts now attacked the state's solution, while the low-wealth districts generally defended the state, although they still pushed for greater funding and challenged the legislature's failure to address the capital facilities issue.

McCown's verdict handed the state its first victory since the Court of Appeals ruling in the first *Edgewood* case (Langford 1991d). It may have been won out of frustration, as McCown openly wondered "if (he had) been assigned to some judicial purgatory where (he) must hear the same case over and over again" (*Edgewood* [III] 1993 trial opinion at 36, cited in *Edgewood* [III] 1992:526). He upheld the CED plan if fully funded, which the state's leaders promised to do. Regarding redistribution, he relied on the Court's opinion in *Edgewood* II that appeared to sanction transfer of property and tax base consolidation. In essence, he argued that the Court had given the legislature "permission" to enact this plan. The rich districts vowed to appeal.

On January 30, 1992, the Supreme Court overruled the trial court, declaring the school finance system unconstitutional for the third time (*Edgewood* (III) 1992). However, the Court set an extended deadline for compliance: June 1993, eighteen months away. The majority opinion written by Justice Raul Gonzalez began by evidencing concern for the frustration expressed by the state's politicians. Gonzalez wrote: "We do not suggest that the Legislature has failed to act in good faith; we hold only that it has failed to enact a constitutional school finance system" (*Edgewood* [III] 1992:493). The system was void for the reasons argued by the rich districts: the CED plan was a state property tax and it transferred tax resources without local voter approval (see *Love v. City of Dallas* [1931]).

On the issue of a state property tax, the Court majority argued that because the state mandated the total amount of revenue raised by each CED, the formula for calculating the tax rate needed to raise that money was fixed, and the CED had no other function. The CED essentially was a subterfuge of the legislature for avoiding the constitutional bar. Gonzalez wrote: "CEDs are mere puppets; the State is pulling all the strings. Though the hands collecting the tax be Esau's, the voice of authority is unmistakably Jacob's" (*Edgewood* [III] 1992:501). Concerning voter approval, the majority held that the CEDs exceeded the legislature's authority by creating new districts that transferred property without voter approval. If the legislature had merely altered district boundaries, that would be different, but the CEDs were an entirely new animal. Voters were denied a voice in the setting of their local tax rate, a prerogative that the Texas Constitution clearly granted them. The transfer of property to other existing districts further violated the Court's previous ruling in *Love*. The CEDs could not stand.

Gonzalez then defended the Court against the charge that it had misled the legislature by "pre-approving" the CEDs, insisting that the Court had refrained from prescribing any particular system in *Edgewood* II and IIA; it had merely listed possible options.

On tax base consolidation, the majority argued, "We did not say that tax base consolidation *could not* be unconstitutional; all we said was that it *could* be constitutional" (*Edgewood* [III] 1992:512). The sense of betrayal that policymakers felt after the CED system was voided showed how seriously they had taken the Court in the first place. To illustrate the depth of frustration at this time (perhaps the low point in all of the *Edgewood* saga), the *Houston Chronicle*, a relatively liberal newspaper by Texas standards, editorialized that "(the) Texas Supreme Court is playing games with the Legislature and the system of financing the state's public schools—the only rational way to stop this comic opera is to amend the state constitution to remove the undefinable jurisdiction on which the Court has acted in the insoluble *Edgewood v. Kirby* case" (*Houston Chronicle* 1992).

State representative John Culberson (R-Houston) had proposed a constitutional amendment to accomplish just what the *Chronicle* suggested (United Press International 1988c). Culberson's amendment enshrined the Court's standard of "substantially equal access to similar revenues at similar levels of tax effort" in the Constitution. It also created a constitutional presumption in favor of the legislature, though, and required the Court to apply a "rational basis" test to any challenged school plan. If the plan were "rational," it had to pass Court muster. In other words, the amendment would weaken the Court's authority. Culberson proposed this amendment soon after the first *Edgewood* decision, but had not been taken seriously for a variety of reasons, including the Republicans' minority status, his inexperience as a legislator (he was not on the Education Committee) and Democratic opposition, from a policy perspective and a concern for the separation of powers. Now, though, as frustration with the Court in the legislature built, the Culberson amendment increasingly became relevant as an option to end the *Edgewood* suit.

The legislature would have to find a solution in the 1993 regular session before the June 1 Court deadline. The legislative leadership significantly differed from that of the previous sessions. Bullock still ruled the Senate with an iron hand, but he appointed a new Education Committee chair, Republican Bill Ratliff (R-Mount Pleasant), after Parker resigned his chairmanship due to frustration and fatigue. Ratliff was a moderate, and respected by all sides in the debates for his expertise with school issues.[7] Parker called Ratliff "about like watching a haircut," but perhaps that is what the legislature needed (Walt 1995). In the House, Glossbrenner passed her Education Committee chair to Libby Linebarger (D-Manchaca), another fairly liberal Democrat and supporter of equalization. The new Speaker, Pete Laney (D-Big Spring), was also ideologically similar to his predecessor, Lewis, but Laney wanted to remove partisanship from his office, acting as an "honest broker" for all members. The new leaders, especially Ratliff and Linebarger, were able to piece together a new plan in a relatively short time, perhaps because the options were so well-known and limited at this point. The renamed "Fair Share" plan would legalize the CEDs by constitutional amendment and recapture $400 million from the richest districts (Rugeley and Markley 1993a; Rugeley 1993b).

This plan passed the Senate easily, but the House resisted, led by Republicans who disagreed ideologically with the plan but who also wanted to embarrass Richards, perhaps by closing the public schools for a couple of days (Robison 1993a). The Republicans increasingly rallied around the Culberson amendment as the best solution. Minority Leader Tom Craddick (R-Midland) said: "We do need an amendment to clarify the role of judges and impose guidelines that restrict their ability to meddle in areas reserved for the elected representatives of the people" (Craddick 1993). Eventually, though, in a test of Laney's leadership, he was able to convince enough moderate Republicans to vote for the Fair Share plan that it would appear on a May 1 ballot, just one month before the Court deadline. He was quoted as saying: "I think . . . the realization that the schools were going to close had a lot to do with it," a claim supported by some of the Republican legislators he persuaded (Stutz 1993a).

Therefore, the voters of Texas would be asked directly for their views for the first (and only) time on the school funding question. Both supporters and opponents of the Fair Share/"Robin Hood" plan relied on fear tactics to persuade the voters to vote yes/no (Keeton and Rugeley 1993). Supporters claimed that the only possible alternative to legalizing the CEDs was massive district consolidation, which no one supported. Richards, in her biggest test as governor, said on the campaign trail, "What we are doing is asking the people of Texas to tell the courts it's OK for us to do it" (Rugeley 1993c). If the voters turned down the plan, according to Richards, McCown would close the schools. She tried to frame a "yes" choice as a vote "for your children." Opponents of the ballot proposition, by contrast, emphasized the issue of taxes, relying on voter antipathy toward steadily rising local property taxes mandated in part by previous reform laws to fuel opposition to the latest plan. Of course, the constitutional amendment legalizing the CEDs would not affect tax rates by itself, but that was too technical a point for most voters to grasp. Opponents also claimed that the threat of school closure was a smoke screen, and would never happen (Robison 1993b).

Supporters of the plan, including the political leadership and the largest businesses in the state, which had grown very worried at the constant chaos in the school system, heavily outspent opponents in the referendum campaign. Opponents preferred to rely on low-budget methods such as word-of-mouth, talk radio shows, and newspaper opinion articles (Rugeley and Markley 1993b). The national Republican party, though, made a large money contribution near the end of the campaign, in all likelihood for the purpose of handing Richards a serious defeat. The opponents of the referendum turned out to be smashingly successful in persuading Texans not to accept the "Robin Hood" plan. The legalization of the CEDs was defeated 63–37, as were two unrelated ballot questions on school issues.[8] Resistance to property taxes clearly played a role, as did the traditional theory of referendum voting, "If you don't know, vote no" (Stutz 1993b). Whatever the reasons, the legislature had to produce yet another solution to the school finance dilemma.

Paradoxically, because of Court demands, the options the legislature produced were even more redistributive and/or disruptive than the plan the voters had just rejected, showing how desperate the legislature had become to end the *Edgewood* saga. The Senate alternative was proposed by Ratliff; it would transfer, at the discretion of the state commissioner of education, around $40 billion of tax base, meaning around $400–600 million in spending, from rich districts to poor districts, including shopping malls, utilities, oil, gas, and minerals. This idea earned the name "Lop-N-Plop" at the Capitol (Langford 1993a; Rugeley 1993d). The Ratliff plan would be quite equalizing, by most accounts; rich districts, because of the loss of tax base and the still-existing tax rate cap of $1.50 per $100 property value, could raise a maximum of $5800 per student, while the poorest district, if it taxed at its limit, could generate $4900 per student. In a class of twenty-two children, this left a $20,000 gap, but it was still much better than before *Edgewood* (*Dallas Morning News* 1993).

There were two major problems with the "Lop-N-Plop" plan, though. First, it was unclear whether the plan would be constitutional after the Court's ruling in *Edgewood* III. The plan was unique, though, like the CED plan, and so one could gamble again that the Court would find a way to uphold it. Second, because of the configuration of property wealth in Texas, seven rich districts would have to be exempted because they did not possess enough separable large nonresidential assets that could be transferred to put them under the tax base cap. Seven districts in a state containing over one thousand may not seem like a lot, but the level of paranoia, especially on the House side, was such that members were convinced that the Court would not let them take *any* districts completely out of the system (Stutz 1993c). Education Committee member Paul Sadler (D-Henderson) said: "If you leave these districts out of the plan, it is like waving a red flag at the Court" (Stutz 1993d). Democrats also resented these districts for appealing the CED plan in the first place; now, the rich districts were about to face a worse alternative.

The Senate overwhelmingly approved the Ratliff plan 27–4 less than three weeks before the Court deadline. However, the House was unwilling to accept it because of the constitutional and practical problems noted above. The House leaders then proposed another solution, which came to be known as the "multiple-choice" plan. This bill would affect the richest one hundred nine districts, all with a tax base over $280,000 per student. These districts would be given a choice of five options to share their wealth. They could:

1) "buy" students in neighboring districts by purchasing attendance credits from the state;

2) "buy" the same credits statewide by writing a check to the state;

3) voluntarily enter into a CED with neighboring districts, as long as the average tax base of the CED was not over $280,000 per student;

4) voluntarily consolidate with another district;

5) transfer property, as in the Ratliff plan.

If none of these options were selected, the original House plan contained a provision for forced consolidation, but this was later modified to selection of an option by the state commissioner of education using legislative guidelines (Stutz 1993e).

The multiple-choice plan, also known as Senate Bill 7, did possess two distinct advantages. First, it was quite equalizing in structure. Ratliff claimed: "This is by far the flattest curve (with) almost exact yield per penny all the way from the very poorest to the very wealthiest. That's the test. I don't know how anybody can argue with that" (Langford 1993b). Second, the legislature made a gesture toward the Court by including a provision for severability; if any options were struck down by the Court, the remaining options would go into effect. Of course, this also meant that if the Court struck down all the redistributive options, the Court would be mandating district consolidation, a position the Court would be extremely reluctant to take. Because of these advantages, and because there really was no other politically palatable alternative, the legislature passed the multiple-choice plan three days before the June 1 Court deadline. Ratliff received a standing ovation from the Senate (Roberts 1993), and Richards signed the bill into law, sending it to the Travis County courthouse for yet another constitutional test.

When the *Edgewood* IV trial hearing opened before McCown, he faced the nightmare of any judge dealing with "public law" litigation. Besides the named plaintiffs, *eight* groups of plaintiff-intervenors filed challenges to the multiple-choice plan, while one set of defendant-intervenors attempted to help defend the state education commissioner, now Lionel Meno, the putative defendant. The plaintiffs were divided into poor districts and rich districts, who were filing on very different grounds. The high-wealth districts challenged Senate Bill 7 on a long list of constitutional grounds, including the issues raised in *Edgewood* III of a statewide property tax, lack of voter approval, and violation of *Love v. City of Dallas* on district-to-district wealth transfer, among others. The underlying message was that the legislature had accomplished exactly what *Edgewood* III had forbidden, under the fiction of a "choice" of unconstitutional methods of redistribution. The multiple-choice plan was illegally coercive of these districts.

The low-wealth districts, by contrast, raised three different sets of claims. First, they argued, Senate Bill 7 left an unconstitutional gap between the eighty-five percent of districts completely covered by equalization, possessing an effective tax base of $205,000 per student, and the richest districts, who could tax with a base of up to $280,000 per student. At maximum levels of taxation, this would lead to a $600 gap per student, or a $13,000 gap per average classroom, which was significant, the poor districts asserted. Second, the legislature had failed to make adequate provision for education in this law; because of state budget difficulties, the foundation level was actually lowered in Senate Bill 7 from the level of the CEDs, as was the Tier 2 guaranteed yield level. Districts could not pay for an education that would meet state accreditation standards with just Tier 1 foundation money. They had to supplement with Tier 2 guaranteed tax base funds, although these were essentially equalized. The larger point, though, was that because of the state's failure to keep up with expanding enrollments, rising costs, and property values that had still not quite recovered from the savings-and-loan bust, poor districts would only be treading water or losing money under Senate Bill 7, while rich districts could use their greater resources to hold themselves harmless, even if at a higher tax rate. The last claim of the low-wealth districts was that the legislature had failed to equalize funding for capital projects or facilities. Under the multiple-choice plan, districts were allowed to exceed the regular $1.50 per $100 property value tax rate cap by up to an additional $.50 for facilities funding. This extra rate was completely funded by local districts. Therefore, it produced the same disparities in facilities present in regular maintenance and operations before *Edgewood*. For all of these reasons, the poor districts argued, Senate Bill 7 should not be accepted by the courts.

McCown opened his *Edgewood* IV opinion by noting the "universal" unpopularity of the multiple-choice plan (*Edgewood* [IV:trial opinion] 1994); however, it was mostly constitutional. He upheld Senate Bill 7 in every respect except for facilities funding, which the state still had to address. McCown displayed his hostility to the rich districts by noting: "One measure of just how much progress is made under Senate Bill 7 is the ferociousness of the fight of the property-rich districts against it" (ibid.:1–2). Given this position, it is unsurprising that he rejected their claims about redistribution. For example, McCown denied the argument concerning a violation of *Love v. City of Dallas* because *Love* allowed transfer if the "host" district is properly compensated. He argued that the legislature's "just compensation" to the rich districts was not consolidating them.

However, McCown denied most of the claims of the low-wealth districts as well, citing a number of statistics showing the progress in equalization the state had made since the original *Edgewood* decision. He declined to rule on the adequacy argument because it was essentially a legislative judgment, not a proper judicial question, although he did find that the legislature had neglected its duty to fund facilities properly, and enjoined the issuance of any new bonds until the legislature had corrected the problem. The overall message, though, was:

> As for the complaint that the court's remedy is too lenient, the court believes that the progress that has been made should be recognized and the remedy retailored to fit the remaining wrong. . . . Senate Bill 7 is a genuine attempt by the Legislature to fulfill its

very difficult responsibilities under article VII, section 1. The judiciary owes the legislature the respect of giving S.B. 7 a chance to work. Perhaps it will not work. Perhaps it will not be funded. But we cannot say today that it will not. (ibid.:79–80)

Even though the high court heard oral arguments in the *Edgewood* IV case in May 1994, its decision was delayed until after the November elections. Some conservatives, especially those living in the property-rich districts, expected the Court to void Senate Bill 7 as unconstitutionally coercive and redistributive, given an unprecedented Republican Court majority. On January 30, 1995, however, these expectations were dashed as the Court ruled 5-4 that the multiple-choice plan was constitutional, at least for the moment (*Edgewood* [IV] 1995). The majority was an odd combination of Justices at the ideological center of the Court, including Republicans Phillips and John Cornyn, and Democrats Gonzalez, Gammage, and Jack Hightower. Cornyn wrote the majority opinion upholding the system as a whole, including facilities funding. While doing so, he changed the terms of debate in the *Edgewood* case.

In previous opinions, the Court had primarily relied on the standard of "substantially equal access to similar amounts of revenues at similar levels of tax effort," or "fiscal neutrality," to judge the constitutionality of the school finance system, although the Court was always careful to allow room for local supplementation. In *Edgewood* IV, though, Cornyn minimized that standard, instead focusing on whether the legislature had made "suitable provision" for the schools, or in other words, whether the provision was "adequate" to meet state accreditation standards (ibid.:463–64). The arguments of "minimum good schools" and accreditation requirements had not been heard in the *Edgewood* saga since the state's defense of Senate Bill 1 five years earlier. Cornyn used a Texas Education Agency report to argue that the minimum cost of a good education in Texas was around $3400 per student, although the state education commissioner had claimed during trial testimony that that number undermeasured the real costs (ibid.:501). Since each district could raise $3400 per student using equalized revenue, even though Tier 1 alone would not cover these costs, the system was constitutionally "efficient." Even if the richest districts were able to tax beyond that level, the poorest eighty-five percent of districts under Senate Bill 7 could still get an "adequate" education.

Furthermore, one cannot separate the question of facilities from the constitutionality of the broader system, according to the majority. Even though facilities funding was unequalized, the disparities in its funding only amounted to a ratio of 28:1, as opposed to the pre-*Edgewood* disparity of regular funding of 700:1. Besides, the Court argued, there was not enough evidence in the record to say how great the poor districts' facilities needs were. If the state failed to address the facilities question, though, the majority threatened to revisit the issue later (ibid.:480).

Cornyn rejected the arguments of the property-poor districts, but he turned aside the claims of the property-rich districts as well. These districts had argued that the state had overrelied on local property taxes to fund the state's education responsibility, but Cornyn ruled that the question of the relative share of state and local wealth was a political question unsuitable for Court resolution (ibid.:470). Furthermore, Senate Bill 7 did not violate the statewide property tax prohibition or *Love*, and the reasons why were quite similar. Cornyn argued that the districts had a "choice," in the setting of the local tax rate and in the rich districts' choice of options for sharing their wealth. Granted, the options were circumscribed by the state, but not unconstitutionally so, because the rich districts did not have to choose an option that would violate *Love*; they could opt for consolidation, for example. The rich districts tried to argue the doctrine of "unconstitutional conditions," but he rejected this claim, saying that school districts, as creatures of the state, possessed no independent rights (ibid.:470–73). Therefore, Senate Bill 7 was constitutional, although the Court took great pains to warn the legislature not to allow their attention to slip from the school finance issue.

> For too long, the Legislature's response to its constitutional duty to provide for an efficient system has been little more than crisis management. The rationality behind such a complex and unwieldy system is not obvious. We conclude that the system becomes minimally acceptable only when viewed through the prism of history. Surely Texas can and must do better (ibid.:459).

Texas had its first constitutional school finance system in almost eight years, even if no one liked it. Some groups appealed to McCown in a hearing described as "part hearing and part group therapy session," but the judge denied their requests, saying, "So what you all really need to do is work it all out in the Legislature and not come back, all right?" (*Austin-American Statesman* 1995)

Since *Edgewood* IV, politics has continued, of course, with mixed results for the new system. Not content to leave education reform issues alone, the 1995 Legislature passed a massive school-reform bill eliminating many state requirements on local districts concerning curriculum and governance, and creating a limited voucher program (Harp 1995). The legislature did not ignore school funding, however, as it increased the "guaranteed yield" Tier 2 funding for districts, in large part because of a desire to placate the Court, according to some observers. The legislature also appropriated $170 million in state money for facilities funding. In the 1997 session, Governor George W. Bush attempted to fundamentally restructure the state tax system by shifting from local property taxes to state taxes, such as sales. He could not persuade the legislature to agree, though, and had to settle for a smaller property tax cut. Before the 1999 session, poor districts filed another suit, claiming that the funding gap had widened unconstitutionally since *Edgewood* IV.

This suit essentially was a warning to the legislature to account for poor district needs. Although it is unclear how strongly the lawsuit affected deliberations, it is clear that the plaintiff districts received substantially more state funds by the end of the session. Facilities funds were available to low-wealth districts, and all districts in the state received money for a $3,000 salary raise for all teachers and support personnel. As a concession to the wealthier districts, the tax base ceiling was raised from $280,000 per student to $295,000 per student before redistribution was triggered, thereby slightly worsening equity. The plaintiff districts, however, seem relatively satisfied with the new money, making a new suit unlikely (Brooks 1999).

Assessing *Edgewood*

In looking back at the long and tortuous history of court-ordered school finance reform in Texas, it would be understandable to conclude that judicial involvement was a failure. I initially reached this result as well after preliminary analysis of outside commentary. However, as the research progressed, and as I interviewed participants in the school finance debates in Texas, it became increasingly clear that this assessment was overstated or failed to account for the larger picture. Of course, one's assessment of *Edgewood* depends upon what standard one uses to judge the efficacy of judicial involvement.

If one is looking for a case in which a court makes a clear ruling and the political branches immediately comply, then obviously *Edgewood* does not meet that yardstick. One must take a more balanced and realistic view of judicial power, though, especially when dealing with complex "public law" cases.

A better set of questions to ask is: first, How much progress was made toward the Court's stated goals? How "fiscally neutral" is the system today? Second, how reasonable is it to attribute the changes in the system to the Court? Did the political branches pay attention to the Court and make good-faith efforts to comply with its rulings? Would "reform" have happened without the Court's involvement? Third, were there costs to the Court in terms of institutional power or prestige? Did the Court damage its "institutional credit" with the political branches in the process?

How Equal?

The first question this section will attempt to answer is: How much progress did the legislature make in resolving the issues raised by the Court? How "efficient" or fiscally neutral is the Texas school finance system today? Given the complex nature of these issues, it is difficult to reach a definitive conclusion. Analysts examining the same data can interpret it in very different ways according to their normative perspectives and biases.

Similarly, interview respondents gave a wide range of answers when asked, "How equal is the finance system today?" The majority can be differentiated into two sets of responses. One group's evaluation was "very equal; the best it's ever been." Another group claimed that the system was clearly more equal now than when *Edgewood* was first decided, although they hesitated to call the overall system "equal." A few interviewees in both groups said that Texas had one of the most equal systems in the nation.

The relatively few respondents who were more pessimistic about the system also fall into two categories. The first group felt that Senate Bill 1 was a large step toward equity, but since then, no real progress had been made. The second group decried the continued reliance on local property taxes, which still account for over 50% of the average Texas district's budget. The Court had not been able to force the legislature to move away from that system (if that was their goal), although at least one interviewee said that the system would be even worse without the Court.

This varied set of responses can be partially explained by an analysis that takes into account these diverse points of view. It seems fairly clear that Senate Bill 1 put a large amount of new state money into the system, funded by a hike in the state sales tax, and the like. The reform plans after Senate Bill 1, though, relied less on state funding (although the state put some new money in each time) and more on local property tax increases in low-taxing districts and "recaptured" money from the wealthier districts in order to achieve the degree of equity that the system possesses now. The CED system produced a very high degree of equity, while the "multiple-choice" plan suffers by comparison mostly due to an overall lack of funding. The result is a system that although not perfectly equal, is much more "fiscally neutral" than before *Edgewood* (Picus 1995).

A combination of data from McCown's *Edgewood* IV trial opinion and school finance expert Lawrence Picus's (1995) study of the system using Texas Education Agency data illustrates these points. Before *Edgewood*, the ratio in tax base between the richest and poorest district was 700:1, while the state only guaranteed revenue of $2,745 per student for poor districts taxing at the maximum equalized rate. In 1994, by contrast, the tax base ratio had plummeted to 1.16:1 for regular maintenance and operations, while the facilities funding ratio was only 28:1. If poor districts fully took advantage of both Tier 1 and Tier 2 funding, they received a total of $5,023 per student in 1993–1994 (Picus 1995).

McCown cited data showing that the overall level of funding in the system (not accounting for inflation) increased by 30% over the course of *Edgewood*. What is even more significant, though, is where those dollars went; the poorest quartile of districts gained 66% in state aid, while the richest quartile lost 15% in state aid, both unadjusted for inflation. According to McCown, "The students in the bottom half of the wealth scale have enjoyed state aid increases of $1.9 billion while the 50% of students in the top half of the wealth scale have enjoyed only $491 million" (*Edgewood* [IV:trial opinion] 1994: 64–65).

Property tax rates used to widely vary in Texas, and not just due to variations in wealth. Some low-spending districts, especially in rural areas, did not tax at a high rate. These districts have borne much of the recent brunt of finance reform, along with the recapture districts, although the richer districts have won "hold-harmless" provisions from the state guaranteeing them their present level of spending. Tax rates and levels of spending are compressed;

the bottom 85% of taxpayers now share the same level of tax base. The richest districts are inextricably connected with the rest of the system as well, because of the tax rate limit of $1.50 plus $.50 for facilities and the tax base cap of (now) $295,000. McCown said: "The amount of unequalized revenue in the system is no more than 2% of the total revenue in the system. . . . Tax effort at 1993 rates now explains an estimated 80% of the variation in revenue in the system while wealth explains only 3% compared to wealth explaining 56% of the variation in the (original) system declared unconstitutional and tax effort explaining only 14%" (ibid.:62-63). The data show that the amount of unequalized local enrichment has greatly decreased over time and will continue to decrease if districts raise their tax rate to $1.50 per $100 property value to fully take advantage of state aid.

This achievement is even more impressive considering the difficult fiscal conditions that Texas experienced at the time of *Edgewood*. One legislator relates: "Every legislature since 1985 has faced a (state budget) deficit in one form or another" (Cuellar 1993). Furthermore, one must not forget the impact of the savings-and-loan crisis on property values during this period. Picus (1995:13) notes that the average property wealth per student decreased from approximately $231,000 in 1988–1989 to $194,878 in 1992–1993. These difficult economic conditions are a significant reason why the legislature decided to "level down" as well as "level up." These may not be accounted for in aggregate studies using increases in state aid as measures of judicial effectiveness.

These data led Picus to the conclusion that "the distribution of funds in Texas is among the most equitable of all the fifty states" (Picus 1995:26). McCown similarly stated, "We have come a long way" (*Edgewood* [IV:trial opinion] 1994:62). This does not necessarily mean that everyone is satisfied with the system; almost no one is. Poor districts desire closure of the still remaining gap, rich districts greatly resent the caps placed on them by the current laws, and everyone wants further reduction in local property taxes. Yet, Texas has made real progress toward the Court standard of "substantially similar access to similar levels of revenue per pupil at similar levels of tax effort" to "provide for a general diffusion of knowledge" (*Edgewood* [I] 1989:397).

Due To Whom?

In the next several sections, I discuss the relative contributions of multiple actors to the school finance reform process, with the goal of weighing the influence of all other forces versus the influence of the Court.

INTEREST GROUPS

In this section I discuss the alignment of interests concerning the school finance equity issue, that is, which interest groups supported the reform goals of the plaintiff low-wealth districts, which groups opposed the means necessary to achieve these goals, and which groups stood aside or took mixed stands in the debates, to assess how large of an impact outside pressure had on the eventual reform legislation.

In the history of the *Edgewood* case, three pro-plaintiff organizations stand out. First, the Intercultural Development Research Association (IDRA), founded in the 1970s by a former Edgewood superintendent, Jose Cardenas, provided the initial support and personnel for the lawsuit. Another San Antonio organization closely affiliated with IDRA was the Mexican-American Legal Defense and Education Fund (MALDEF.) MALDEF's role was to provide the legal backbone of the *Edgewood* suit, personified by MALDEF's lead lawyer, Albert Kauffman. The third important organization, the Equity Center, was initially part of IDRA, but formally broke with that organization early in the preparations for the lawsuit because of philosophical differences. The Equity Center was founded in 1982 by James Vasquez and James Lehman, but was led by Craig Foster and Richard Kirkpatrick, another former superintendent, and was based in Austin, not San Antonio. The advocates at the Equity Center concentrated on statistical research on school finance disparities in order to bolster the suit. All three groups worked closely together, however, for the common goal of improving the education of children in the poor districts.

The subtle divisions in the pro-equity interest groups were mirrored in the plaintiffs themselves, producing two distinct factions. The first group was associated with MALDEF and consisted of eight heavily Mexican-American districts, although that number eventually grew to thirteen. These districts took the position that they should demand one hundred percent equity from the state. As one advocate said, "How can you say that my kids are only worth ninety percent of what your kids are worth?" This group viewed complete equity as not only a practical issue, but also a moral and racial issue, given past discrimination against Mexican-Americans.

They did not necessarily want to pull down the rich districts, but would not be too displeased if redistribution was necessary to achieve equity. On the other hand, the second group, the plaintiff-intervenor districts, who eventually grew to one hundred twenty-five (out of a thousand) in number, were not primarily Mexican-American, but were largely poor rural districts that did not possess an oil refinery or a nuclear power plant. These districts had no real interest in focusing on race, but instead concentrated on wealth disparities.

The other important difference between the two groups concerned the nature of a fair school funding system. MALDEF believed that if complete equity were achieved, the system would not stagnate because the rich districts would pressure the legislature to raise the level for everyone to boost children in their districts. The plaintiff-intervenors, however, disputed the claim that one hundred percent equity would lead to higher funding levels, pointing to California where spending was equalized by court order but remained at a very low level by national standards. The better alternative, argued these districts, was to equalize all but the very richest districts, but with a "chain" on those districts such that everyone else would be "pulled" up behind them, thus avoiding equalized mediocrity. Otherwise, it would be too easy for the legislature to pull down the rich districts without helping the poor districts, and to rely on inertia to avoid further significant spending increases.

The split between the two plaintiff groups was present throughout the litigation, although it usually was not a real problem for the reform efforts (Cortez 1998). The general goals were the same for both groups, and at least in terms of the advocates' perceptions, the reform acts throughout most of the litigation were not close enough to either group's ideal system that the split became an issue. Given the complexity of the school finance issue, though, the lack of a single clear voice from the plaintiffs cannot have helped the policymakers in constructing a new system.

The high-wealth districts opposed to redistribution were not as tightly organized as the plaintiff groups and did not have an institutional base to rally around. They were united mostly by their dislike of the solutions proposed in the legislature to end the school finance crisis. This relative lack of coordination minimized their influence in the legislature and to a lesser extent in court. At the same time, though, the high-wealth districts did win some significant legal victories (for example, the voiding of the CEDs in *Edgewood* III), even if the final resolution was not to their liking. However, the low-wealth districts also exerted their greatest direct influence through the Court, not the legislature. The plaintiff groups sued the state to begin with because their voice was not taken seriously in the legislature, in part because of their relatively small size. On the other hand, through repeated legal action the plaintiff groups were able to achieve much more equity than they could have through straightforward legislative lobbying. The importance of the court system for these groups is exemplified by the number of intervenors for *both* sides in the final *Edgewood* IV suit.

In contrast to the smaller interests involved in litigation, there were larger interests that generally possessed more direct influence with the legislature, such as the established education groups (for example, the school boards association, the teachers unions, the school administrators association) and larger business concerns that have nearly always found a friendly ear in Texas. These groups, however, were all either internally divided or not directly concerned with the equity issues before the Court and legislature. The education groups all possessed members from both rich and poor school districts. They did not wish to alienate parts of their membership, and so they were reduced to lobbying for more money for the state school system as a whole, a position that became increasingly difficult as tax increases and budget deficits loomed. Furthermore, after Senate Bill 1 was voided by the Court, many legislators lost faith in the ability of these groups to find a constitutional solution. Business groups, such as the Texas Chamber of Commerce, Texas Association of Taxpayers, and Texas Association of Business, also did not enter the school finance debates full force for several reasons, mostly involving conservation of monetary and political resources. These groups were not as concerned with distributional issues as they were with the quality of education future workers were receiving in the public schools. Since the equity and quality issues were separated throughout the litigation, business involvement was minimized. Furthermore, aside from lobbying against targeted business tax increases, these groups did not want to appear anti-education unless necessary. Overall, the lack of influence of business groups is seen in the "multiple-choice" plan, which gives districts the option of transferring some of their largest business property tax base from their low-tax district to a neighboring high-tax poorer district, a solution the businesses themselves would not favor. Therefore, although interest group influence was certainly present in the school finance debates, it was most significantly channeled through the courts and did not by itself control the ultimate resolution of the issue in the legislature.

PUBLIC OPINION

What was the role of the general public in the school finance debates? Considering that the only time that *Edgewood* issues were before the voters, a proposed solution was overwhemingly defeated, one might expect that the public took out its wrath on the legislature, the Court, or both branches because of the mess that occupied the state Capitol for six years. Surprisingly, this was not the case, according to nearly all the interview respondents. When I asked interviewees whether members of the legislature won or lost because of *Edgewood*, some said that "no one" did, while others opined that "a few" gained or lost seats, but could not think of any examples. When one looks at the history of *Edgewood*, one does not see martyrs to voter backlash. Among the leadership, many legislators resigned for various reasons (Glossbrenner, Linebarger, Lewis), but only one, Parker, was defeated at the ballot box. His loss, though, at least according to one interviewee and news articles, was due to his sending signals to the electorate that he was tired and just going through the motions, which was fatal for a Democrat in the Republican year of 1994 (*Dallas Morning News* 1993).

Similarly, on the Court, no interviewee specifically attributed any election gain or loss to *Edgewood*. There was high turnover on the Court during this period, but issues besides *Edgewood*, such as "the need to put a woman on the Court" (Spector over Cook) and tort law (Enoch over Mauzy), led to the only electoral defeats of sitting Justices. In general, the interviewees said, Court elections were (and are) determined by the conflict between business defendants and plaintiff lawyers on civil law issues; school finance was only a minor player. This is not to say that *Edgewood* had *no* effect on Court races. Specific areas of Texas, especially the Dallas suburbs, have not forgiven Phillips for joining the first two *Edgewood* opinions and voting to uphold the "multiple-choice" redistributive plan. The *Dallas Morning News*, for example, after *Edgewood* IV was handed down, threatened that Phillips and Cornyn, who also sanctioned Senate Bill 7, would have primary opponents in 1996 as a result (*Dallas Morning News* 1995). These challenges never took shape, however, and so the effect on reelection of these Justices was only the loss of a few votes and contributions in Dallas.

Ironically, the politician who might have been the most significant victim of *Edgewood* was not a major player in producing a legislative solution. Richards put her credibility on the line in selling the ratification of the CEDs by constitutional amendment. When the amendment was overwhelmingly defeated by the public under the label "Robin Hood," she lost credibility with the voters. Certainly her narrow loss to Bush in 1994 can be attributed to a number of different explanations, but *Edgewood* must be reckoned among these reasons.

In general, though, there does not seem to be a significant backlash against the legislature or the Court in the general public because of *Edgewood*. How can one explain this result? Three reasons stand out. First, public knowledge about the complexities of school finance was low, according to most interviewees. The public's views were very generalized and inchoate. One interviewee described the results of focus groups done during *Edgewood* as an initially positive reaction to the principle that "everyone should have an equal shot at an education," but as time wore on, property taxes rose, redistributive solutions were proposed, and the "Robin Hood" label became more salient, the public turned against the "mess" at the Capitol. Still, though, there was no clear target for this resentment (except perhaps Richards,) and so resentment remained at an underdeveloped stage. Second, no Court decision on *Edgewood* was issued right before a major election, probably not by chance. If people wanted to vote based on school finance, they would have to recollect the rulings of Justices months before. Similarly, regular sessions of the legislature convene at the start of odd-numbered years while elections are held at the end of even-numbered years. Voters would have to keep their resentment of any reform law passed for a relatively long time before expending it at the ballot box. Third, according to one interviewee, "members (generally) played their roles." In other words, legislators from property-wealthy districts opposed reform laws, while members from property-poor districts supported equalization. This sentiment is reflected in the statements of several interviewees that members were extremely influenced by the computer printouts that analyzed whether their district would gain or lose by any particular solution. The alternatives were constructed by the leadership within Court guidelines, but the actual votes were largely determined by the printouts. Since members generally followed their districts in this manner, voter backlash was minimized.

This is not to say that the general public had no influence on the *Edgewood* debates. Legislators certainly knew that several options were foreclosed to them as possible solutions, such as massive district consolidation or a state income tax (also constitutionally barred.) Backlash was strong and swift whenever either of these options was seriously mentioned. Within those broader constraints, however, lawmakers (and Justices) had significant flexibility in designing remedies for the constitutional problems of the school funding system.

THE MEDIA

The state's major newspapers also played a role in the school funding debates, although much less so than in Kentucky, as we shall see in chapter 4. The primary function of the media was to publicize the school finance equity issue and keep it on the legislative agenda. This is not to say that the legislature would not have debated and acted without media coverage, but that the coverage and the legislative debates were mutually reinforcing, as the newspapers were glad to cover conflict over an important issue. The media's role did not go far beyond coverage, though. Unlike in Kentucky, where the state's major newspapers pushed in a unified direction for certain solutions, the media in Texas were divided. Some newspapers, such as the *Austin-American Statesman* and the *Houston Chronicle*, were fairly sympathetic to the claims of the plaintiff low-wealth districts, although the *Chronicle* eventually became quite frustrated with the Court. The *Dallas Morning News*, on the other hand, attacked most, if not all, of the redistributive solutions proposed to end the school finance battles, and editorially lamented the seemingly exclusive focus on money instead of discussion of educational quality issues (*Dallas Morning News* 1993b).

Also unlike in Kentucky, the state's major newspapers did not take on a strong "muckraker" role in exposing faults in the funding system and recommending change, focusing instead on the debates in the legislature. On the other hand, these debates were covered in-depth and almost daily. Very few, if any, other state policy issues received as much newspaper attention as public school finance did from the time of the first *Edgewood* decision in 1989 to the eventual declaration of constitutionality in 1995, and coverage has certainly not ceased since then. The constant attention may have heightened legislative willingness to deal with the issue (Smith 1994). It is difficult to imagine, however, that the legislature would have completely sidestepped the issue even without media coverage, given the number of people affected and the large dollar amounts involved. Furthermore, as noted above, the coverage in itself did not point the legislature toward any one solution, given the divisions within the media. Therefore, the media played a role in the school finance debates, but should not be given responsibility for the move toward equity.

THE GOVERNOR AND EXECUTIVE BRANCH

Ordinarily, one might assume that the substantial progress in school finance equity must have resulted from hand-in-hand cooperation between the legislative and executive branches. Otherwise, how could so important and substantial an undertaking be accomplished? The evidence shows, though, that such cooperation was either minimal or unorthodox. This section will focus on the role of the executive branch in reaching school finance consensus. In most states, the governor is the undisputed leader of the executive branch. In title, this is true in Texas as well. Under the Texas Constitution, however, the lieutenant governor is the presiding officer of the Senate in an extremely legislatively driven system. The lieutenant governor has the power to appoint committee chairs in that body and essentially controls the flow of bills on the floor. The governor, by contrast, has only limited power over the executive bureaucracy because many officials are separately elected, and really plays a role in the policy process only in suggesting ideas to the legislature and vetoing bills as a last resort (Kraemer and Newell 1984:199).

Regarding the governors, executive-legislative relations during the time of *Edgewood* started off poorly and only marginally improved over time. When *Edgewood* I was handed down in 1989, Clements was serving his second nonconsecutive term as governor, in part because of his "no new taxes" pledge in his last campaign. Clements, initially "dismayed" by the court ruling, soon warned that it would lead to the destruction of local control and elected school boards, and vowed to keep his campaign pledge in spite of the ruling (United Press International 1987; Dittrick 1988). Moreover, although he appointed a 15-member commission to study the issues, he called for a constitutional amendment to remove jurisdiction over school finance issues from the court system (United Press International 1988a). Clements claimed he wanted reform, but not change led by the judiciary. "We're not turning our schools over to the judicial system. . . . That's what the constitutional amendment is all about—to put it back in the hands of the Legislature where it belongs" (United Press International 1988b).

Another reason why Clements was willing to remove judicial authority to review the case was that he did not trust the Court, and Mauzy in particular, to rule in a way Clements considered impartial. Mauzy had moved from the Senate Education Committee chairmanship to the Court a few years before, and the two were not on good terms. Clements publicly accused Mauzy of already having written his opinion upholding Clark even before the appeal

(United Press International 1988c). Mauzy responded by asking whether Clements' hand was on the Bible when he made the accusation.[9] Clements' relationship with the legislature was little better, which is one reason why it took five special sessions to get Senate Bill 1 passed. Even given the mutual distrust between all three branches of government in this period, though, the political system produced a law that increased taxes (no mean feat in Texas), set equity goals, and appropriated $555 million.

In November 1990, Democrat Ann Richards was elected Governor, defeating Republican Clayton Williams in a hard-fought campaign. During the campaign, she had supported only modest attempts to ameliorate the school finance problem, and there is not much evidence that the issue played a significant role in her election (Langford 1990a). She found the issue quite complex and difficult, as exemplified by this quote: "School finance is like dividing up your sweet old aunt's estate. Someone is always going to get coffee mugs when they really wanted the roll-top desk" (Rugeley 1992c). After her election, she expressed support for the goal of equalization, but did not play a leading role in crafting a solution. Partly this may have been due to her relative inexperience with the issue and the office, but also traditional legislative territorial pride may have been involved, especially regarding the first woman governor in sixty years in a male-dominated political system.

Even though Richards supported equalization, this did not mean that she necessarily had a good relationship with the Court. For example, during the *Edgewood* crisis she expressed her frustration with the Court this way: "We have reached a point in this country that literally you can't take action unless you end up in one court or another. . . . My impulse is, let them have it." She later continued, "The absurdity of it is that the court is supposed to give you the general outline and the parameters of what they believe the law is. You move and perform in a responsible fashion to comply with that direction and then find out that wasn't really what they had in mind. So why not let them do it at the outset? Let them go ahead and do their own plan" (United Press International 1991b; Rugeley 1991b). The only Richards solution was to tax business and mineral interests statewide instead of in local districts. The proceeds from these property taxes would then be used to equalize funding. Local districts could still tax residential and agricultural property (Rugeley 1992a). Unfortunately for the governor, this idea was also unpopular, especially with business groups and the school boards association. The business groups did not want to separate their tax rate from that of residences, for fear that their rate would be significantly higher, while the school boards feared losing their most valuable assets from their tax bases. Richards did not strongly lobby against this opposition, and so the plan was rejected. It should be noted that she did lobby strongly for the "Fair Share" plan when it went to a statewide popular referendum. The measure went down to a convincing defeat, though, and did not signal an upturn in the governor's relations with the legislature, which were wary overall.

In the Governor's race of 1994, Bush outpolled Richards in a close election. During the campaign, he assessed the multiple-choice plan in this way at the Republican state convention: "It is not a plan that robs from the rich and gives to the poor. It is a plan that robs Texas of its future by making the whole state poor" (Selby 1994). In fairness, though, he did not make opposition to the multiple-choice plan a major issue in his campaign (Walt 1994). Therefore, all three governors during this period were either hostile to the goals of *Edgewood* or not strong proponents of the decisions.

As noted above, however, in Texas the governor arguably does not have as great a role in the policy-making process as the lieutenant governor, who during the *Edgewood* period was first Bill Hobby, then former state comptroller Bob Bullock. Bullock's leadership was key to the eventual progress concerning school finance reform. He ran the Senate like a semibenevolent dictatorship, making deals in private and producing unanimous or near unanimous votes in public (Ramsey and Rugeley 1993; McKenzie 1993). One legislator joked, "voting 'no' in the Senate is closing your eyes while saying 'yes.'" An interviewee said of Bullock, "He only believes in one branch of government with three departments." Another respondent, echoing this sentiment, said that Bullock was the "driving force," the "major player" behind school finance reform. The "force of his will could not be overstated." Bullock's power did not come from his knowledge of technical details or formulation of solutions (although his staff provided much of the legislative expertise), but from his determination to do *something*, not to let the process fail because he thought it was the right thing to do. Nonresponse was not an option. If Bullock got a gut feeling that something had to be done, according to this interviewee, "you'd better help or get out of the way." On the school finance issue, Bullock felt that every child ought to have an equal opportunity and that everyone else was greedy and was missing the point.

Therefore, Bullock's influence was necessary. It was not sufficient, though, to achieve school finance equity. First, Bullock only controlled the Senate, not the House. Second, his power only came into play once the school finance issue had been firmly planted on the political agenda by the Court and the litigants. At that point, Bullock rose to the challenge to legislative capability. It seems unlikely, however, that the lieutenant governor on his own would have spearheaded changes that would cost substantial amounts of money and alienate a fair number of voters. When Bullock at one point in the process suggested a state income tax in order to pay for *Edgewood*, the negative reaction was sharp and swift, and he backed off immediately. Therefore, the influence of the lieutenant governor was perhaps necessary to school finance reform, but was not the only spur.

Before leaving the executive branch, one should not neglect the role of the Texas Education Agency (TEA), especially since its head, the state education commissioner, was the putative defendant in the *Edgewood* litigation. In reality, the TEA played the part of an "honest broker." The agency was split between a desire for more money for education and its role as agent of the state that was being sued. Therefore, it decided to provide common data to both sides of the lawsuit. In this "public law" case, the real disputes concerned the meaning of the numbers, not the data. The agency also gave technical assistance. For example, the CED plan that was the second solution to the *Edgewood* crisis was originally developed by the TEA, although substantially modified in legislation.

THE LEGISLATURE

The Texas legislature that the Court charged to fix the school funding system was in transition from a good-old-boy conservative Democrat bastion to a more diverse body, in several senses. To generalize, the most significant trends in Texas politics over the last twenty or thirty years have been: first, a significant increase in the Hispanic voting population, which has led to the formation of a significant Hispanic voting bloc in both houses of the legislature. Second, the Republican Party, accentuated by the popularity of Ronald Reagan has gained influence. Legislative Republicans were largely ignored before the 1980s; today, they constitute a formidable force in the House and a majority in the Senate, although the Democrats still retained majority status during most of the *Edgewood* debates.

The Republicans constituted one of three groups roughly equal in power in the legislature on the issue of school finance reform. Of course, the relative strength of these groups waxed and waned over time. The "open space" for policymaking left by the Court in the *Edgewood* ruling meant that each of these legislative groups, plus the outsiders pressuring them, could interpret the decision in the way that best reflected their own interests. One group, mostly liberal white and Hispanic Democrats, strongly supported the *Edgewood* ruling, and may have even wanted the Court to go further. They saw *Edgewood* as a once-in-a-lifetime opportunity to restructure the system for equity.

Another group, conservative Republicans, thought that the Court had illegitimately usurped power by declaring the school finance system unconstitutional in 1989 on the basis of a single word, "efficiency," that had been in the constitution for almost one hundred twenty years without such an interpretation. A third group, mostly white Democrats and containing many of the leaders in the legislature, favored school finance reform in the abstract, but wanted to make sure change would not be disruptive, costly, and protracted. None of these groups could act alone; they needed the cooperation of at least some of the activists on either side.

A further complicating factor was that the distribution of power between the three groups varied by chamber. The Senate tended to favor the more liberal and moderate interests, although the Hispanic caucus was smaller. Senate Republicans were either ideologically isolated or often cooperated with the Democratic leadership. Eventual Senate Education Committee chair Ratliff, appointed by a Democratic lieutenant governor, was the best example of the latter Republican position. One reason why the Senate tended toward a moderately liberal position was that most senatorial districts were large enough to contain rich and poor school districts, with the poor districts often outnumbering the rich in voting power, if not financial resources. In the House, on the other hand, districts were small enough that a representative could more fairly be said to come from a "rich district" or a "poor district." Thus, on the school finance issue, the chamber was much more internally divided than the Senate. The three-group split was clearly present in the House, with a roughly equal division of power, although the House Republicans started weak but grew stronger as the school finance debate continued.

In the semistructured interviews with policymakers, most respondents said that the legislature took the court decisions quite seriously and acted in basic accordance with the Court's directives, even if the members did not necessarily understand what each ruling meant. Parker was quoted by one interviewee as saying, "We want to surrender, but we just don't know where to turn ourselves in." This assessment should be qualified. When one says "the legislature" took the Court seriously, in essence, one is referring to the legislative leadership, meaning the institutional leaders such as the Lieutenant Governor, Speaker of the House, and minority leaders to a lesser extent, plus members of the education committees in both chambers. The Texas Legislature is quite elite-driven, as reported by interviewees, and so these specific policymakers made most of the key decisions. The only "back-bencher" to have much impact on the process was Culberson, and his Court-weakening amendment was ultimately defeated.

It is clear that the legislative leadership paid a lot of attention to the court rulings. Numerous hearings were held where testimony was taken from many different legal commentators and experts as to the implications of the *Edgewood* decisions and what the constitutional consequences would be of various solutions considered. The legislature did not always follow the advice of the legal experts, especially when there was no consensus among them. The legislature was willing to gamble with the Court, and usually tried to do the minimum necessary, as reported by many interviewees. But it never openly tried to contradict what it thought was a Court requirement. One can also see legislative willingness to respond in the numerous attempts to comply with court-imposed deadlines, even though the legislature did not always meet those due dates. It is true that this compliance was not due solely to legislative altruism, as McCown's threat of a plan drawn up by a court-appointed special master influenced legislative deal-making. The success of the master threats, though, certainly shows the effect that the courts had on the legislative process. Overall, then, it is fair to say that the legislature made "good-faith efforts" to comply with the Court's decisions, to the extent that the legislature understood the Court. No one except for a few Republicans wanted to engage in "massive resistance."

This assessment leads to the question of why the legislature decided to essentially comply with the Court over the course of the *Edgewood* litigation. There are many different possible explanations, especially since one cannot treat the legislature as a monolith. For example, the liberal group in the legislature had an incentive to comply with the Court orders, especially the early rulings, because their poorer constituents would be clear beneficiaries. On the other side, the conservative Republicans, although usually not urging open defiance of the Court, clearly wanted to nullify the effects of the Court's decisions by use of the Culberson amendment, not least because their wealthier constituents might be harmed by legislative "solutions" to the school finance problem. Therefore, when one is discussing willingness to comply, the group that is most interesting is the mostly Democratic centrist leadership. They were the "swing votes," and could have chosen from a multitude of options depending upon where they believed their maximum political advantage lay. Why did they choose grudging compliance with the Court?

One interviewee explains this attitude toward court orders as being generational, as many of the leaders, especially the newer leadership of the 1990s, experienced the civil rights struggles as children and did not want to repeat that experience, making "massive resistance" an unpalatable option. Another experience these leaders had shared, however (and still were sharing at the time of *Edgewood*) was federal court takeover of the state prison system and state mental health facilities. This experience did not necessarily lead legislators to deplore the Court's role in school finance, though. When asked what effect these other dealings with courts had on the *Edgewood* response, answers were quite mixed. Most interviewees differentiated the issues, saying that each controversy posed its own set of challenges. One major difference was that in the prison and mental health cases, a federal judge was ordering improvements as opposed to the state supreme court. The respondents said that there was quite a bit of "fear and loathing" of the federal courts.[10] Many former colleagues sat on the state supreme court, by contrast, and the state court had to face the same electorate that the legislature did, producing more of a "comfort zone" on the part of the legislature.

Deeper explanations for the leadership's decision to comply with the Court, though, lie in two sources: first, the lack of an effective alternative because of Court threats, and second, ideological agreement with the basic principles of the court orders on the part of most of the leadership, even if the leaders did not necessarily agree that the courtroom was the proper forum to resolve these issues. The judicial system effectively foreclosed the option of nonresponse by threatening implementation of the "master" plan (McCown's strategy), and threatening closure of the school system by cutting off state aid to local districts. When I asked the policymakers about the likelihood of Court-ordered school closure, answers varied by partisan position. The more conservative interviewees were generally convinced that the threat of school closure was a "smoke screen" designed to shoehorn the legislature into solutions that would never pass otherwise, such as a state income tax. The more liberal respondents reported that they took the threat of school closure very seriously, especially because of the activism of McCown. Of course, this position helped them make their argument for redistributive solutions.

Those in the ideological middle and outside the legislature took a more moderate position on school closure. They were more likely to say that the legislature wasn't sure whether the Court would close the schools or not, but they did not want to take the chance. One interviewee said: "The Court and the legislature were playing chicken with each other, but both blinked a bit . . . the Court was scared to death of non-response . . . (while) the legislature was scared to death the Court might actually do it (close the schools.)" Another respondent said, "everybody knew that when push came to shove, it wasn't going to happen" because "nobody wanted to victimize the children and teachers—there were too many stakeholders." In other words, neither side was willing to gamble with closure.

Another reason why the legislature was not willing to risk school closure is that when asked who the general public would blame if the schools closed, most respondents named either the legislature solely or both the legislature and the Court. Very few, except for one Justice and one executive branch official, said that the Court would take most of the blame. The legislature would be faulted by the public because the members were closer to the people and it was seen as their job to construct the school system, not the Court's job. Therefore, the legislature could not pass the buck if worse came to worst, at least according to the perceptions of many of its members. The only way to remove the possibility of school closure would be to pass the Culberson amendment weakening the authority of the Court on school finance issues. As noted in the initial discussion of the Culberson option, however, legislative opposition to this solution stemmed from moderate-to-liberal legislators who felt that poor school districts would lose if the status quo were ratified and from a concern for separation of powers if the legislature stripped the Court of some authority. In the words of one respondent, it would be "a fundamental change in our system of government." During a legislative debate over a similar amendment, Ratliff said, "I suppose I'm corny. I believe in the American system of separation of powers" (Rugeley 1993a). This reasoning was likely not the major reason the Culberson amendment was defeated, but it furnished some of the deciding votes.

Therefore, the legislature was "in a box" in dealing with the Court orders because of Court foreclosure of other options. The second reason why the leadership decided to at least do the minimum required by the Court is that many leaders truly believed that the Court had identified a problem that needed correcting. This was clearly true of all of the chairs of the education committees, including Glossbrenner and Linebarger in the House, and Parker and Ratliff in the Senate. The Speakers of the House were more mixed on this issue, but not necessarily opposed to equalization. Bullock's influence over the Senate is noted above. The lack of strong ideological opposition within the leadership created an "open space" for court-ordered policy change.

Because of the support of so many key leaders ideologically for equalization, it would be tempting to conclude that the Court's role was minimal in that the legislature would have equalized to the present extent without the Court. According to the interviewees, this was not the case, however. When respondents were asked whether the legislature would have made significant changes in the school funding system without the Court, a strong majority agreed that the Court was a major influence for equalization, while some called the Court the "only influence" in that direction. This assessment was true across institutional position, from legislator to executive branch official to interest group leader to lawyer to Justice (Note: This finding is consistent with a smaller interview study in Texas [Carr and Fuhrman 1999].)

Some more conservative interviewees disputed calling the changes "progress," but most were willing to give the Court "responsibility" for moving the system. One legislator explained this assessment by saying, "That's the way the Texas Legislature operates. . . . Until (there's a) gun to the head, (it) won't do anything unpopular." Another added, "The Court gets most of the credit. . . . Otherwise, members would have just voted their districts." One nonliberal Justice agreed, saying: "We were a catalyst—nothing was going to happen without the Court." Some interviewees said that the level of funding would be somewhat similar but the distribution would not have nearly been as equal, while others claimed the reverse, but nearly all gave the Court the major share of responsibility for moving the system. In the words of a couple of respondents, "The Court drove the system."

No interviewee specifically contradicted this evaluation and claimed that the Court had no real impact on the process. A few maintained that even though the Court sped reform at the beginning, the Court then slowed the process down, starting with *Edge-wood* IIA, the motion for rehearing. Another argued that even though the Court inspired some progress on finance, at least at the beginning, the "costs of uncertainty" and chaos in the system grew intolerably high by the end of litigation. Policymakers were not allowed to deal with quality issues because they had to spend so much time on finance. Glossbrenner said: "(I've) serve(d) four years as chairman of the House Committee on public school finance and have never been allowed to chair the House Committee on Public Education" (Dubose 1993). On the other hand, the legislature was able to make significant changes to the curriculum and governance structure in 1984 with the passage of H.B. 72 centralizing state control and in 1995 concerning the new Senate Bill 1, which transferred power back to local districts. Many of the finance laws contained accountability provisions as well.

Furthermore, one should not ask more of the Court than what it promised. The *Edgewood* opinions only dealt with finance issues, in part because the plaintiff districts were not seeking changes in curriculum or governance. These districts merely wanted more money or a more equal distribution of existing resources. Once that was achieved, "local control" could be a reality for them. All other issues were separate. No one in the process thought the Court was institutionally capable of dealing with "quality" issues, including the Justices themselves. The Court set for itself a relatively quantifiable target of fiscal equalization in the *Edgewood* case. Even though it hinted at other possible reforms, the real bottom-line standard was either "fiscal neutrality" at the beginning or "adequacy" measured by dollar inputs at the end. Given that this was the standard, most policymakers reported that the Court was effective in persuading the legislature to make significant progress toward that goal. Even this more limited finding is notable as a sign of Court power.

THE SUPREME COURT

The Texas Supreme Court that pressured the legislature was itself a court in transition. Before the 1980s the Court was known as a conservative institution that overwhelmingly supported business interests against plaintiffs claiming injury. The Court rarely intruded into "politics" or major areas of public policy outside civil justice (Murchison 1994). In the 1980s, though, the Court began to change. Individual plaintiffs began to win more often and receive larger awards, and many legal doctrines that previously had precluded recovery were turned aside. Of course, at least one interviewee claimed that Texas was just "catching up" to the national trends, but there still is no question that there was a difference from the past. Another reason the Court might have been more willing to challenge established doctrines was that there were a preponderance of former legislators on the Court, including former Senate Education chair Mauzy. Six of the nine Justices at the time of the first *Edgewood* case had spent some time in the Capitol as a Representative or a Senator. This law-making experience may have given the Court more confidence to go beyond what the law had been to what the justices thought it should be.

Unfortunately, this shift was also accompanied by scandal, touched off when the television program *60 Minutes* ran a story entitled "Justice For Sale." The story strongly implied that the Court's decisions were being "bought" by campaign contributions from large interests, usually plaintiffs' groups but not exclusively so. In Texas, state supreme court Justices have to run in partisan competitive races every six years, with the costs of election seemingly increasing each year. The *60 Minutes* story had a devastating effect on the Court. Even ten years later, many interviewees mentioned that story without prompting when discussing the Court's reputation. One Justice was forced to resign, and a second was disciplined. All the Justices serving at the time, though, had a taint left on them because of the scandal. The Court was still recovering from that debacle at the time of *Edgewood* (Champagne 1988).

The other lasting effect of the *60 Minutes* story was to open an opportunity for the newly emergent Republican Party in Texas (Borges and Elder 1988). Because of the seats left open by resignation, the Republicans gained three Justices in the 1988 elections. These included Associate Justices Eugene Cook and Nathan Hecht, and also the Chief Justice, Thomas Phillips.[11] Phillips soundly defeated Mauzy in a nasty and ideological campaign to win the chief's job, although Mauzy retained his Associate Justice seat. Therefore, the Court was badly in need of some internal fence-mending. Phillips was quoted later as saying "We are still groping together for new solutions" due to the problems of turnover (Borges 1991).

In the early stages of the *Edgewood* litigation, it appeared that the Court had overcome these hurdles to send a clear and unified message to the legislature. The willingness of Phillips and his Republican colleagues to sign on to opinions voiding the school funding system contributed greatly to this consensus. There are a few different possible explanations for these actions, and probably the truth is a combination of all. Phillips was relatively young for a Justice, and "fact-oriented," in the words of one interviewee. He could see the disparities present, and found it hard to say that this system was rational. Another factor in his vote and authorship, according to another respondent, may have been a desire to consolidate his leadership of the Court. Whatever the motivation, Phillips's name on the opinion led policymakers to believe that the Court was serious and unified on the school finance question.

However, as the *Edgewood* litigation continued, and increasingly legally creative and redistributive solutions were proposed and enacted, the Court consensus fractured. The Court increasingly appeared to be "negotiating" with the political branches, especially after *Edgewood* IIA, the last-minute opinion on the motion for rehearing. This action raised serious separation of powers problems for liberals such as Justice Lloyd Doggett. His statement on that issue spoke to the larger question of the proper role of the judiciary in resolving such complex "public law" cases, especially when a court takes a "negotiator" role. "Undoubtedly, to some there is a certain allure to the notion of this court working hand-in-hand with the Legislature as different drafts are submitted for review. Each chapter, section, and sentence could enjoy the careful scrutiny of this court. We could negotiate away any misunderstanding about constitutional requisites perhaps at the same time that the Legislature was resolving the court's budget" (*Edgewood* [IIA] 1991:505).

Of course, this debate over the proper judicial role also had a partisan tinge to it, as conservative Phillips in that opinion discouraged tax base redistribution while liberal Doggett defended it. Finally, in *Edgewood IV*, the relative moderates on the Court united to end the lawsuit and defeat both liberal and conservative opponents of the "multiple-choice" plan. The Court partly acted to preserve its legitimacy and independence, as drastic measures such as the Culberson jurisdiction-weakening amendment would have been taken more seriously if the Court had forced the legislature to remake public school finance yet again.

Perhaps paradoxically, however, the long-running debate over *Edgewood* actually seemed to increase the attractiveness of service on the high court, as prospective candidates realized what power the Court potentially could wield. Each of the judicial races in 1994 illustrated how the perceived power of the Court had grown over the years. Gonzalez, a conservative Democrat who had written the *Edgewood* III majority opinion voiding the CEDs, faced a difficult primary battle against Rene Haas, a candidate strongly backed by civil litigation plaintiffs' lawyers. Gonzalez had also angered Democrats when he voted with Republicans on the state's recent legislative redistricting plan. The costs of this bitter, personal, and ideological primary race eventually reached almost $5 million, unheard of in Court history, with Gonzalez victorious (Nichols 1994). Another seat was contested by a candidate who had turned down a lifetime federal district court appointment to make the ultimately unsuccessful race (Robison 1994). The third contested seat was vacated by Doggett, who was able to make the Court a stepping-stone to Congress.

Since I have argued so far that the judicial system convinced policymakers to pass laws that they would not have otherwise by a mixture of persuasion and threat, it becomes a fair question to ask: Was there a "backlash" against the Court within the policy community, specifically the legislature, as a result of *Edgewood?* Did the Court lose any long-term power or prestige, which also could be defined as "institutional capital?" The question of backlash is especially relevant because of a news article written after *Edgewood*, titled "At the Capitol, Court Wore a Dunce's Cap; Hamstrung by *Edgewood* Backlash" (Elliott 1993). The article cited various incidents to show legislative resentment at the Court, including defeat of a plan proposed by Phillips to consolidate the Supreme Court and Court of Criminal Appeals, set up a single level of trial courts, and equalize the appellate court workload. Furthermore, the legislature cut some judicial education funds and transferred others to the criminal court. The State of the Judiciary speech was abolished, and Phillips was thrown off the floor of the House as a visitor during a debate on a judicial districting settlement (ibid.).

On the other hand, some interviewees discounted these actions as either trivial or unrelated to *Edgewood*. For example, according to some, the judicial reform plan lost because of state bar opposition and because members resented Phillips's appearing to dictate legislation to them. Another interviewee stated that even though the judicial education funds were cut, the Court got its full allotment of regular maintenance and operations funding from the legislature. Similarly, some interviewees discounted the cancellation of the State of the Judiciary speech, saying that "no one ever went anyway—it was just a waste of time." Furthermore, some respondents agreed that there was resentment against the Court in the legislature, but that *Edgewood* was only one factor, and that the Court's civil law decisions were a greater influence. Along the same lines, when I asked some Justices about legislative backlash—they tended to minimize it. One Justice said, "After *Edgewood* I and II, they realized we were over here; after *Edgewood* III, they were sorry we were here; after *Edgewood* IV, they were just relieved. (There was) not much if any backlash—they thought we were honestly doing our job (without) an agenda—the only (problem) was they didn't want to make the political pick—they wanted us to spell it out, but that's their job, not our job."

Given these diverse assessments, which side is right, if either, about the extent of resentment against the Court in the legislature because of *Edgewood*? On the question of gain/loss of "institutional capital," one must separate the concepts of "power" or "prestige" because some interviewees did in their responses. Answers varied greatly on this question. Some claimed that this variation in evaluation was due to ideology, as according to one interviewee, "people have opinions based on ideological compatibility with the Court, not the Court as an institution." Another echoed this sentiment, saying "half liked it, half didn't." However, at least in the sample of interviewees, this was not necessarily the case. For example, one liberal respondent said, "(The Court) totally lost prestige—these people don't know what they're doing—they're yanking our chain and don't want to write (a) plan themselves." One more conservative interviewee, on the other hand, discounted any backlash and even opined that "the Court gained power because it forced the legislature to do what it didn't want to do—it moved property taxes." Other interviewees across the ideological spectrum agreed with this more positive assessment of legislative reaction, saying, for example, "(the Court) probably gained credibility with the legislature . . . (they) showed they would stand their ground." Another said "the Court gained because they were perceived as a threat—there was a major sense of court takeover of (legislative) functions."

This assessment of the Court gaining credibility was certainly not universal, however. The major criticism that reocurred in the interviews was of the Court's lack of expertise on the school finance issue, as noted in the earlier comment about "yanking (the legislature's) chain" without a plan. Another lawmaker said, "(the court) is a less equal branch of government because it's not as respected and honored—(we) don't take them as seriously—they were a paper tiger (that) never did anything" when deadlines were missed. Another respondent said on the expertise issue, "they didn't understand what they were about." Unwillingness to set clear standards really frustrated this group of interviewees.

A third subset of respondents did not necessarily agree with either group, saying that *Edgewood* had little effect either way on legislative-judicial relations. For example, one said that "there was a lot of talk and blustering" but "no real long-term effects." Another claimed there was no backlash because "legislators expect this out of courts." Similarly, "the legislature has never liked the Court because of the separation of powers and because the Court can set deadlines." To sum up this assessment, one legislative interviewee said "I'm not sure the legislature respected the Court to begin with—they have their branch and we have ours."

How can one explain the lack of a serious legislative backlash according to a number of interviewees? Two possible related explanations stand out. First, regardless of variance in the answers of the elite interviewees, for the average member of the legislature, assessment of the Court probably depended upon ideology and whether his/her district gained or lost because of *Edgewood*. Given the general increase in funding, and because the number of rich districts harmed by recapture only represented 10% of the state, one might assume that almost 90% of legislators would either see an increase in funding or a break-even result for their districts, although general state fiscal conditions of rising local property taxes and increasing costs of education are cautions on that point. At the very least, though, this distribution pattern should dampen resentment of the Court.

Second, one cannot treat the Court as a monolith anymore than one can regard the legislature in that manner. The Court was growing increasingly conservative over time, eventually producing a solid Republican majority of Justices. This conservative Republican track paralleled the partisan and ideological shift in the legislature from a solidly Democratic body to a conservative two-party system. It would make more sense for the legislature to start a backlash if the Court was the same body that in the mid-1980s revised tort law in a more liberal direction. Given the ideology of the present Court, however, backlash may not seem as necessary.

Conclusions

The "standard civic model" of a court's role in government is that court decisions promulgate clear principles and standards for judging the legality of legislative and executive actions. Once court decisions are issued, the political branches promptly comply. Recent revisionist thinking challenges this model, arguing that there is a "disconnect" between the courts and the legislature and executive in that the political branches feel free to ignore court decisions when these rulings will be politically costly to comply with (Rosenberg 1991). In the case of Texas school finance, I argue that neither of these models fit. First, one can see that the Court struggled mightily to formulate principles to guide the legislature in its deliberations without becoming overly prescriptive or over-reaching past its own level of expertise with the issues. Further-more, the constant problem of reaching a consensus on difficult issues among strong-minded jurists plagued the Court throughout. As one Justice said, "We are not constituted to be clear." Another legal source said: "The problem wasn't that the judges knew how to solve (the problem) and the legislature didn't, the question was how much the legislature could get done."

On the part of the "political" branches, we see neither rapid acceptance of Court decisions nor "massive resistance" or indiffer-ence to the Court. The legislature, as noted throughout, is not a monolithic entity. The Court energized certain forces already pres-ent in the legislature and altered the incentives for others because of its threats of sanctions. The Court was not able to persuade an unbreakable majority to follow its policies because it did not have a clear vision itself of an "efficient" system and because of legitimate disagreement in the legislature with the Court's goals. This com-plexity is likely present in most legislative bodies that courts have to deal with, and is something that no study of judicial impact can afford to ignore.

When both sides had established their positions, according to one interviewee, a "certain hydraulic" set in, leading the partici-pants to do things that they would not have at the start, such as the U.S. Supreme Court eventually sanctioning busing as a means of compliance with *Brown* (1954; see *Swann*, 1971). This particular interviewee was not sanguine about this "hydraulic," stating that it led people to "dig in their heels," and criticize each other unneces-sarily. On the other hand, another interviewee also noted this ten-dency, but was much more positive in evaluation. This respondent described a semiconspiracy between some legislative leaders, the plaintiff groups, the Texas Education Agency, and the like, to speed the process along. He said of this group: "We all like each other." Whatever the outcome, it was better to face the issue "serially and rapidly" rather than trying to achieve everything as a result of one court decision. The result was a "delicate waltz" between the Court and legislature. The Court aided the cause of the reformers prima-rily in that its decisions were usually not specific enough to pro-duce a single outcome (and the process broke down when the Court tried), but it issued decisions very quickly and set deadlines, forcing relatively swift legislative response. After all, three different reform laws and four state supreme court decisions (five if one counts the motion for rehearing) were promulgated in the space of six years. In the words of another respondent, "there was no breathing room."

Whether one sees this "conspiracy" or "hydraulic" as a positive good depends in part on one's normative perspective. Many conservative Republicans saw this same dynamic as a conspiracy, but with the eventual goal of a state income tax. One Republican respondent called the *Edgewood* decisions a "Trojan horse" constructed to serve Mauzy and the education establishment, and argued that the decisions were a "black hole" that no amount of money could satisfy. On the other hand, many liberal respondents were quite pleased with the outcome, even if they wished the process could have continued further. From a more ideologically neutral standpoint, one can view this case study as real evidence of the potential importance of the courts in the policy-making process. In direct response to court decisions, the legislative and executive branches produced numerous solutions that ultimately led to a system that met the Court's initial goal of "fiscal neutrality." Texas now has one of the most "equal" school finance systems in the nation, without a serious and sustained backlash against the Court in the legislature or in the general public.

It is important to recognize that the school finance system today is not one that anyone in particular supports. It is extremely unwieldy and complex. As noted above, liberals want even more equalization, while conservatives would like nothing better than to repeal the various caps on rich districts. Even the Court is not necessarily pleased with this system, upholding it mostly because of the long history of the case. This should not detract from the overall conclusion of judicial effectiveness, however. The process of constructing a new system of funding public education was extremely difficult and complex, as most "public law" litigation is likely to be. Notwithstanding, the Court was instrumental in producing a new resolution.

CHAPTER 4

~

Kentucky: "The Courts Made Us Do It"

When Americans think of Kentucky, two images generally come to mind: one is of horse racing, as the Kentucky Derby is perhaps the preeminent horse race in America, if not the world; the other is of impoverished miners living in small, rural communities, isolated from the rest of the nation. These images are reflected in geography. Horse racing occurs in the bluegrass region, in the north-central part of the state. Louisville and Lexington are there, as are most of the state power centers, including its largest businesses, its major newspapers, its namesake university, and its Capitol in Frankfort. Mining takes place in eastern Kentucky, abutting Virginia and West Virginia. In contrast to the relative prosperity of the residents of the bluegrass region, the population of eastern Kentucky struggles to survive in a rugged and unforgiving land dominated by two sources of employment, the mines and the schools. These two very different regions and cultures were to unite, however, behind a movement to improve the education of their children.

For most of its history, Kentucky was not known as a leader in educational policymaking, to put it mildly. In 1990, however, the legislature passed and the governor signed a sweeping reform law known as the Kentucky Education Reform Act (KERA), which restructured nearly every aspect of schools, including finance, curriculum, and governance. The legislature appropriated over $1.2 billion in the act, with the bulk going toward various components of the educational system from the primary schools to higher education. Although there is still resistance to certain aspects of the act, Kentucky is known nationwide in education policy circles as one of the leaders in innovative thinking (Appelbome 1996). How can one explain such a dramatic turnaround? How could a state that had, in the words of one commentator, "changed the least of any state in the

111

Union," take a giant leap toward innovation in one of its most important policy areas? (Barone and Ujifusa 1992). This chapter will attempt to provide some answers, keeping in mind that there are no simple explanations for collective decision-making. Multiple forces converged, and to paraphrase several interviewees, "the stars were in alignment." Complexity of causation, though, should not obscure the significant role of the Kentucky Supreme Court, whose decision declaring the entire state public school system to be unconstitutional acted as a "catalyst" for the reforms (*Rose* 1989).

Chronology of Reform

Education in Kentucky

As in most other American states, the educational system has evolved slowly in Kentucky. At the time of the adoption of the U.S. Constitution in 1789, schools in Kentucky were almost completely private and scattered. It was not until 1838 that the legislature created the first free statewide public school system, which was not fully operational until 1850 (Alexander et al. 1989). Over the next two generations of Civil War and Reconstruction, numerous state constitutions were promulgated, concluding in 1891, when the present one was adopted. This constitution was designed for twin purposes: to limit the power of the legislature in favor of that of the governor, and to curb the influence of large commercial concerns, especially the railroads, which had been linked to various scandals involving legislative corruption (Miller 1994). One of the few exceptions to the general legislative weakness was the section concerning public education. Section 183 states, "The General Assembly shall, by appropriate legislation, provide for an efficient system of common schools throughout the state." The key word in this rather terse provision is "efficient," a term in vogue in 1891 because of the early American Industrial Revolution. The Kentucky Supreme Court would seize on this word almost one hundred years later to declare the entire Kentucky school system unconstitutional. The other notable point in this section is that the legislature, and no other body, is given the responsibility and duty to construct this "system of common schools." This constitutional charge became significant in the struggle between the legislature and governor over school reform.

In 1908, the legislature required districts to levy local property taxes to receive state money for education. The required amount of local money was quite low, though, until 1990, with the passage of KERA. By the 1920s, the population included over one hundred thousand total illiterates (Garrett 1989a). In 1953, the legislature passed a minimum foundation program, similar to that of other states in that the state guaranteed a "floor" of per-pupil spending for every child regardless of wealth, assuming a minimum local tax effort (ibid.). Of course, as elsewhere, richer districts were free to tax and spend above the foundation amount, and a substantial amount of the state funds were distributed to rich districts as well as poor, an unequal result. Even this foundation program was not truly funded until 1960 when Governor Bert Combs pushed through the legislature and a public referendum a three-cent state sales tax, sold under the slogan "One Cent for Soldier Boy, Two Cents for Johnny Boy," combining school aid with a veterans' bonus (ibid.). The tax earned Combs the nickname of the "education governor." We shall see Combs's continuing impact later.

In 1965, the Kentucky Court of Appeals seemingly handed education supporters a victory by requiring all property in the state to be assessed at full market value (*Russman* 1965). Many districts were not assessing at anywhere near market value, severely limiting the funds available to schools from local property taxes. The statewide median assessment was 27% of market value (*Rose* 1989:194).[1] The court ruling held out the promise of greater revenue from local school taxes. This hope was dashed, however, when the legislature promptly passed a law rolling back local property taxes so they would earn no more revenue than under the old assessments (*Rose* 1989: 195). Furthermore, the Court was never really able to enforce its ruling, so poor assessment remained a problem until the reform act of 1990 (Wolfson 1989). The final blow resulted from the property tax limitation movement of the late 1970s sparked by Proposition 13 in California. In 1979, the legislature passed House Bill 44, which capped the rate of increase of local property tax revenue at 4% per year unless voters approved a larger increase. This law further limited the options of the poorest districts, although their tax base was so low that larger tax increases would not be worthwhile. Still, the average local property tax rate declined 33% from 1979 to 1981 as a result of HB44 (*Rose* 1989:196).

By the 1980s, therefore, the outlook for education was bleak. On the financing side, as the Supreme Court noted later, "If one were to summarize the history of school funding in Kentucky, one might well say that every forward step taken to provide funds to local districts and to equalize money spent for the poor districts

has been countered by one backward step" (*Rose* 1989:196). Overall, in per-pupil expenditures, Kentucky ranked fortieth in the nation
(*Rose* 1989:197). Few, if any, of the one hundred seventy-six school
districts in the state even spent at the national average (Dove 1991).
Furthermore, disparities among the richest and poorest school districts were significant, as the tax base ratio was 10:1 richest to
poorest, and the high-low spending ratio approached 3:1, with the
rest of the districts in between (Goetz and Debertin 1992; Dove
1991). These financial problems were coupled with serious deficiencies in adminstration and governance of several districts. In
some parts of the state, mostly in eastern Kentucky, superintendents ran their districts as personal fiefdoms. In these districts, the
school system often was the largest employer. Superintendents
could create "machines" by putting relatives and friends on the
payroll as a janitor, cafeteria worker, teacher, with little state supervision. Education itself was secondary, and any change or innovation
was to be feared (*Lexington Herald-Leader* 1988; Garrett 1989c).

Money is not everything, of course, and various studies have
failed to find a link between increased spending on children and
higher test scores (Hanushek 1989, 1991). Unfortunately, there is
an abundance of proof that children were suffering under the Kentucky system. First, lack of money was reflected in deficient facilities in the poorest districts in eastern Kentucky. Many were forced
to hold classes in run-down buildings without the money to buy up-
to-date textbooks, while the richest districts bought computers for
their students housed in clean and modern buildings. Course offerings varied widely, with the poorest districts unable to offer advanced
classes in science, English, or math, and completely neglecting foreign language, music, and art (Dove 1991). Students in these districts
often had a difficult time preparing for any type of higher education
(Howington 1989a).

Second, the "products" or "outcomes" of the system were sub-
standard. Student achievement test scores varied from rich to poor,
and the overall state average on the American College Test (ACT)
lagged behind those of its immediate neighbors (*Rose* 1989:197).
Kentucky ranked fiftieth in the nation in the percentage of adults
with a high school diploma, and forty-ninth in the proportion of
adults with a college degree, but first in the percentage of adult
illiterates (Davis 1995). The statistic that explains the most about
the Kentucky public school system, however, was that statewide,
only 68.2% of ninth-grade students ever graduated from high school
(*Rose* 1989:197). In a global economy in which survival is increas-

ingly linked with education, Kentucky was falling far behind. This point was driven home in the mid-1980s, when Governor Martha Layne Collins persuaded the Toyota car company to locate a large factory in the bluegrass region. Toyota needed to hire a large number of skilled workers to operate its plant, yet was forced to turn away applicant after applicant because of lack of training (Wilkinson 1995:286). If poor education inhibited job creation in the richest part of the state, the rest of Kentucky could expect an even worse fate.

The sorry state of Kentucky public education became a cause célèbre for various interests. Business groups were clearly worried that their work forces would be unskilled compared with foreign competitors'. Most education groups strongly supported increased school funding. Leading newspapers took up the issue of education quality, running stories nearly every day on some aspect of educational corruption or failure. Another factor spurring change was a movement for education reform that was sweeping the South in the 1980s (Howington 1989b). After the struggles over civil rights, a new generation of leaders was trying to build the "New South" of a high-wage, high-growth, forward-looking economy, an effort to which education was central. At the forefront were governors such as Lamar Alexander in Tennessee, Richard Riley in South Carolina, and Bill Clinton in Arkansas.[2] Clinton was particularly notable because of his persuasive appearance at the Kentucky Capitol in the mid-1980s at the start of the reform debates in the legislature. Because of the convergence of these efforts, school reform was bound to become an issue in Kentucky politics in the 1980s. Still, the movement needed a focal point.

The Lawsuit: Rose v. Council for Better Education

In John Kingdon's (1984) terminology, the "policy entrepreneur" responsible for bringing all these various reform forces to a head was a former employee at the state Department of Education, Arnold Guess. He had been involved with education issues for years, but after he was dismissed from his job for political reasons, he had time on his hands to ponder a long-standing idea of his—a lawsuit against the state for greater equity in funding (Dove 1991: 88). Guess consulted with various friends around the state, mostly representing poorer districts in eastern Kentucky, and got encouragement for a lawsuit. He decided to hold a meeting of the newly formed Council For Better Education in May 1984 in Frankfort. The council decided to secure legal counsel and to ask its members' school boards for the tax revenue to finance a suit against the state (Dove 1991:88–89). The goal of this litigation was rather simple; superintendents of poorer districts wanted greater financial equity with the rest of the state, which could be accomplished only with more state money, as no one believed that taking money from the richer districts was politically possible or desirable, unlike in Texas (Dove 1991:115).

Reaction to the proposed lawsuit was swift and sharp. The chairmen of both education committees in the legislature, Senator Nelson Allen (D-Bellefonte) and Representative Jody Richards (D-Bowling Green), issued a statement saying that they thought the issue should be resolved legislatively, not in the courts (UPI 1984). State school superintendent Alice McDonald went even further, stating her opposition to the suit and vowing to go to court for an injunction against "misappropriation of funds" (Warren 1984). It was especially inappropriate, she argued, for these particular super-intendents, most of whom came from eastern Kentucky, with its reputation for corruption, to try to take the high ground in asking for more money. Several plaintiff districts were singled out for state audits as a form of intimidation, although no particular improprieties were found (Executive Editor 1989:135). The general legislative reaction was not much more positive. Because of the lack of emphasis on structural reform, the council could not even secure the support of the Prichard Committee for Academic Excellence, a prominent business and education group that had been pushing for reform for years (Dove 1991:111; Cropper 1988d). The council needed some instant credibility or its lawsuit would surely founder, in the courts or in the legislature (Dove 1991:89).

Guess's solution was to persuade one of his friends, former Governor Bert Combs, to become the lead attorney for the plaintiffs. Combs was born in a poor section of eastern Kentucky and was all too familiar with the problems of the state school system. Also, he had held a number of high-profile positions besides governor, including Justice of the Kentucky Court of Appeals (the state's high court at the time) and co-founder of what became the leading state law firm of Wyatt, Tarrant, and Combs (Dove 1991:89–90). Combs was quite reluctant to sue the General Assembly. As he later put it, he needed this suit "about as much as a hog needs a side saddle" (Combs 1991). The council, however, reminded Combs that he still claimed to be the "education governor" and a top-notch lawyer and related to him the sorry state of Kentucky education (ibid.). Once sixty-six state school districts had joined the council, a "critical mass," Combs was persuaded to take the case. According to many interviewees, Combs's name on the suit helped the council immensely in terms of popular perception and credibility with the policy-making community (Dove 1991:112). His direct influence on the legislature was limited, but he seemed to know every prominent Kentucky politician fairly well. The media and the interest groups were quite impressed that one of the leading Kentuckians would get involved in this suit. He was not just a figurehead, either, as his mind for legal and political strategy was still quite sharp (Dove 1991:116). Combs's participation was one more brick in the construction of school reform.

The most difficult legal problem Combs faced was that of naming the defendants (Combs 1991:371). He decided to take a kitchen sink approach in that he named all the policy actors with some control over the education budget, including the governor, the superintendent of public instruction, the state board of education, and the state treasurer. The legislature, of course, possessed the ultimate authority, but suing it presented a conundrum: How does one sue the legislature for not acting? Does one have to name all the members? Can the suit be confined to lawmakers' representative capacity, not their personal liability? Combs decided to name just the presiding officers of each body, Senator John "Eck" Rose (D-Winchester) and House Speaker Donald Blandford (D-Philpot), in their representative capacities. His reasoning is very important because it illuminates the limited goals of the lawsuit, which was intended to bring pressure on the legislature, but not to force court-ordered change. Combs related:

> We never expected this case to reach the point of confrontation between the General Assembly and the judiciary. We were concerned that if this should occur, the controversy between the court and the General Assembly would overshadow the merits of the plaintiffs' demands for improvement of the school system. Our objective was to obtain a declaratory judgment by Kentucky's highest court that the state's school system was inadequate and inefficient to the point of being unconstitutional, and that the oath of the members of the General Assembly required that body to establish and maintain a system that was constitutional.
>
> Our concept of the plaintiffs' case was that such a declaration by the supreme court would generate sufficient awareness of the dire needs of the public schools that the pressure of public opinion would spur the General Assembly into action. We thought, too,

that a supreme court decision could act as a buffer for those more timid members of the General Assembly ("limber twigs," in Kentucky vernacular) who panicked when the word "taxes" was even mentioned. (ibid.:372) [new paragraph added]

Because of this strategy, Combs decided to file the lawsuit in 1985, then wait and see what the legislature would do about it.

"A Mutual Failing"

The state political leadership took notice of the various forces converging for school reform. As Combs had hoped, something had to be done to address the concerns about the school system; in the words of one interviewee, "it was an issue whose time had come." In 1985, Collins called a special legislative session to deal with education, resulting in a new $300 million commitment, financed mostly through a corporate income tax. One of the major goals of this legislation was to reduce class sizes. This change was important, but nowhere near the massive structural reform that many, including the Prichard Committee, were advocating, and did not commit enough money to satisfy the poorer districts represented by the council, which was more displeased when the legislature did not appropriate the promised funds in the 1986 regular session (Dove 1991:93). In the 1986 session, the attitude of the legislature toward the council became even more hostile. Even Combs took some criticism from legislators who thought that the 1985 changes had satisfied the need for education reform. Furthermore, the Senate passed a bill that would bar the poorer school districts from using school funds to sue the state. The bill died in the Assembly Education Committee, but the message was clear. Also, the legislature hired attorney William Scent to defend it in court (Dove 1991:94–95).

The simplest explanation for the reluctance of the legislature to implement far-reaching reform is lack of political will to raise taxes. Collins, as all her immediate predecessors had done, had campaigned on a promise of "no new taxes." Once in office, she made it clear that she supported school reform in general, but like Ann Richards in Texas, did not aggressively push for a specific program in the legislature. She was not willing to take the political heat of a tax increase off the legislature, leadership that was seen as necessary in a traditionally gubernatorial-centered system. The legislature itself was split on the issue. Many lawmakers did not support a tax increase under any circumstances, although the "limber twigs" did not yet sense the type of broad-based consensus that would allow them to support any kind of significant reform. One interviewee sympathetic to the school reform cause termed this period a "mutual failing."

The 1987 gubernatorial race proved extremely significant for education reform. The real election was in the Democratic primary, as Kentucky was still essentially a one-party state.[3] The surprise winner of the primary and the general election was eastern Kentucky businessman Wallace Wilkinson, who had never held public office. Wilkinson had run an aggressive campaign touting the idea of a state lottery, instead of new taxes, to pay for education reform. He also stressed the need for structural change in the school system that would place greater emphasis on goals and accountability, but the lottery was the theme that resonated with the voters (ibid.). Because of Wilkinson's outsider status and his stated lack of enthusiasm for a large tax increase for education, many in the establishment were suspicious of him when he took office. The media, at least according to Wilkinson in his autobiography, portrayed him as a "backwoods Bubba" who would dash the hopes of those trying to make Kentucky schools respectable again (Wilkinson 1995:57). The Prichard Committee, which might have been a natural ally on his restructuring proposals, was quite nervous because of his reluctance to commit any money to reform (ibid.:137). Professional education groups also focused on his opposition to taxes and did not like the sound of whatever "accountability" measures he proposed (ibid.:48).

During the 1988 regular legislative session, the legislature and governor began suspicious of one another, and relations deteriorated from there. Regarding education issues, the first priority of the legislature was guaranteeing that the 1985 class size reductions would be fully funded, whereas Wilkinson did not want to be locked into such a commitment. He wanted the legislature to pass his ideas concerning goal-setting and school accountability before he would agree to their funding, but the leadership wanted Wilkinson's commitment to a large tax increase before considering his school restructuring proposals. The immediate effect was near complete gridlock. The central issue was the timing of the tax increase. Wilkinson tried to assure legislators in private that he would be willing to support a tax increase when the time was right, yet his public rhetoric spoke to the contrary. Given the basic lack of trust between the legislative leadership and the governor, it is unsurprising that when Wilkinson said he would agree to a tax increase, in the words of one interviewee, "no one believed him." Therefore, the result of the 1988 session was the status quo; the 1985 reforms were fully funded, but no other changes were made. The lawsuit was progressing through the legal system, however, and holding the promise of breaking the political impasse.

The Corns Decision

As noted, Combs[4] decided to file the suit in Franklin County Circuit Court, whose jurisdiction included Frankfort. Fortunately for the plaintiffs, the case, called *Council for Better Education v. Collins et al.* (1988) (soon to be renamed *Council v. Rose*), drew Judge Raymond Corns for the trial hearing in 1987. Corns had served in numerous posts in state government, including as a legal advisor to Combs during Combs's gubernatorial term. Corns also had considerable experience with education issues, as he had acted as chief legal counsel for the state department of education for fifteen years, and had assisted Combs's deputy attorney Theodore Lavit, and plaintiff adviser Kern Alexander in filing a suit in 1972 against the federal government for unequal distribution of Title I education funds. Because of these connections between the plaintiffs and the judge, one might expect that questions would be raised concerning a possible conflict of interest. It appears that the issue was discussed among the parties, but quickly dismissed. The benefits of Corns's participation, it was felt, outweighed the disadvantages. Given the complex nature of the factual issues, Corns would not have to be "brought up to speed," as a more inexperienced judge would. Corns also promised to be impartial, and given the connections between most Kentucky political figures, there might not have been a better alternative. Finally, both sides knew that the case would eventually reach the state Supreme Court regardless of what Corns decided (Dove 1991:96).

The trial was short. Combs focused on the low quality of education provided to children in the poorest districts, arguing that it was not "efficient" under the Kentucky constitution. Numerous education experts testified to the inadequacies of the system and the disparities among the rich and poor school districts. As a summarizing touch, Combs put in the record photographs of the deteriorating facilities in the poorest schools in Eastern Kentucky (ibid.). Scent responded to Combs's arguments on a variety of grounds. First, he argued that the plaintiffs had no standing to sue, as school districts were "creatures of the state" under long-established law.

Second, the plaintiffs improperly chose specific legislators as defendants. Third, the legislature, not the judiciary, had sole responsibility for maintaining the school system. Fourth, the legislature had been making changes in the system to discharge its constitutional duty, including the 1985 special session reforms. Fifth, mismanagement and waste in the poor districts, not inadequate funding, cause the problems. If the poor districts would just use their resources better, their children could excel as well (Commonwealth of Kentucky [Brief for Defendants]).

After both sides were heard, Corns took a six-month recess, coinciding with the 1988 legislative session, to issue an opinion. The impasse of the 1988 session cannot have encouraged Corns about the possibility of the legislative and executive branches resolving the issues on their own. It was still a surprise to many when Corns declared the state school finance mechanism unconstitutional. His opinion detailed the long list of problems with the school system, not only including finance, although his actual ruling was confined to that issue. Schoolchildren, he said, were "suffering from an extreme case of educational malnutrition" (Dove 1991:98). Because of his childhood in a poor district, Corns said, "I am a representative of inequity." He declared education to be a fundamental right under the Kentucky constitution and ruled that the present system was nowhere near "efficient" under Section 183. Furthermore, Corns promulgated seven "capacities" that each child in the Kentucky school system should possess after high school graduation, a list that would become a central part of the Supreme Court opinion. Each child should have:

i)   sufficient oral and written communication skills to enable students to function in a complex and rapidly changing civilization;

ii) sufficient knowledge of economic, social, and political systems to enable the student to make informed choices;

iii) sufficient understanding of governmental processes to enable the student to understand the issues that affect his or her community, state, and nation;

iv) sufficient self-knowledge and knowledge of his or her mental and physical wellness;

v)   sufficient grounding in the arts to enable each student to appreciate his or her cultural and historical heritage;

vi) sufficient training or preparation for advanced training in either academic or vocational fields so as to enable each child to choose and pursue life work intelligently;

vii) sufficient levels of academic or vocational skills to enable public school students to compete favorably with their counterparts in surrounding states, in academics or in the job market. (Dove 1991:100)

Beyond these guidelines, Corns did not offer the legislature many specifics on remedying the situation. He did not explicitly order the legislature to raise taxes, yet he stated that redistribution of funds from the richest to the poorest districts was unacceptable. Therefore, more money was needed, just as the plaintiff districts had asked (Cropper 1988c).

Corns retained jurisdiction of the case to allow time for the political branches to construct a solution to the problems. In another controversial move, he decided to appoint a five-member commission to study the issues and issue a public report that he would use in his final order. All the members had educational backgrounds and were sympathetic to the need for school reform (Cropper 1988b). Judging from the interview data, however, it appears that the real purpose of the commission was to increase the pressure for reform by holding public hearings around the state that the media would cover. The report would also serve this purpose, as it would be one more document chronicling the deficiencies in Kentucky education. Finally, the commission would buy time for the reform movement to gain strength and for the pro-change message to sink in with the political branches.

The targets of this public relations campaign, the legislature and governor, did not present a unified reaction to the Corns ruling. Surprisingly to some, Wilkinson said he agreed with the ruling and asked that his name be removed from the case. His meetings with commission member Kern Alexander to make sure that the two agreed on the need for restructuring, not just more money, might have played a role in this decision (Dove 1991:99). Wilkinson still did not agree to new taxes, however.

In the legislature, reaction was split between two significant groups. The first primarily consisted of the named defendants, Rose and Blandford, who did not appreciate being known as the "obstacles" to education reform. Rose and Blandford, in the words of some interviewees, were quite angry at the Corns decision because of what they saw as the judge's usurpation of legislative prerogatives.

They had addressed education in the 1985 session, and who was a circuit judge to second-guess them? According to some interviewees, the legislative leadership also felt that Corns was part of the "old-boys network" of eastern Kentucky. Combs had manufactured this decision on behalf of the most corrupt superintendents in the state. Publicly, Blandford vowed to appeal:

> We feel the legislature of Kentucky has done a good job, based on the economy of Kentucky. . . . We don't know what (the ruling) says. . . . We need some interpretation. . . . I feel like we've done a respectable job with what we've had to work with. . . . I don't think we need a court or a judge or some kind of special commission out there telling us what our job is. We have a serious question as to whether the court system has the authority to legislate to the degree that we feel like they're doing in this decision. (Cropper 1988a)

Other legislators saw the ruling as a real opportunity for change. Prominent in this set of lawmakers was a group informally known as the "Young Turks." These House members were relatively youthful, bright, and experienced in educational issues. Many had served as teachers, school board members, and/or had spouses who were educators. Their reaction to the court decision was quite positive overall, typified by House Public Education Committee chair Roger Noe (D-Harlan), who said, "We are not going to wait till we're told to do something in this process. We want to be a leader and a partner in whatever decision is made. . . . (The court ruling) could be the stick that is being used to publicly force the legislature into additional action" (Cropper 1988c).

Because the General Assembly was not scheduled to convene again until January 1990, and because Wilkinson did not want to call a special session until after the Supreme Court had ruled on the case, education reform remained at the talking stage among policymakers. The commission report, which called for greater state involvement in education, in September 1988 did not seem to have much impact on those deliberations. In fact, several interviewees did not even recall the commission or the report until pressed. After the report was issued, Corns made his ruling final on October 14, 1988.

The Supreme Court Rules: A "Huge Gamble"

Scent wanted to expedite the appeal to the Supreme Court, bypassing the Court of Appeals. Combs acquiesced, as both parties knew the case would end there anyway. The Supreme Court was willing to hear the case as well, setting oral arguments for December 1988. Because of the relatively short time since the trial court ruling, the claims that both sides presented were essentially the same as those argued at the trial level. Combs and Debra Dawahare for the plaintiffs asserted that the Kentucky school system did not meet the standard of "efficiency" under Section 183 of the Kentucky constitution. Scent highlighted potential process flaws, such as standing and improper naming of defendants. Scent also defended the legislature in maintaining the school system, arguing that it was doing the best it could to live up to the constitutional standard (Dove 1991:101–2).

While the Supreme Court deliberated, a majority of legislators stated in an anonymous *Louisville Courier-Journal* poll that they were willing to raise taxes to pay for school reform, but only if the governor publicly supported this effort (Johnson 1989). A sales tax increase was seen as the best available alternative. A poll of the public showed that Kentuckians were willing to pay increased taxes if the money would go toward education, a result that "shocked" legislators (Johnson 1989). Also around this time, a legislatively commissioned study of the school system called for a significant increase in funding, although very little restructuring or increased accountability was contemplated (Wilkinson 1995:216). In April 1989, the legislature and governor were moving toward a general agreement on a package for education. Wilkinson's accountability measures were included, with more funding of the 1985–1986 class size reforms and other programs. The total cost was projected at $350 million. If the Supreme Court had not been ready to make a ruling, Wilkinson might have called a special legislative session to pass this plan. Instead, the impending ruling convinced him to wait and see what the judicial branch would contribute (Wilkinson 1995:190–91).

The Supreme Court, especially Chief Justice Robert Stephens,[5] was faced with several difficult choices in resolving *Rose*. Should Corns be upheld? If so, should the opinion focus on the finance equity issues as Corns had, or should it expand the scope of litigation to include all the problems with Kentucky schools? What kind of remedy could the Court order, and would the legislature go along? How would the remedy be enforced? Regardless of the various factors that went into the opinion (more on this below), Stephens answered the questions in a manner that surprised just about everyone in the Kentucky policy-making community. In an opinion issued on June 2, 1989, he not only upheld Corns's opinion, but greatly expanded it (*Rose* 1989). Stephens did not declare just the school financing method unconstitutional. He voided the *entire Kentucky school system* as not meeting the standard of "an efficient system of public schools" in Section 183 of the Kentucky constitution. Stephens wrote:

> The issue we decide on this appeal is whether the Kentucky General Assembly has complied with its constitutional mandate to "provide an efficient system of common schools throughout the state."
>
> In deciding that it has not, we intend no criticism of the substantial efforts made by the present General Assembly and by its predecessors, nor do we intend to substitute our judicial authority for the authority and discretion of the General Assembly. We are, rather, exercising our constitutional duty in declaring that, when we consider the evidence in the record, and when we apply the constitutional requirement of Section 183 to that evidence, it is crystal clear that the General Assembly has fallen short of its duty to enact legislation to provide for an efficient system of common schools throughout the state. (*Rose* 1989:189)

Stephens then proceeded to detail the inadequacies in the educational system. Regarding this evidence, he stated, "The tidal wave of the appellees' evidence literally engulfs that of the appellants" (*Rose* 1989:197). Therefore, "the total local and state effort in education in Kentucky's primary and secondary education is inadequate and lacking in uniformity. It is discriminatory as to the children living in 80% of our local school districts" (*Rose* 1989:198).

Stephens then dealt with the procedural issues of standing, and a proper class action. He argued that the school districts had standing because they had a real interest in the performance of the state school system as it affected them. Stephens conceded that there was not a proper class action on behalf of all Kentucky schoolchildren, but maintained that this was irrelevant, as the children whose parents did sue were being harmed by state actions. That only one of these children testified at the trial did not matter either (*Rose* 1989: 199-203). Regarding the naming of certain legislators as defendants, he cited cases from other jurisdictions in which this practice was accepted, although he agreed that it was not a proper claim. Yet "This case of major statewide importance has been tried and practiced vigorously by all parties and was decided on the merits by the trial court. We will not now initiate useless circuity of action by requiring the cumbersome process of serving all members of the General Assembly" (*Rose* 1989:204–5).

Stephens then examined the debates in the 1891 Constitution concerning Section 183 and the definition of "efficiency," with subsequent interpretations. The result of this historical perusal was a list of nine characteristics that an "efficient" system of common schools must possess:

1) The establishment, maintenance, and funding of common schools in Kentucky is the sole responsibility of the General Assembly.

2) Common schools shall be free to all.

3) Common schools shall be available to all Kentucky schoolchildren.

4) Common schools shall be substantially uniform throughout the state.

5) Common schools shall provide equal educational opportunities to all Kentucky children, regardless of place of residence or economic circumstances.

6) Common schools shall be monitored by the General Assembly to assure that they are operated with no waste, no duplication, no mismanagement, and with no political influence.

7) The premise for the existence of common schools is that all children have a constitutional right to an adequate education.

8) The General Assembly shall provide funding which is sufficient to provide each child in Kentucky an adequate education.

9) An adequate education is one which has as its goal the development of the seven capacities recited (in Judge Corns' opinion noted above [Rose 1989:212–13].)

Stephens closed his opinion by emphasizing the sweeping nature of the ruling. He wanted to make the opinion quite clear as to the legislative duty:

> Lest there be any doubt, the result of our decision is that Kentucky's entire system of common schools is unconstitutional. . . . Just as the bricks and mortar used in the construction of a schoolhouse, while contributing to the building's facade, do not ensure the overall structural adequacy of the schoolhouse, particular statutes drafted by the legislature in crafting and designing the current school system are not unconstitutional in and of themselves. Like the crumbling schoolhouse which must be redesigned and revitalized for more more efficient use . . . statutes relating to education may be reenacted as components of a constitutional system if they

combine with other component statutes to form an efficient and thereby constitutional system. . . . Section 183 places an absolute duty on the General Assembly to re-create, re-establish a new system of common schools in the Commonwealth. (*Rose* 1989:215)

According to the Court, the new "schoolhouse" must be built by the end of the next regular session of the General Assembly convening in January 1990, only seven months away. Stephens did not remand the case to Franklin County Circuit Court for Corns to supervise, but made no provision for rehearing, placing the burden for constructing the system solely and squarely on the General Assembly. At least one interviewee speculated that Stephens might have been worried that Corns, in concert with the eastern Kentucky superintendents, might try to narrow the scope of litigation again to concern only the financial issues. In any event, Stephens was taking a "huge gamble," in the words of one interviewee, that the legislature would act on its own.

Two Justices concurred in the ruling and two dissented. Justice Charles Leibson filed the dissent that was most noted in the broader policy-making community. This result was perhaps ironic in that Leibson was a strong proponent of independent examination of the Kentucky constitution, as the majority had done, but he also firmly believed in judicial restraint and observance of legal procedures, which he felt were being ignored in this case. His attack on the majority encompassed a number of different issues. First and foremost, even though he agreed in principle that the Kentucky school system was not "efficient," Leibson argued that the issue of efficiency was a "political question" not subject to judicial resolution. The "political" nature of these issues, Leibson said, was most apparent in the majority ruling that declared the entire school system unconstitutional, yet refusing to find any specific statutes null and void. This ruling went far beyond what the plaintiffs had asked for. In fact, according to Leibson, if one took this language seriously, the districts had just succeeded in persuading the Court to declare their own existence unconstitutional (*Rose* 1989:224).

Turning to the parties, Leibson claimed that the plaintiff districts had no standing to sue because they were subject to change or abolition at the discretion of the General Assembly. The schoolchildren were not proper parties because they had alleged no specific harm, aside from one student's testimony that there was a computer class she would have liked to have taken if her school had offered it. Nevertheless, the Court treated this small group of students as representative of the entire state student population, which Leibson felt was a serious mistake (*Rose* 1989:226).

Concerning the defendants, Leibson noted that the only true defendants were the legislators, because they were the only parties charged with carrying out the remedy. But how can two legislators elected at the last regular session "represent" the entire General Assembly? Leibson argued that the legislature has no existence outside the laws it passes, and that once it adjourns, it ceases to be until its next session. How can the majority bind future General Assemblies through an order directed to two individuals? He called this part of the majority opinion "pure fiction, not (just) legal fiction . . . This is a lawsuit with no defendants" (*Rose* 1989:227).

Leibson concluded (supplemented by comments on a motion for rehearing):

> An appreciation of the difference between legislative and judicial lawmaking is essential to maintaining constitutionally mandated separation of powers. . . . This (decision) is more than a vain act or a bad precedent. The result may well create havoc in the educational process. . . . (On rehearing) Since publication of the initial Majority Opinion three months ago, the predominant reaction from the public, the press, and the politicians, has been that our decision provides the Governor and General Assembly an unprecedented opportunity to reform a deficient educational process. . . . Unfortunately, providing opportunities at the expense of the integrity of the judicial process is not a traditional item on the judicial agenda, nor in my view an appropriate role for the courts. . . . We have now become part of the problem when we intend to be part of the solution (*Rose* 1989:224, 227–28).

"Building a New Schoolhouse": The Construction of KERA

As Leibson noted, the predominant reaction in the Kentucky policy-making community to the Supreme Court decision was a combination of shock, worry, and hope that can be synthesized in the word "opportunity," which policymakers used again and again in the interviews to describe the consequences of the ruling. The Court, according to one legislator, had "turned us loose" to solve the problems in the educational system without the usual political constraints, specifically those against raising taxes. Another legislator agreed, saying the political limits were temporarily lifted, creating a "freedom of the moment."

After the decision, the key players in school finance reform were Wilkinson, Rose, and Blandford. If school reform were to succeed, all three would have to reach agreement. They started building consensus early, meeting at the governor's mansion the day after *Rose* was announced (Wilkinson 1995:199). The results of this meeting were general agreement on the goals of the political response and the process necessary to achieve those ends. Publicly, Wilkinson said:

> The Supreme Court has given us an opportunity to start with a clean slate. Those of us in the executive and legislative branches are in agreement that we need to start from scratch. It is no longer a question of my plan or their plan. As of today, it's our plan. We will begin immediately to take up the issue of what kind of school system we can devise that meets the Supreme Court's guidelines of adequacy and uniformity. We are not looking back. . . . I want to make this final pledge. . . . When we can say to the people of this Commonwealth that we've built a better school system . . . a system, in other words, that provides equal opportunity for an adequate education, I will support the necessary revenue measures to pay for it (ibid.:200).

Wilkinson appeared finally willing to publicly commit to new taxes, as he felt the timing was right. He could be much more confident that his ideas about accountability would be part of the reform legislation because "The principles of public policy contained in the court's opinion were the same ones underlying the restructuring policy assumptions I championed" (ibid.:195). Wilkinson and legislators debated the size and composition of the tax increase until the very end, however.

Rose and Blandford also noted the sea change that had taken place because of the Court opinion, although they were a little more cautious than Wilkinson. Rose argued that special interests no longer had to protect their turf, because "there no longer is any turf. . . . We're beyond politics now" (UPI 1989; Bleiberg 1989). Blandford stated: "I think we need to take some time to decipher, to determine exactly what it is the court is suggesting and directing, and go back to the drawing board. . . . We need to build an entire system from the ground up. . . . There are no longer any sacred cows" (Bleiberg 1989; Voskuhl 1989). Even though these leaders might have felt that the Court had gone too far, they were not willing to criticize the Court or offer resistance because of the momentum for change (Wilkinson 1995:193).

Rose, Blandford, and Wilkinson decided in the meeting at the mansion to construct the reform act outside the normal legislative process. Their goal was to keep tight control over the final product, as so much, including their political futures, was riding on the success of school reform. In the words of one participant, "We have to control this." Similarly, a legislator reported that the general feeling was "The ones who create have to be the ones who pass." Their solution was to create a joint legislative-executive task force (ibid.:201). The task force, according to most interviewees, was structured to minimize the influence, but not the input, of interest groups, namely the professional educator groups such as the Kentucky Education Association, the Kentucky School Boards Association, and the Kentucky Association of School Administrators, and the business-led or civic groups such as the Prichard Committee and the Chamber of Commerce. The "Young Turks" on the House and Senate education committees were also excluded from full participation, although the chairs of both committees were later added to the task force. The leadership felt that their ties to the professional education groups were too strong to allow them votes. One legislator noted that as the task force was originally set up, there were no women, no ethnic minorities, no Republicans, and no teachers (although a Republican was added later). After much deliberation, Wilkinson also decided not to become a formal member of the task force. He was concerned that if he were not a participant, he might have to sign something he disagreed with, but overriding that worry was the analysis that if he were a member, the media would focus on any conflict between him and the legislature instead of the work of the task force itself (ibid.:202–3). Given that legislative-executive relations were not completely harmonious even during this period (more below), Wilkinson probably made the right decision.

The sixteen legislators and five executive branch representatives on the task force all had fairly close ties to the leadership. The process valued unity over openness; decisions were to be made by consensus, not formal voting, whenever possible (ibid.:203–4). There were public meetings of the task force at which all interested parties could speak, but much of the most important work was conducted behind closed doors, according to respondents. The task force (see Jennings 1989a for a list of members) was divided into three subcommittees, each charged with reforming a different aspect of the educational system, including curriculum, governance, and finance. Rose and Blandford were the chairs of each subcommittee, but many interviewees reported that they avoided most of the deliberations, increasing their involvement only when the package was ready to be put together into formal legislation. The "real" leaders of each subcommittee were Senator Mike Moloney (D-Lexington), Representative Joe Clarke (D-Danville), and Representative Joe Barrows (D-Versailles) on finance, Senator David Karem (D-Louisville) and Representative Jody Richards (D-Bowling Green; later speaker) on curriculum, and Senator Joe Wright (D-Harned) and Representative Kenny Rapier (D-Bardstown) on governance.

The task force leaders also made the key decision that outside consultants were needed to incorporate the latest ideas in national education circles into the new school system. In the words of one participant, "We needed thinking outside the box." As it turned out, the selection of the consultants was the point in the process at which Wilkinson had the most direct influence. He was very concerned about the ideas that would be incorporated because of his firm desire for greater accountability and restructuring. To that end, he sent his close adviser and secretary of education, Jack Foster, to a meeting with experts from the National Governors' Association, the National Conference on State Legislatures, and the Education Committee of the States to discuss consultant candidates. Foster selected David Hornbeck for the curriculum committee, as it appeared his views were closest to Wilkinson's, and accepted the experts' recommendation of John Augenblick for finance (Wilkinson 1995:204). Legislators vetted and approved both candidates, and also added the husband-and-wife team of Luvern Cunningham and Lila Carol to consult with the governance subcommittee.

Over the next few months, the three subcommittees held numerous meetings, public and private, to work through the various reform options. The legislators and executive branch representatives considered ideas from a number of different sources, varying by subcommittee. The curriculum subcommittee was the focus of the majority of attention of the outside actors for several reasons, not least of which was that this panel was supposed to report first with its outline of what children should be expected to learn in the new school system and how best to achieve these outcomes (Jennings 1989c). Governance and especially finance would then follow from the needs of the curriculum program. As it turned out, the panels worked mostly independently, but with increasing coordination as the time for constructing a package drew closer.

The result of all this input was a significantly altered curriculum. Perhaps the most drastic change was that grades 1–3 were reorganized into what became known as the "ungraded primary."

Students were to learn at their own pace, with their progress being measured by skills tests, not by the older system of letter grades and near-automatic promotion from one grade to the next. Beginning in the fourth grade, student ability would be assessed by periodic statewide tests putting heavy emphasis on problem-solving ability, instead of the traditional multiple-choice exams. So-called writing portfolios also assumed a central place, forcing students to write more frequently and more adeptly than ever. The state Department of Education was charged with promulgating standards and guidelines for the assessment tests, eventually known as the Kentucky Instructional Results Information System (KIRIS). The results of these exams would have real consequences for the schools, as Hornbeck advocated. Hornbeck's original idea tied teacher pay to the test results, but the subcommittee modified the plan to make the monetary "rewards" for good results schoolwide, whereas schools that performed badly for more than one year would be declared "schools in crisis," ripe for state takeover (Jennings 1990a).

The general theme of the governance subcommittee recommendations was to transfer power from the elected local school boards that patronage appointments and, in the words of the Court, "political influence" had compromised, to the state level or the school itself. For example, the subcommittee endorsed "site-based management," or the idea that schools should be free to run their own affairs, including hiring, firing, and some aspects of curriculum, as long as they were accountable to state standards and limited by an overall budget set by the local school board. Other recommendations included replacement of the elected state superintendent of public instruction with an appointed state school commissioner, or "education czar"; creation of an agency charged with monitoring schools for waste and corruption (eventually known as the Office of Education Accountability); and a statewide ban on nepotism in school hiring (Jennings 1989d).

Ironically, the finance subcommittee, which was charged with remedying the problems that led to the lawsuit, received comparatively the least attention from the various interests, although certainly every group, including the plaintiff districts, the Kentucky School Boards Association, the Kentucky Education Association, and the Prichard Committee were interested in seeing what conclusions the panel reached. The largest districts in the state, including Louisville and Lexington, were also concerned about the recommendations. Complicating equity matters, these districts were also among the richest in the state. They were quite fearful that the panel might attempt to achieve fiscal equality by "leveling down" their programs to the level of the poorer rural districts (Miller 1989). The urban districts also strongly pointed out to the legislators that underassessment of property was still a significant problem in many counties, although not theirs. Furthermore, the poorest districts also tended to levy lower tax rates than the Louisville and Lexington districts, whose rates were relatively high. The excuse for the poor districts until now was that a rate increase would do no good because of their miniscule tax base. The legislators, in consultation with Augenblick, concluded that the poorest districts would have to accept a greater tax burden in return for more finance equity (Thompson 1989).

Augenblick and the legislative leadership, mostly Moloney and Clarke, supported a significant funding increase to allow local districts to pay for a "bare-bones" program. Every district, however, would be required to make a contribution through a minimum local tax rate of 25 cents per $100 of assessed value, plus 5 cents for facilities. If the district could not meet the foundation level at this tax rate, the state would make up the difference. Again, accountability was required; property assessments would have to be at full market value, and state investigators would be charged with supervising the local assessors to see that the rules were followed. Many districts in the state, including the largest, taxed well beyond the minimum rate of 30 cents per $100 value. The finance panel agreed that they should be able to continue these higher rates. Furthermore, up to a certain level (set at 15% over the base amount), they would not be subject to the restrictions of House Bill 44, which capped the revenue increase in any one year to 4%. Within this level, known as Tier 1, the state would provide matching funds for rate increases in individual districts, equalizing tax bases.

State funds were not unlimited, though, and a few districts, including Louisville and Lexington, taxed even higher than the Tier 1 matching amounts. Therefore, the leaders had to decide whether to "level down" these districts, the eventual result in Texas. The leaders and Augenblick agreed that districts should be able to go beyond the Tier 1 level to meet local needs and preferences, and that the Supreme Court would be willing to tolerate some equity discrepancies between districts. What they did not know was the line between permissible and impermissible inequity. Augenblick argued for less discrepancy, but the legislators wanted more tolerance. The result was a compromise, an overall cap on spending set at such a high level (30% over Tier 1) that most districts would not reach it for a long time. House Bill 44 would apply to Tier 2, capping the rate of revenue increase for any district at 4% and, it was hoped, restraining the richest districts from forging too far ahead of the poorest districts. Thus, in Kentucky, the politicians made a different choice from their Texas counterparts, deciding to let the richest districts keep their tax rate and return, although with some restrictions (Wilson 1990a).

There are a number of reasons for this difference. First, as noted in the discussion of the Court and "local enrichment," the Court was not clear on where the line was between acceptable and unacceptable inequality. Therefore, the political leaders gambled that the Court would tolerate some disparity in the name of a newer and better system. This "gamble" is rather similar to the risk the Texas legislature took in passing Senate Bill 1, the first (unsuccessful) attempt to achieve equity, yet in Texas, reforms were limited to the finance issue. Second, in Texas, the richest districts in the state were generally small areas containing oil, gas, or nuclear facilities or rich suburban enclaves. In Kentucky, the richest districts were the largest, educating about fifteen percent of the total school population of the state. "Leveling-down" such a significant number of children seemed wrong from a political and policy standpoint, leading legislators to opt for comparatively more inequity.

The package of school system changes, to be known as the Kentucky Education Reform Act (KERA), was in the final stages of construction when the General Assembly opened its regular session in January 1990.

Passing the Kentucky Education Reform Act

Unfortunately for the cause of reform, relations between Wilkinson and the legislative leadership, which had seemed to be improving in the summer, were nosediving even lower than in the stalemated 1988 session. After appearing to support a tax increase subsequent to the meeting at the mansion, Wilkinson retreated a bit, stating that only relatively minor tax changes were needed, such as repeal of the deductibility of federal income taxes from state income tax returns. This thinking ran counter to the legislators' support of a one-cent increase in the state sales tax to six percent (Loftus 1989; Jennings 1989e). Furthermore, personality intruded. In late January, Wilkinson adviser James Carville, who had assisted the governor in his 1987 campaign, made an obscene remark about Kentucky legislators to a reporter in a conversation that Carville thought was off the record (Cross 1991b), poisoning interbranch relations for weeks. Wilkinson contributed to the conflict by running television ads criticizing the legislature for its allegedly corrupt insider ways, hinting that lawmakers were about to divert state lottery proceeds into "their General Fund" (Loftus 1990a). He defended this action, saying it was the only way to make legislators pay attention to his ideas (Wilkinson 1995:311), but the short-term effect was increased tension. Also hanging over the proceedings was Wilkinson's push for a constitutional amendment allowing him to succeed himself as governor (Loftus 1990a). The constitution limited governors to one four-year term, a provision that was not removed until 1992.

Eventually, though, the spirit of compromise prevailed. In a bold move, Wilkinson's final revenue package increased taxes by over $1 billion through a combination of repeal of federal deductibility, a sales tax on services, and rises in the cigarette tax and business income tax. Wilkinson's justification was that he was not increasing the tax rate of any general tax, just the rates of targeted taxes (Wilkinson 1995:239–40). The billion-dollar price tag was a large step in the direction of reform, as it would more than pay for the changes that the task force proposed (Loftus 1990b). The legislature was still committed to a one-cent increase in the sales tax, however, feeling that the public would think that a sales tax rise was more fair because everyone paid it. Also, legislators might not have been eager to offend powerful interests, such as lawyers, doctors, and newspapers, which the services sales tax would have affected. In fact, the *Louisville Courier-Journal*, generally one of the leaders in support of school reform, editorialized against application of the sales tax to newspaper advertising (Wilkinson 1995: 248). Faced with a choice between the one-cent general sales tax rise or no package, Wilkinson relented, in what he later said was a bitter disappointment (ibid.:253). There were not nearly enough votes in the House to make the sweeping changes he wanted in the tax structure. In return, though, Wilkinson did get a road-bond issue that he wanted, and a guarantee from leadership that the education reform package would be passed intact (ibid.:251). Days after the switch, Wilkinson said, "I determined I had to do something to make something happen. . . . It was getting so late that I felt I had to break this thing loose" (Cross and Loftus 1990). On the legislative side, there was incentive for compromise as well. Rapier said the legislature had to pass something because "our credibility was on the line" (ibid.).

After Wilkinson and legislative leaders agreed on the general outlines for the revenue package, the task became to sell school reform, and especially the tax increase, to the legislature as a whole. The job of assembling a majority in the legislature was usually carried out by the governor for major bills or by the majority whips on more minor legislation. In the case of KERA, though, the speaker took on the task (Loftus 1990c). One interviewee even reported that before the vote Blandford visited each legislative office with a clipboard pad full of desired projects and asked each member how he or she would vote. The vote determined whether projects were circled or crossed off. (At least one Democratic committee chair lost his post because of his vote against KERA [Cross 1996]. It seems clear that at this point, horse-trading was the theme of the day (Cross 1990a).

There were a few different sources of opposition to KERA at the time of the vote. Primarily, many members were opposed to the tax increase, not only the sales tax rise but also the required rise in the minimum effort of many low-taxing districts. Republicans in particular saw the tax issue as a golden opportunity to use in the next election to break the Democratic stranglehold on the General Assembly. Others opposed the education reforms because they went too far, too fast, or greatly resented how the task force had excluded rank-and-file legislators from decision-making. On the floor, Rep. Joe Barrows, who disagreed with the local tax increase, said, "This whole process has been fast-forwarded about as fast-forward as you've ever seen it" (Loftus and Jennings 1990).

Amendments that would weaken the minimum required local effort and the minimum revenue increase for each district were rebuffed. The House then adopted KERA, 58–42, and the Senate passed a similar bill, 30–8, days later. The bill then returned to the House for final passage (Howington, Jennings, and Wilson 1990; Jennings and Howington 1990). One of the more notable speeches in the KERA debates was given in the House before the final vote by Rep. Greg Stumbo (D-Prestonsburg), a member of the leadership who hailed from eastern Kentucky, where he had received only a minimal education as a child. (In fact, many of the participants in the battles over KERA, such as Guess, Combs, Corns, Blandford, Rose, and Wilkinson could tell similar stories of the lack of good formal schooling as children. It is possible that this experience helped motivate their support for KERA.) Stumbo began his emotional speech by admitting that he did not agree with all the aspects of KERA, but stated that that was probably a good thing.

Furthermore, "when you look at the part of the state that I come from, and the fact that kids all too often start out behind in life and all they do is get farther behind, and I think that what we have a chance to do today is to see that that never happens again— that no child in Kentucky will ever have to look back and say that he or she didn't receive the full education that he or she was entitled by the constitution of this state." As the national spotlight focused on Kentucky, "we're not going to be a follower any more. We're going to be a leader" (Howington and Jennings 1990; Stumbo 1990). Stumbo then received a standing ovation from his colleagues.

After the House repassed the bill, Wilkinson signed it on April 11, 1990. He touched on the same themes as Stumbo had, noting the poor education that had kept him from college. He ended by saying, "Now Kentucky leads" (Jennings 1990c). The leading newspapers in the state were similarly proud of the law. The *Louisville Courier-Journal*, in an editorial entitled "For the History Books," called KERA the "best hope for Kentucky's children" and a "watershed in Kentucky (and in) the evolution of the Legislature." It had the "potential to bring about the most profound change in education since one-room schoolhouses began to pop up in Kentucky's villages and hollows" (*LCJ* 1990).

The "Outcome" of KERA

It was probably inevitable that such a sweeping change in public policy, especially one championed by liberal newspapers in a conservative state, would provoke a backlash against the pro-KERA "establishment," centered on the legislature. Larry Forgy, a former law partner of Bert Combs and member of the Corns panel, led the charge. Forgy was not necessarily opposed to school reform, but believed that the legislature and governor had ventured far beyond what the court decision had required of the political branches. According to Forgy, a $200 million increase in funding to the poorest districts would have satisfied the Court, instead of the $1.2 billion tax increase used for primary and secondary education and for many noneducational areas of state government. Beyond the monetary issue, the reforms mandated in KERA were too experimental, according to Forgy. It was "imprudent" to uproot an entire school system overnight, he said (Forgy 1990). Furthermore, below the surface opposition was growing to what one conservative Republican interviewee called the "social engineering" of KERA. There were two major interconnected sources of opposition, spearheaded by largely conservative Christian groups and including many worried parents and harried teachers.

The first source resisted a perceived lack of emphasis on basic skills in the new system, a special concern of the parents. One parent was quoted as saying: "My child is not challenged. Everything is writing. There is no right and wrong" (Malone 1994). In a Bluegrass State Poll, a clear majority labeled the reforms "too experimental" (Schaver 1996c). Christian groups were also quite concerned about a perceived emphasis on "value relativism," which might result from less black-and-white standardized answers (Harp 1994) and "outcomes-based education." The second major source of opposition was educators who felt left out of the creation of the reforms that they were required to implement in their classrooms. Senator Ed Ford admitted: "One of the shortfalls of KERA was the attention that we gave to professional development, particularly for the teachers that were in the system. I've never seen an unhappy parent whose child was in the class of a happy teacher" (ibid.).

The president of the Kentucky Education Association, Marnel Moorman, said: "I wish 'stress' could be in large letters and underlined. A lot of it is caused by lack of support and correct information. It seems like there is always another hurdle we have to go through" (ibid.). The lack of training and development was also a problem, according to most interviewees, even those supportive of KERA. One blamed these difficulties on the way KERA was passed, with an insulated task force determined to make all the necessary changes in one package and to brook no disagreement. In a related vein, Penny Sanders, the first head of the Office of Education Accountability, made this assessment:

> There was no safety valve for legitimate criticism, and we have needed to create an arena where people can air their criticism without feeling like they're breaching the orthodoxy. We gave the impression KERA was written in stone, and it wasn't. We need to build reservoirs of goodwill that allow us some room for adjustments, and we don't have it yet. (ibid.)

Because of increasing opposition to the social reforms, many observers expected the 1995 gubernatorial race to be a referendum on KERA. This feeling heightened when Forgy won the Republican nomination and faced Democratic Lieutenant Governor Paul Patton, who was strongly backed by the Kentucky Education Association and who thought that KERA needed some adjustment, but not a major overhaul (Loftus 1995b). According to some interviewees, a split in the business community over KERA harmed Forgy. Small businesses generally agreed with him on the need to change certain aspects of the law, including the ungraded primary and the testing system, and to roll back some of the tax increase. Yet larger businesses generally supported KERA as their best chance to create an educated workforce. In fact, a business group known as the Partnership for Kentucky Education Reform ran television commercials during the campaign in favor of KERA and, implicitly, of Patton (*Louisville Courier-Journal* 1995). Patton faced division in his ranks over KERA as well. A significant number of teachers opposed the law because it had made their jobs much more difficult. The "writing portfolios" were time-consuming to deal with; grades were not as simple and direct as "A," "B," and "C" anymore. Lesson plans that had been used for twenty years in some cases had to be completely redone, which was not easy for many veteran educators (Harp 1994). According to some interviewees, though, a majority of teachers generally supported KERA because of the increased funding and greater classroom flexibility.

In the end, KERA might not have decided the election. Patton won narrowly, but according to most news reports, his success stemmed from his late-campaign attacks on U. S. House Speaker Newt Gingrich and the Republican Congress on issues such as Medicare and abortion. Patton assembled a coalition of liberals, teachers, racial minorities, women, and the elderly that topped Forgy's support from small business and the religious right (Garrett 1995c). Still, to the extent that KERA was an issue, some interviewees reported that it favored Forgy, although not by a large margin. At the same time, there was little evidence that the public wanted to scrap the law, as not even Forgy took that tactic.

Since 1995, the legislature has made some changes to KERA in response to criticism. The ungraded primary for the youngest students was adjusted. The KIRIS testing system was dropped, replaced by the Commonwealth Accountability Testing System (CATS), although the basic concept of low-performing schools facing state takeover remains (Harp 1999). Yet the essential structure of KERA remains intact. Overall, KERA still enjoys support from the groups that advocated reform in the first place, such as the Prichard Committee, the elite business community represented by the Partnership for Kentucky Education Reform, and the Chamber of Commerce, and the media. Many parents and teachers also are quite happy with the results of KERA for their schools and welcome the challenge of reform.

The impact of the reforms in curriculum and governance has been difficult to measure, but the effects of KERA on school financing have been relatively clear. KERA produced a significant increase in funding for the poorest districts and granted the richest districts a much more modest increase in state aid. Overall, combined state and local revenue for districts rose nearly 40% from 1989–1990 to 1993–1994, from $3,079 to $4,291 (Appelbome 1996). Nationally, Kentucky moved from forty-fifth in state and local spending in 1990 to a level much nearer the national average (Anthony and Hickrod 1993; Davis 1995). Increases in state aid account for some of this rise, although many districts are contributing a much greater local property tax effort than ever. Moreover, full assessment of local property seems finally to be a reality in Kentucky (Loftus 1994). The tax rate increase and assessment reform have increased revenue substantially, yet they have provoked some voter backlash.

The equity gap also appears to be closing. Many interviewees cited a 1995 Office of Education Accountability report, which presented the best data on spending in Kentucky schools (OEA 1995; also see Goetz and Debertin 1992). It claimed that the spending disparities between the richest and poorest school districts narrowed 52% since KERA was enacted (OEA 1995:263; Davis 1995). The Kentucky financing system is still not perfectly equal; the tax rate cap is still so high that it does not restrain the richest districts, although HB44 limiting the rate of revenue increase in any one year is still a significant obstacle (OEA 1995:270). The Kentucky system might not pass the muster of the Texas Supreme Court in its early *Edgewood* decisions. The gap between rich and poor, however, is definitely narrower than before KERA.

Politically, support for equalization has remained strong. Even the more conservative interviewees I talked with did not necessarily oppose the financing reforms, unlike their Texas counterparts. Of course, redistribution in Kentucky was much less (if it even existed) than in Texas. In the first couple of years of KERA, the SEEK program (the name for the state aid distribution mechanism) was underfunded because many more districts raised their local tax rates than anticipated (Jennings 1990f).

The state has slowly been making up the difference, however, although the funding amounts have not risen quite as much as originally envisioned because of tight state budgets (Schaver 1996a). Also, institutional inertia is beginning to become a positive factor for KERA, according to some interviewees. If it were going to be overhauled, the time would have already come, according to these respondents, yet strong Senate leadership has prevented major changes in the law. One commentator made this assessment during the 1996 legislative session: "It's increasingly clear that the question is no longer whether KERA will survive, but whether it will restore confidence in the public schools" (Garrett 1996). Therefore, the results of the overall political struggle are still unclear.

Rating *Rose*: Due to Whom?

In this section, I discuss the contributions of each of the primary actors inside and outside the political system to school reform in Kentucky. The role of the Supreme Court will be presented last, but the nature and relative weight of its influence will inform the discussion of the parts of the other participants. As I did in the Texas case, I argue that although multiple forces were responsible for the changes, the Court took a key part in moving the system toward reform.

Interest Groups

As related, in the early to mid-1980s numerous forces for educational change in Kentucky began to take shape. One force consisted of the elite in the business community, which was becoming concerned about the global competitiveness of the state. Many of these leaders were involved with the Prichard Committee, which evolved out of a state commission formed in 1980 to study and recommend solutions to problems in higher education (Dove 1991: 110). The commission concluded that many of the problems in the Kentucky university system stemmed from defects in student preparation for college. Its members created an organization to mount a public relations campaign for reform in elementary and secondary education (Parrish, "The Prichard Committee . . . ").

The committee contained many more business leaders than it did professional educators, and the solutions that it advocated reflected this membership. The committee did not place its major emphasis on finance reform and equity, although it certainly supported those goals. Just as important were calls for increased accountability of schools to statewide performance standards and an end to the "old-boys" network of school superintendent patronage, especially in eastern Kentucky. Merely pouring more money into the same old system was not acceptable. Through grassroots organization, the committee was able to hold a joint set of one hundred forty town meetings on the evening of November 15, 1984, concerning the state of Kentucky education. Even though the weather was generally poor, nearly twenty thousand people across the state attended, which was a surprise to almost everyone (Dove 1991:111). The turnout got the attention of the legislature, which became important later in members' assessment of the possible public reaction to the reform legislation.

One should not ignore the role of professional educators in supporting change in the school systems. Interest groups such as the Kentucky Education Association, representing teachers, the Kentucky School Boards Association, and the Kentucky Association of School Administrators favored increased school funding, although they split on the usefulness of various "accountability" measures. No one wanted to work in a school system consistently below the national average. Some districts had become patronage fiefdoms, but a majority genuinely wanted more resources to do their job of teaching children better. Still, the task force charged with promulgating reform after the Supreme Court decision, according to most interviewees, was structured to minimize the influence, if not the input, of interest groups, namely the professional educator groups such as the KEA, KSBA, KASA, and the business-led or civic groups such as the Prichard Committee and the Chamber of Commerce. The interest groups involved were able to make their voices heard, though: they concentrated most of their attention on the curriculum subcommittee, rather than governance or finance. The business community in particular was concerned about the results of this panel because curriculum drove the skills of future workers available to Kentucky businesses. These groups focused on student achievement and outcomes rather than finance or governance problems, which they believed were more isolated to eastern Kentucky or not as directly connected with learning.

The Prichard Committee was similarly concerned about student outcomes. For years the committee had listed recommendations for what a successful school system should teach (Prichard Committee 1985). In the new political climate, these suggestions finally had a chance of becoming law. In fact, the guidelines formed the foundation for the work of the curriculum subcommittee, with

Hornbeck's ideas as an overlay to these policy prescriptions. The curriculum panel also received input, funneled through the professional education groups, from sources outside Kentucky, including the Southern Regional Education Board and the National Governors' Association. (As noted earlier in the chapter, leaders interested in building the New South had been experimenting with education reforms throughout the 1980s.) Both organizations, and others, promulgated lists of desirable components of a modern school system. As one legislator said, "The bullets were there . . . everybody had the list but no one (until now) was executing."

Assessing the work of the task force, one sees that pressure groups were consulted for their input, but they did not have a direct formal role in the process. This was worrisome to the groups, which were not only concerned about the public reaction to whatever might emerge, but also fearful of what the legislature might produce, left to its own devices. At the same time, most interests decided that it was worth the risk to support reform. One interest group representative said: "It would have been a better process if it had involved (us), but we realized the legislature was going to take responsibility. We chose to support them and make (our) concerns known."

Another noted "conflicting feelings" about the task force, in that "the upside was the comprehensive package with the tax dollars to fund it and get votes; the downside was that the local . . . communities were locked out." A third stated that the decision to exclude the interest groups was "good, because otherwise nothing would have been done." One way that the various interests attempted to counter the legislative tendency toward isolation was to confer to see what ideas they could all agree on. These could then be presented jointly to the task force, presumably making a greater impact than single suggestions (Sexton 1993). The groups also attempted to assess which issues were the "hot-button" ones for individual interests (for example, teacher tenure for the KEA), so they knew to avoid those when dealing with legislators.

It should also be noted that all consultants, especially Hornbeck, possessed significant power in that they were mostly responsible for shaping the alternatives presented to legislators and executive branch officials who were not experts in school-related issues. This is not to say that they abused their power—many legislators praised Hornbeck for his ability to give them various options—but this does not eliminate the agenda-setting role. The legislators were so worried about consultant power, according to one interviewee, that the consultants were not allowed to meet together to talk about issues (although such meetings did take place informally). The legislators were evidently afraid that the consultants would unify and then present them with a fait accompli.

The final notable interest group was the one that began the litigation, the Council for Better Education (CBE). Ironically, the council had comparatively less influence on the shaping of KERA than many of the other interests. The council focused much of its attention on finance rather than curriculum, although even in that area its power seems to have been limited. State aid increased significantly, which is what the council wanted, but required a dramatic increase in local taxes. Some members of the eastern Kentucky-dominated council also must not have been thrilled at some of the governance reforms in KERA, such as the nepotism ban. Nonetheless, the council remains a force in education politics, mostly through its occasional threats to relitigate the *Rose* issues if poorer school districts fall too far behind their richer suburban counterparts. Because the general political perception is that KERA was a major step forward, however, these threats are not taken as seriously as they might be in Texas, for example. It still appears, though, that the benefits to the council districts of going to court exceeded the costs involved. Litigation was not a "hollow hope" (in fact, the opposite for better and worse) for the plaintiffs.

Overall, therefore, interest group influence was present in Kentucky school reform, and likely was even necessary to spur change. Groups such as the Prichard Committee laid the groundwork to prepare the public for the need for a large departure from the old school system, and were ready to step in with ideas once the "window of opportunity" opened after the Supreme Court decision. One should not think that the reform movement by itself would have produced change, though (a point to which I shall return.) The committee and others had lobbied the legislature for years without success before the Court decision. It was the combination of forces that made reform possible.

THE MEDIA

Another force for change was the advocacy of leading newspapers. Two major newspapers, the *Louisville Courier-Journal* and the *Lexington Herald-Leader*, dominate the state, with the *Kentucky Post* in Covington (northern Kentucky) trailing in circulation. All these papers, especially the Lexington and Louisville journals, were very supportive of education reform. This attitude was a source of great consternation to opponents of certain aspects of the reform law, who saw a "conspiracy" between the reformers and the media to pass and implement the law with no public criticism.

The leading newspapers extensively covered the activities of the Prichard Committee, including the town forums in 1984. Even before the meetings, the *Courier-Journal* had published a long series of articles detailing the corruption in the school administrations of eastern Kentucky. The *Herald-Leader* was not to be outdone, though, in exposing the deficiencies of the old Kentucky system. In the fall of 1989, as the task force was deliberating, the paper ran a series of stories entitled "Cheating Our Children," which won a Pulitzer Prize (Dove 1991:84). The series explored the corruption and nepotism in some eastern Kentucky districts, increasing the pressure on the governance subcommittee. Additionally, the paper focused on the property assessment problem, which caught the eye of the finance panel. Stories displayed pictures of the houses of local political leaders next to the assessed values of those homes, which were ridiculously lower than what the photographs suggested. This investigative reporting spurred the public pressure on the task force members to correct these abuses (also see Wolfson 1989).

Day after day, these newspapers would run stories dealing with aspects of Kentucky education (Dove 1991:112). This barrage, some interviewees said, was necessary to get education on the public mind and to overcome entrenched resistance to change. The attitude that "If it was good enough for Pap, it's good enough for me," in the words of one Kentucky historian, needed to be uprooted if reform were to succeed (Dove 1991:87 quoting Robert Sexton quoting historian Thomas Clark). According to many interviewees, the media played just that role in keeping pressure on the legislature.

THE PUBLIC

Generalizations about public opinion in Kentucky around the time of KERA are difficult because of the lack of comprehensive data. The *Courier-Journal* conducted occasional Bluegrass State Polls on various issues facing the state, but even these surveys were not detailed. The available evidence shows some influence of public opinion (or at least perceived public opinion) on the education reform process, however.

One of the principal tasks of the Prichard Committee, among other interest groups, and the media was to spotlight the deficiencies in the educational system to argue for reform. Overcoming opposition to reform was difficult, especially because restructuring would cost a substantial amount of money, mostly paid for by taxes. The efforts of the committee, exemplified by the statewide "town meeting" in 1984, began to bear fruit, though. Polls showed that Kentuckians believed that the school system was the largest problem in the state. Legislators also much noted a poll in 1989 before the Supreme Court decision concluding that people would pay higher taxes for better schools (Dove 1991:87).

Furthermore, political and judicial leaders looking for a sign of the public mood could note the 1989 Supreme Court election barely one month before oral arguments on the *Rose* case: in an eastern Kentucky district, Court of Appeals Judge Dan Jack Combs (no relation to Bert Combs) defeated Justice James Stephenson. Stephenson was known as a judicial conservative on civil and criminal law issues. Combs, by contrast, was relatively pro-plaintiff and pro-defendant, and more flamboyant than Stephenson; for example, Combs knowingly violated the Kentucky Code of Judicial Conduct prohibition against campaigning on specific issues, as he attacked Stephenson's decisions that supported big businesses against injured plaintiffs (Keesler 1988; Lawson 1988). The larger significance of this race is that if Justices were looking for a signal about voters' preferences, the election of Dan Jack Combs would tell them that the public (or at least the public that voted in Supreme Court elections) was in a relatively liberal mood. On an even more concrete level, Combs's victory likely took one vote from the state defendants in *Rose* and handed it to the plaintiff districts.

Nor was state public opinion the only opinion that mattered. National attention was focused on Kentucky because of the Supreme Court decision; newspapers such as *The New York Times* were following the Kentucky education story (Combs 1991). The political leadership did not want to be portrayed yet again as backward and resistant to change. According to one interviewee, "we would be a laughingstock" if change were not made. On the other hand, if politicians did make substantial reforms, they had a chance to be "heroes around the country," as one respondent reported. As it turned out, in education circles, Kentucky politicians are highly sought after for advice because of KERA (Jennings 1990e; Cross 1990c; Bodie 1994; Holland 1995; Davis 1995; Appelbome 1996).

The perceived shift in public opinion emboldened legislators to take the chance that their constituents would support the taxes necessary to pay for KERA. But many legislators lived in fear of an anti-KERA backlash beginning in 1990, the first election cycle after the law was passed. Some legislators feared a "bloodbath," as had happened after Republican Governor Louie Nunn had increased the state sales tax from Bert Combs's three cents to five cents in 1968. Now that the legislature had raised it to six cents, many members were terrified of public reprisal (Wilson 1990). Yet, there was no "bloodbath," in the primary elections or in the general elections in November 1990, even though the tax increase might have played some role in defeating a few electorally marginal legislators. Fourteen legislators, mostly Senators, who voted for KERA lost reelection bids, including Nelson Allen, the chair of the Senate Education Committee. Seven lawmakers who opposed KERA also were defeated, however (Howington and Bryant 1990; Loftus and Wilson 1990). Broader partisan shifts might have contributed to these results.

The Kentucky Republican Party spent an unprecedented amount of money on legislative races and "snuck up" on the Democrats in many instances (Ellers 1990b). Given the large Democratic majorities in both chambers, especially the Senate, by the law of averages it is perhaps unsurprising that a significant number of Democratic KERA supporters would be defeated. Even so, Democrats still enjoyed a 27–11 edge in the Senate and a 68–32 majority in the Assembly (ibid.). In short, KERA probably played some role in the elections, but was not by itself the cause of a large backlash.

A public opinion poll after the elections provided evidence to confirm this assessment. The Bluegrass State Poll, the major state survey, asked 829 adults what was the state's main problem. Without any prompting, twenty-six percent replied "education" or "schools," which was the single most popular answer, but down from thirty-eight percent in a similar poll in July 1989 after the Supreme Court decision (Kaukas 1990). These results can be interpreted as showing a strong public awareness of the need for education reform, but that people thought the state had made strides in addressing the problem. Similarly, Bert Combs had predicted before the election that backlash would be minimized because the public generally supported school reform, at least in principle (Wilson 1990).

The 1992 and 1994 legislative elections largely replicated the results of 1990. A fair number of legislators retired or were defeated, most notably Roger Noe, the chair of the House Education Committee (Jennings 1992; Jennings and Wolfson 1992; Walfoot 1992; Garrett 1994). Some interviewees reported that a few of these losses were attributable to KERA, although many also blamed "local factors."

The tax increases, especially the local property tax increases, were the major visible irritant to the voters, but growing opposition to what one conservative Republican interviewee called the "social engineering" of KERA might have played a role as well. According to most sources, few, if any, legislators have lost solely because of social issues surrounding KERA. One conservative interviewee, nonetheless, maintained that many Republican candidates have been motivated to run for office because of their opposition to KERA, even if the school issue is not dominant in the campaign.

Yet multiple factors could explain these outcomes. A general trend toward the Republican Party was sweeping the South, especially in 1994, when Republicans elected a majority to the Kentucky congressional delegation for the first time since 1928. The state legislature was no exception to that movement, although the Republicans did not gain a majority in either chamber until 1999 (Loftus 1999). General anti-incumbent sentiment also seems to have been a factor in some elections, as several supporters of KERA lost, as did a fair number of opponents. This trend was exacerbated by one of the worst scandals in recent Kentucky history, the arrest and conviction of almost twenty legislators, including Blandford, for acceptance of kickbacks in return for horse racing legislation in an FBI sting operation (Loftus 1995a; Garrett 1992). Voters might have felt it was better to "throw all the bums out," regardless of their position on school reform. Furthermore, quite a few of the legislators responsible for KERA were veterans who were getting ready to retire in any event. In fact, some interviewees said that school reform was more palatable to these legislators because it was their "one last chance" to do something for the state before leaving the legislature.

The third branch of government, the judiciary, also felt no real electoral impact from KERA, even though there were two contested Supreme Court races in 1990. Because of rules of judicial conduct that prohibit campaigning on specific issues, Kentucky judicial campaigns, in the words of one interviewee, are "issueless wonders." These campaigns often are decided in clashes between civil plaintiff trial attorneys and business defendants, although not with the same big-money contributions as Texas Supreme Court races (Ellers 1990a). It appears that KERA did nothing to change this pattern, in 1990 or later. Because of retirements and death, the Court membership has changed significantly since the *Rose* case, but according to most interviewees, the shifts have not affected Court views on the *Rose* decision.

Polls show significant strengths of KERA, but also important weaknesses. On the plus side for KERA, a majority of Kentuckians in a 1996 survey agreed that they did not want to return to the traditional system. Asked whether they supported KERA as a whole, though, 49% opposed the law and only 40% supported it. On whether they thought schools were generally getting better, respondents evenly divided between improvement and decline (Schaver 1996c). It is not surprising that such a large and comprehensive reform passed with relatively little public input would engender mixed feelings in the body politic. Some aspects of KERA, such as the ungraded primary, might not survive this opposition.

Overall, however, the voice of public opinion was important, if somewhat muted in the KERA process. Certainly, the perceived shift in public attitudes toward education reform and its financing played a significant role in moving the legislature toward change. There is little to no evidence that the public specifically desired the changes mandated in KERA, though. The public could help set the general direction, yet was largely uninvolved in the detailed blueprints of the proposed school system. Even the public mood might not have become a factor without the prodding of the reform coalition and the Court decision. Lastly, the lack of KERA electoral backlash again suggests that the role of the public was general and diffuse, not specifically focused on the construction of KERA. To explain more fully the outcomes of the reform process, I will have to examine more closely the institutions specifically charged with living up to the Court mandate.

THE GOVERNOR

The legislative-gubernatorial relationship during this period is one of the fascinating aspects of Kentucky school reform. Some scholarship on court success in implementing decisions suggests that courts can be effective only when the legislative and executive branches are in harmony (Rosenberg 1991). In Kentucky, however, this "relationship" was bitter and contentious at best, encompassing the gamut of personal differences, policy disagreements, and institutional rivalries. The roots of this conflict were deeper than one particular administration. The Kentucky constitution provided for a relatively weak legislature, exemplified by the sixty-day limit on biennial legislative sessions. The governor, although limited to one term, exerted relatively greater power, even appointing legislative committee chairs until 1979.

But since 1979, the legislature had claimed increased authority, aided by state Supreme Court decisions granting it greater discretion to pass laws for the general welfare and primary authority over the state budget. The legislature was quite possessive of its new authority, by most accounts, and was very sensitive to any attempts by governors to reclaim any sway over legislative deliberations. In the words of one legislator, the general mood was "We're never going back."

Given this attitude, the election of Wilkinson was like lighting a pool of gasoline. Wilkinson's political style was quite aggressive and confrontational, yet as he pointed out, the legislative leadership had no shortage of ego as well. He had run as an outsider against the political establishment in Frankfort, which essentially was the legislature and its allies. More specifically, Wilkinson believed that the legislature had gone too far and that it was attempting to usurp powers legitimately belonging to the governor, such as control over the state budget and a proposed constitutional amendment giving the legislature a veto over administrative regulations (Wilkinson 1995:11). Furthermore, Wilkinson believed that the rise to power of the legislature made it even more necessary for the gubernatorial term limit to be lifted, preferably including himself, a move that the legislature strongly resisted (ibid.:11–2).

Regarding education reform, Wilkinson claimed in his autobiography that he was always willing to agree to a significant tax increase for education, thinking it was necessary. Nevertheless, he wanted to show the legislature that he could not be pushed around. His greatest fear was that the legislature would raise taxes, blame him for it, and then ignore the restructuring proposals, such as giving rewards for successful schools, that he favored. Such an outcome would effectively end his political career. The only solution, Wilkinson felt, was to hold the line strongly on taxes until he could feel sure that the rest of his package would get through the legislature (ibid. 165–8). The upcoming judicial resolution of the school funding issue played a significant role in this thinking. He believed that the best time to make the necessary funding changes (and likely tax increases) was after the ruling, when the stage would be set for such a change. Optimally, the restructuring proposals would already be in place, but under no circumstances should taxes be raised before restructuring and before the Court decision (ibid.:165–6).

Wilkinson's overall beliefs on education reform remain complex. Clearly, Wilkinson wanted structural reform and accountability in education. He pushed for those changes throughout his administration, and many of them ended up in KERA, although the law went beyond his proposals in some cases. On the revenue measures, the record is more mixed. He waited until the last year and a half of his four-year term to propose a tax increase, but when he did, it was much larger than anyone, including legislators, expected. Before the Court decision, he and lawmakers were about to agree to a $350 million package. After the decision, the price went up to $1.3 billion (ibid.:190; Appelbome 1996). Therefore, we can see the role of ideological compatibility with the decision, but also independent Court influence.

Even so, the relationship between the legislative and executive branches during the Wilkinson administration can be summed up by this quote from the governor:

> From a practical standpoint, I really had no other option than to enter into open political warfare with the legislature. As uncomfortable as this political style made some people feel, it was the only effective way to deal with a defiant Kentucky legislature. I was under no illusion that I could somehow intimidate or coerce the legislature into enacting my agenda into law. The legislature had grown independent enough that a governor no longer could directly force it to do anything it didn't want to do. (Wilkinson 1995:300–301).

As for the legislature, even after passage of KERA, one lawmaker was quoted as saying of Wilkinson, "I don't know how long people can sit by and not say something about the farces he perpetuates on state government" (Cross 1991a). After the session, Rose said, "Relations between the two branches hit an all-time low as far as I can remember, so low that I doubt we'll see it again in the foreseeable future" (Loftus 1990c). An editorial writer later called the Wilkinson years "Kentucky's most tumultous administration since the Civil War" (Cross 1991b).

At the same time, in the 1990 session the General Assembly passed one of the most significant laws in twentieth-century Kentucky history. How can one explain this seeming contradiction? Some interviewees thought that the rivalry between the branches might have aided the cause of school reform. Neither branch wanted the other to take full credit for the package, but neither desired to be seen as solely responsible for the tax increase. Once the Court had set the gears in motion for school reform, each side needed the other. Other interviewees were more skeptical, stating that the broader public movement for reform and leadership on both sides, at least on this issue, were more responsible for KERA than petty jealousy and blame-avoidance. In any event, this case study should provoke further thought on the necessary institutional dynamics for court success.

THE LEGISLATURE

Without a doubt, in passing KERA the legislature complied with the basic principles of the *Rose* decision, although there is dispute concerning specifics. A set of interrelated questions thus emerges. First, what was the reaction to the Court decision in the legislature? Was it uniform or varied? Second, why did the legislature go as far as it did in complying with the decision, even going beyond the court mandate on certain issues? Third, would the legislature have enacted these reforms without the decision?

Concerning the overall legislative reaction, the results are varied. One explanation for political movement in Texas was that of ideological compatibility within the leadership with the substance of the Court ruling. There is no question that compatibility played a role in Kentucky as well, although the issue is complex. To generalize, the Democrats[6] in the legislature could be divided into three groups: conservatives who wanted to preserve the status quo and block tax increases; "Young Turks" on the House Education Committee who wanted tax increases but few "accountability" reforms; and leaders such as Moloney and Clarke, who supported tax increases for services such as education and insisted on fundamental structural changes in return. The Court decision affected each of these groups differently. For the conservatives, there was almost nothing in the decision to like, because both tax increases and accountability reforms were mandated, explaining why many of them voted against KERA. The "Young Turks" had to be pleased with the prospect of more money and finance reform, but nervous about any structural changes, the reason that the leadership wanted to exclude them from the task force.

The Moloney-Clarke group had to be quite satisfied with the ruling, although perhaps a little dismayed at the loss of institutional prerogative. Essentially, the Court had given it the opportunity to do exactly what it wanted: raise taxes for government services and reform what it considered to be corrupt power bases in eastern Kentucky. The comment of one interviewee, "The legislature was glad (the Court) told them to do it," probably applied best to this group of legislators. The sweeping nature of the decision was especially useful to this group of legislators. As one legislator said, "the Court saw the issue of money would be difficult to address—but if it freed up the General Assembly to address other issues. . . ." Similarly, an interest group representative supportive of accountability told legislators, "This is your chance to make Kentucky different." Another interest group leader stated that the Court decision "eliminated some reasons for obstinacy." A third claimed it was "an opportunity to start fresh" and a "unique political situation."

At the head of the legislature, the named defendants, Rose and Blandford, were not necessarily opposed to education reform. Their interest seems to have been more political than policy-oriented, however. Once the Supreme Court gave them a direction, and they could see that the political winds were moving in that direction, they acted quickly to get out in front of the movement and were essential in assembling the final coalition. In other words, the Court shifted the balance of power in the legislature, and leadership responded.

One might think that one reason the legislature complied with the Court was clarity of the decision. Perhaps the Court gave the legislature a blueprint of the new system, and all lawmakers had to do was follow through; this was not the case, though. Here, I shall focus on the work of the task force. Concerning the curriculum subcommittee, for example, the decision provided a little help. The Court had identified what it believed were the nine attributes of an "efficient" school system and the seven capacities that each child in the Kentucky schools should possess upon graduation. According to interviewees, the decision was somewhat useful in providing a general blueprint from which they could begin working. Wright said at the time, "I think the Supreme Court established the guidelines about what a child should know. . . . And so I think we can move right on through these issues" (Jennings 1989b). On the other hand, some interviewees found the Court guidelines vague. What does it mean, they wondered, to create an "adequate" school system that is "substantially uniform" with "no political influence"? One observer went so far as to call the Court standards "platitudinous hogwash." A prominent legislator admitted that at no time during the process did the question "Will this satisfy the Court?" ever arise. This assessment might be an exaggeration, but it is fairly clear that the task force members did not feel overly constrained by the Court decision. Still, they never explicitly contradicted the Court language.

Regarding the work of the other two subcommittees, governance and finance, the story is much the same. The Court had ordered the governance subcommittee to take "political influence" out of the schools, but the panel was not specifically ordered to ban nepotism in district hiring, which it did. As noted concerning the finance subcommittee, the Court was not clear on the line between acceptable and unacceptable inequality. Thus, the political leaders decided to gamble that the Court would tolerate some disparity. (This "gamble" is similar to the risk the Texas legislature took in passing Senate Bill 1, the first attempt to achieve equity, although of course in Texas, reforms were limited to just the finance issue.) Mostly the decision was useful in articulating a general premise, such as "no political influence" or "equality of opportunity," and then leaving the task force maximum flexibility in constructing means of achieving this goal. The decision itself does not seem to have been central in shaping the specific alternatives presented, but it certainly provided an outline for the task force. The tone and breadth of the decision, however, were much more important in the reform debates, as noted below.

Another reason the legislature complied with the Court decision might be fear of judicial retribution, one could argue. In Texas, fear of retribution from the supreme court in the form of a school closure order helped persuade the legislature to at least attempt to comply with the court decisions. Concerning the issue of the court as threat in Kentucky, when I asked interviewees what they thought would happen if the legislature and the governor could not reach agreement and did not comply with the court order, there was no consensus on a response. A few mentioned the possibility that the Court would write its own plan. Other interviewees, plus Senator Moloney (Dove 1991:107–8), thought school closure would be the Court response; in his words, "The concept of Junior staying home all year long got the Legislature determined to pass something" (ibid.). Still others reported rumors that legislators would be held in contempt of court and possibly jailed. The variety of these responses and their relative implausibility suggests, with other interviewee comments, that most never really thought about the issue for very long. Respondents reported that once the Court decision was issued, it was very clear that the legislature would have to make some kind of response; massive resistance was never even considered. According to one interviewee, "The whole thing (school reform) had been held back for so long . . . it was reaching a crescendo." The Court power of sanction, then, was not really a factor in producing legislative action.

What other factors might explain legislators' willingness to revamp education? One that must have weighed heavily on the minds of legislative leaders was the prestige of the General Assembly. The legislature had broken free of the direct control of the governor barely a decade before, and the Court had placed the responsibility for constructing the new school system squarely on the shoulders of the General Assembly. Failure would be deeply embarrassing. Moloney, who had long championed legislative independence, said, "It'll make or break us as an institution, in my judgment" (Garrett 1989b). Noe argued that school reform was a test of "whether we can act with the acumen that an experienced, full-time legislature would have" (ibid.).

Some interviewees said the legislature had gained power because of its success in passing this reform law, claiming that the legislature had shown that it could respond to a major state problem with courage and skill. Contemporaneous media reports also expressed this view of a stronger institution that proved it could stand up to an aggressive governor (Cross 1990b). Still, other interviewees maintained that the power shift had already taken place, that the legislature had declared its independence before KERA. The education reform law was just a consequence, not a cause, of legislative power. The sobering aftermath of the FBI sting operation noted above, which might have hurt the public perception of the legislature as much as KERA helped it, also fueled this view. Regardless of one's policy views, though, the complete restructuring of the schools in KERA in and of itself should be seen as quite an accomplishment for a part-time legislative body.

So far, I have offered a partial explanation as to why the political leadership complied with the Court decision: ideological compatibility coupled with a challenge to legislative policymaking capability. Other factors must have been involved, however, considering the nature of elected officials. According to one legislative source, left to legislators' own devices, "we do what we're told . . . going beyond (the political consensus) is not the way policy gets made . . . (normally) we run schools based on finance formulas." Similarly, a legislator stressed the difficult position of one-term governors who want a political future, meaning that they do not want to be remembered as the "taxing governor," and legislators who increasingly see politics as a career. Each of these actors has real incentives for slow, incremental change. Yet the legislature went well beyond what was expected in passing KERA. Three interrelated reasons stand out, described in increasing order of importance. First, recall the national attention focused on Kentucky because of the Court decision. The political leadership did not want to be portrayed again as backward and resistant to change. According to one interviewee, "we would be a laughingstock" if change were not made.

Second, immediately after the Court decision was handed down, the most common reaction word was "opportunity." It was "a unique political situation," "an opportunity to start fresh," when "everything came together at once" and "two moons collided." According to one senior legislator, "(the Court) opened a window the legislature had never seen before." The sweeping nature of the decision, which under other circumstances could have been seen as a vast overreach of judicial power, might have helped the reform cause. One interviewee said that because the entire "schoolhouse," in Stephens's terms, had to be reconstructed, "the Court gave the time, resources, and opportunity to put everything together." Another said, "The Court raised the institutional stakes for everyone (including the Court itself.)" A third noted that when the legislature thinks there is a "global mandate . . . there's a different mindset when they know they have to do something big. . . . It takes on a life of its own."

The third reason was perhaps the most commonly cited: the legislature could use the Court as a "shield" behind which it could act. One interviewee said that "reverence for Court decisions" was not really a motivation, but the public opinion climate was such that "the Court had the legislature over a barrel." If that was true, the best strategy the legislature could adopt would be to comply with the decision and blame any negative results on the Court. Thus, according to one interviewee, "they had a perfect explanation—(the public knows) judges can order people to do things. . . . It made it more palatable." Another said, "It allowed leaders to say to followers 'We have to do this.'" According to a third, "The Court became the whipping boy." A fourth stated, "(the legislature) said, 'The Supreme Court says it has to be done' . . . (there was) no choice." Another said, "The General Assembly was off the hook, considering the unpopularity of taxes . . . there was no courage otherwise . . . (they could say) 'the devil made me do it'." A lawmaker stated that the decision was "a great opportunity" especially because it was so broad. A second legislator, although he voted against KERA, noted the theme of his colleagues: "the Court justified the action . . . the courts made us do it." It is useful to recall

Bert Combs's statements about the goals of the suit. He wanted the Court to issue a declaratory judgment that would help build enough political momentum so the "limber twigs" in the legislature could employ just this strategy of "blame the Court" (Combs 1991). In terms of forcing the legislature and governor to act, Combs's plan worked just as he hoped it would, although his clients might not have agreed with the results.

Of course, as I have shown, ultimately this strategy enjoyed mixed success. Some lawmakers were defeated at the polls. One could argue, however, that the backlash would have been worse if the legislature had enacted KERA on its own without the decision as a "shield." These professional politicians certainly thought the Court decision was quite useful to them electorally. Without the political consensus among interest groups, the media, and certain legislators, nothing would have happened, probably even with a court decision.

But this conclusion does not answer the question of whether the Court decision was necessary for passage of the law, at least in its present form. According to virtually every interviewee, the answer was a resounding "yes." In other words, the Court was indispensable. Asked whether the legislature would have acted without the decision, interviewee after interviewee, from legislator to executive branch official to judge to interest group leader to outside observer, gave answers ranging from "no" to "absolutely not" and "never." One legislator conceded that perhaps the changes would have been made in thirty years, but not sooner. The uniformity of response was striking.

This is not to say that the legislature by itself was unimportant. It seems fairly clear that much of the actual work product was attributable to the efforts of the task force members themselves and their overworked staffs. In the words of one interviewee, the legislature "took ownership." According to another interviewee, the Court "put the ball on the field," but the political leadership "kicked it in the goal." One should not ignore the role of any of these institutions in producing social reform, for in the end, the branches worked hand in hand to make changes in the school system. In Kentucky, there was no "disconnect" between the Court and the legislature.

THE SUPREME COURT

If the legislature had experienced a significant increase in power in the 1970s, the same was true for the judicial system. The

1891 Constitution provided for a court system that was haphazard and sprawling, composed of various lower courts known as circuit courts, county courts, quarterly courts, justice courts, and so forth, with varied jurisdiction. There was a seven-member Court of Appeals, but this court could hear only cases that began in Circuit Court (Miller 1994:153). In 1975, a constitutional amendment was proposed to "unify" the court system by creation of a structure with which most Americans are more familiar: a four-level hierarchical system beginning with a District Court for relatively minor civil and criminal cases; a Circuit Court for appeals from District Court and more serious original jurisdiction civil and criminal cases; a Court of Appeals for appeals from Circuit Court; and, at the top, a seven-member Supreme Court that normally hears appeals from the Court of Appeals, although not in the *Rose* case. In one giant leap, "Kentucky moved from the ranks of the nation's most outdated judicial systems to one of its most progressive" (ibid.).

The seven-member Supreme Court was now elected from districts across the state roughly corresponding to U.S. House district boundaries. Court elections, which were staggered, were also nonpartisan. At the beginning of each term, the seven Justices chose their Chief by vote. Stephens, who led the Court that heard the *Rose* case, had served in a number of government posts, including state attorney general, before winning election to the Court. He had served as a clerk for a previous Chief Justice for the old Court of Appeals, and so was generally familiar with the workings of the Court. Stephens was also quite connected with the political establishment, including his friendships with a number of prominent legislators. In the words of one interviewee, one of the reasons Stephens became Chief Justice was that he "knew how to deal with political people." This was not necessarily true of the other Justices; by contrast with Texas, in which many Justices had moved from the legislature, none of the serving Court members had spent any time in the legislature.

The other prominent Justice on the Kentucky Supreme Court at that time was Charles Leibson. He had a reputation as the sharpest legal mind on the Court, although he was not as talented as Stephens in coalition-building. Although no one claimed that the other Justices were unskilled, more than one interviewee maintained that Leibson's intelligence improved the work product of those around him, making Court output more professional and legally sophisticated, which was quite a contribution to a relatively new institution. From a policy standpoint, Leibson pushed the Court to expand the remedies available to civil plaintiffs and urged justices to take the Kentucky constitution more seriously in their rulings.

Before Leibson's arrival in 1984, the Court decisions themselves could be characterized by two themes. First, in civil law, the Court had a conservative reputation similar to that of the Texas Supreme Court before the 1980s (although information is scarce in this particular area because of lack of media coverage). The second theme was "judicial stretching" (ibid.:158). According to one scholar, "A pattern can be seen in judicial decisions to step aside and allow government to function—even despite apparent constitutional obstacles" (ibid.). The 1891 constitution contained so many limits on the legislature that the Court often has felt compelled to "stretch" the words of the constitution to allow the legislature to act. For example, when faced with a constitutional salary cap on government officials, the Court issued what became known as the "rubber dollar" decision, ruling that the salary must be adjusted for inflation (*Matthews* 1962).

In another case, the Court ruled that the city of Lexington could merge with its county, Fayette, even though the constitution contained strict limits on local government and the constitutional framers never contemplated a city-county merger (*Holsclaw* 1973). Stephens, not yet Chief Justice at the time, was familiar with this type of "stretching," as he was a party to the Lexington case and supported the merger (Wolfson 1993). Because of decisions such as these, Charles Johnson and Bradley Canon (1984:237–39) said that the general role of the Court has been that of a "legitimizer" of state government. Therefore, one might have expected the Court to have "legitimized" the state school system as well, especially given the rather vague constitutional charge that the system be "efficient." Stephens decided to take the opposite road, however. It is impossible, of course, to know exactly what thoughts crossed his mind when deliberating *Rose*. One can attempt only a reasonable guess, using all available evidence.

The most common analysis of the interview sources concerned the "rising tide" for educational change in Kentucky. The combination of media pressure, public opinion turnaround, interest group support, and the like, had created a groundswell of support for reform. Interviewees speculated that the Court did not want to be perceived as the obstacle to this movement, just as the legislative leaders resented their role as defendants. On a broader scale, *Rose* was an opportunity for the relatively new Court to do something truly important, to make a mark in history. As it turned out, many interviewees said the decision was one of the most significant court rulings in the twentieth century in Kentucky. The decision also gained national attention and often is given credit for having sparked the so-called "third wave" of court rulings on school finance systems nationwide (Thro 1990).

There might also have been a more specific motive behind the *Rose* opinion. Several interviewees noted the close personal relationship between Stephens and Moloney, the chair of the powerful Senate Appropriations and Revenue Committee. The two had grown up together and, by all accounts, were good friends; Moloney, also a lawyer, had even handled Stephens's divorce case. Forgy, during his 1995 gubernatorial campaign, maintained that the Court ruling "represented to some extent the Court's closeness to the financial barons of the General Assembly, namely Clarke and Moloney" (Garrett 1995b). Forgy was not alone in expressing this opinion. Many interviewees, liberal and conservative, representing a number of institutional positions, speculated that Moloney, possibly in concert with Clarke, the House Appropriations and Revenue chair, informed Stephens of what a great opportunity the Court had to expand Corns's ruling to create more systematic reform. The political timing was right for the legislature to act.

Regardless of any communication with the Court, it is clear that Moloney and Clarke did not want to risk political capital over a tax increase just to pour money into the old system, which would benefit the superintendents these legislators felt were part of the problem in the first place, without achieving any structural reform. Therefore, Moloney and possibly Clarke could have raised the possibility with Stephens of going beyond the Corns ruling to address systemwide issues. One could dismiss these comments as typical rumor-mongering around the Capitol, but the number of interviewees who mentioned the story, especially one respondent with close personal knowledge of the situation, led me to believe there is some truth to it.

It is very important to note, however, that Stephens and Moloney have always vigorously denied that any such communication took place, and there is no "smoking gun" to decide the matter. Furthermore, no one implied that Moloney dictated the opinion to Stephens. It is fairly clear that Stephens believed what he wrote in the *Rose* case and felt that the constitution compelled the result. There was no question of coercion or threat. If the story does have merit, it illustrates the possiblities for interbranch policy-making between the "political" branches and the judiciary. To note one of the broader themes of this book, to treat these political and legal institutions as hermetically sealed off from one another is a real mistake. "Dialogue" is a better description than "separation."

Because of retirements and death, the Court membership has changed significantly since the *Rose* case, but according to most interviewees, the shifts have not affected Court views on the general principles of the decision. Pressure has not been felt from the initial plaintiffs, however (more on this below). In Texas, of course, the passage of the first reform law was just the beginning of the court-legislature dialogue. In Kentucky, though, the Council for Better Education decided to leave well enough alone. Regarding future legal action, in a significant understatement, Bert Combs declined a further suit, saying "I think this (KERA) will meet the mandate of the court" (Associated Press 1990). Similarly, Rose stated that "we went probably beyond what the court mandated that we do and beyond what the court would expect" (Jennings 1990d).

The Court has had to deal with suits regarding KERA, but they have all been confined to relatively specific issues. In the only successful legal challenge to KERA, the Court in the summer of 1992 narrowly voided the ban on teacher political participation in school board races, yet only on grounds of "vagueness" and "overbreadth" in restricting the important First Amendment rights involved (*State Board* 1992). Concerning the most frequent target of litigation, the Court has held firm on the constitutionality of the nepotism ban in hiring and personnel practices despite First Amendment and equal protection claims by school board members whose relatives worked for the district (*Chapman* 1992; *Kentucky Department of Education* 1996). The Court ruled that there was no fundamental right to school board candidacy and that this exclusion, which the Court noted could be removed if the relatives left their school jobs, did not violate voters' rights.

The Court played a background role, though, in one of the toughest tests for the finance reforms in KERA to date. In return for strong Kentucky Education Association support in his 1995 campaign, Governor Patton proposed in his budget a mandatory 2.6% statewide raise in teacher salaries (*Louisville Courier-Journal* 1996), which raised two problems in terms of KERA goals. First, a statewide mandate for teacher salary increases detracted from the authority of the local school councils and district school boards to make their own decisions about spending state funds. Second, a salary increase for all teachers could have a potentially disequalizing effect. Because the funds would be appropriated outside the normal formula and distributed regardless of wealth, the richest districts in the state would receive just as much money (or more if their teacher salaries were higher) than the poorest districts would, as opposed to the money being appropriated in the regular formula, in which the funding increases would be proportionate to district wealth.

Patton claimed that the local control and equity effects would be minimal, but the plan encountered strong resistance in the legislature. Senate leaders such as Moloney, soon to retire, were especially vociferous in their opposition (Schaver 1996b). Eventually, the raise was removed from the budget, although language was inserted, strongly recommending to districts that they offer the increase anyway (Loftus 1996b). The raise lost in significant part because the political consensus for finance equity was still strong six years after KERA was passed. Interestingly for the purposes of this study, Rose used the *Rose* decision as an argument against the Patton plan. He warned that if the raise were passed and nothing were done to remedy the equity effects, the courts would return to the school funding question and issue more mandates that the legislature would not like (Loftus 1996a). This showed the potential use of courts as threats in the normal legislative process, dovetailing with the work of Michael McCann (1994). In this situation, however, the threat of Court intervention was fairly hollow.

When I asked interviewees whether they thought the legislature had to be careful in its education spending decisions because the Court might return otherwise, most were skeptical. One said, "I can't imagine why the Court would want to wade into that again." Other interviewees noted all the progress the state had made toward equity and the remaining consensus for finance reform as reasons why the Court would not reintervene. A number of interviewees also mentioned that for the Court to issue a new ruling, some group, probably rich or poor districts, would have to file a case. Most respondents, including those sympathetic with the poorer districts, thought that that possiblity was unlikely soon because the original plaintiffs have been relatively satisfied with KERA, at least in terms of financing, if not governance.

Of course, in Texas it was the richest districts that kept the lawsuit going for its last few years because of their opposition to redistribution of their tax base. In Kentucky, occasionally there are some rumblings from the wealthier districts, especially ones with rapidly growing enrollments, about a suit. Some districts, in fact, commissioned a study in 1992 as an exploration of just that question. Nothing has surfaced as yet, though, and most interviewees discounted that possibility. Furthermore, to illustrate the switch in Kentucky attitudes toward rich and poor since KERA, first recall the legislative defense strategy at the *Rose* trial to blame the problems of poor districts on mismanagement and waste. Now consider this quote from Moloney after some relatively wealthy districts complained about having to tread water financially under KERA: "(They) just want more money. You can never satisfy that need. You can open up Fort Knox . . . and they would spend it all the first year" (Jennings 1992a). The issue had turned one hundred eighty degrees.

Beyond the school issue, one notable legal consequence of the *Rose* decision might be emerging. When one examines the Kentucky Supreme Court cases in which *Rose* is cited, one sees an increasing willingness of the Court to use *Rose* as justification for allowing the legislature to be sued in its representative capacity for failure to comply with legal mandates (e.g. *Philpot* 1992; *Kraus* 1994; *Jones* 1995). The legislature itself has occasionally invited these suits, but this trend could be troubling for legislators concerned with institutional prerogatives. Overall, though, when one considers Leibson's warning that "we have now become part of the problem when we intend to be part of the solution (*Rose* 1989:229)" and the protracted legal fights in Texas, the aftermath of the *Rose* decision appears relatively tranquil, at least for the Kentucky Supreme Court. When I asked respondents whether there was any legislative backlash against the Court from the *Rose* decision, all agreed that there was none. Some reported that some legislators were happy that the Court had given them the opportunity to reform, so there was no real reason to resent the Court. Even the conservative backlash against KERA centers more on certain aspects of the law rather than the Court decision. Nothing like the Culberson jurisdiction-weakening amendment in Texas was ever proposed in Kentucky. Many legislators do resent the Court, but because of its invalidation of a legislative redistricting plan in 1994, not because of school reform.

Despite the relative confidence that the Court will not intervene further on finance issues, people still remember that the Court is "out there" somewhere as a potential player in school reform. If the Justices' goals were not already being met, the threat of judicial intervention would seem much more real. One respondent said, "The Court is holding everything together." Rose's use of the threat of the Court against the Patton plan is only the best example of this undercurrent. As another interviewee put it, the Court is still "on call."

Conclusions

What conclusions can one draw concerning court power from this case study of Kentucky school reform? First, courts cannot succeed in such a high-stakes "public law" case without strong backing from outside the institution. In Kentucky, the movement for better schools had been percolating over a decade. Much of the sifting and winnowing of reform ideas had taken place, so the interest groups were ready to make recommendations to the task force. The effects of the perceived shift in public opinion partly because of the media should not be underestimated. Also, many politicians were sympathetic with at least the principle of school reform. Without this broader political movement, the Court decision would have been received much more harshly in the political branches.

Second, though, this case study suggests that courts can succeed even when the legislative and executive branches are feuding. It is hard to imagine a more contentious relationship than that between the Kentucky legislature and Wilkinson, yet the Court was able to persuade both combatants to work together, at least on this issue. Perhaps this was because of a mutual desire to avoid blame or take credit, but whatever the motivation, the Court succeeded in producing a rare consensus.

Third, unlike in Texas, judicial power did not result from a meticulous examination of the wording of the Court decision. The task force essentially used the broad principles articulated in the decision but did not actively consult the decision to resolve contentious issues, again unlike in Texas. The decision itself was very effective precisely because of its scope and breadth. It was broad enough for legislators and Wilkinson to put their own ideas into and then blame the Court for any political fallout. Gerald Rosenberg in *The Hollow Hope* argues that courts can be effective when leaders can say to the "implementing populations" that the courts are to blame for unpopular policies, not the leaders themselves (Rosenberg 1991:34–35). This "shift-the-blame" strategy was definitely a factor in Kentucky compliance. Even this formulation understates judicial power as the Kentucky Supreme Court exhibited in this case, however. Before the ruling, almost *no one* expected the breadth of the decision declaring the entire state public school system unconstitutional. It was not the case that there was a consensus to reform the system completely and the Court merely gave the politicians an excuse to do it. Instead, the Court dramatically shifted the alternatives, the possibilities, and the worldview of the politicians.

Lastly, even though the court has not played nearly as strong a role as the Texas Supreme Court has in following up the Justices' initial decision, the Court still seems to be a presence, albeit reduced, in decisions on education issues even to this day. Court influence does not end with the ruling itself. Most of the political actors currently discount the Court as a major force, but that is only because so much of what the Court wanted is already on the statute books. The real controversies now are over maintaining that consensus, not pushing further to meet new Court mandates. If the state were to retreat seriously on KERA, it is very likely that the discussion of possible Court action would reopen immediately.

In the introduction to this chapter, I described the role of the Court in *Rose* as a "catalyst." By "catalyst" I mean an entity that assembles forces present in the environment and fuses them into something very new and different, with more power than what each of these forces possessed individually. This type of change is not always positive. Many people, including parents, teachers, administrators, and legislators, have serious and legitimate complaints concerning the substance of KERA and the way in which it was passed with relatively little discussion, input, or criticism. The "catalyzed" entity, the pro-KERA consensus, seems unable to incorporate healthy criticism without threatening to destroy the whole, a defect that perhaps stems partly from the sweeping language of the Court decision. This intolerance might yet doom certain aspects of the reform law. In fact, some interviewees said that the pro-KERA consensus is slowly weakening, although others disputed that assessment. Whatever the ultimate resolution (if there ever is one) of the issues that KERA presented, though, one cannot ignore the role of the Kentucky Supreme Court, with many other forces for change, in producing this historic reform. In this way, the Court succeeded.

CHAPTER 5

❧

North Dakota: "We'll Give You One More Chance"

The state of North Dakota, at first glance, appears to have little in common with the other two states chosen for this book. Unlike Texas, North Dakota's population is small and relatively equally distributed, with the exceptions of the "big cities" of Fargo (population approx. 75,000) and the capital, Bismarck (approx. 50,000). Unlike Kentucky pre-KERA, the North Dakota public schools are generally considered successful—the state's students regularly score near or at the top on nationwide achievement tests. North Dakota does share a bond with these other two states, however—a hard-fought battle over school funding that the state high court attempted to resolve.

In the previous two chapters, state supreme courts have taken strongly active roles in dealing with the political branches on school funding issues, either through multiple court orders as in Texas or one comprehensive order as in Kentucky. The experience of North Dakota with school finance reform displays a different role for a state high court, that of "threat." In 1994, the state Supreme Court narrowly upheld the constitutionality of the state's plan for public education finance, but a concurring opinion by the Chief Justice sent a clear message to the legislature and governor that the present system was only marginally acceptable; the Court desired change.

The response to the Court's warning is at the heart of this chapter. How successful can courts be when they merely threaten action? In the case of the North Dakota Supreme Court's school finance order, the answer seems to be: "somewhat successful." A clear majority of interviewees reported that the legislature did take some steps to comply with what lawmakers believed the Court wanted, although the length of those steps is much debated, and certainly did not extend to comprehensive reform, as in Kentucky.

This chapter will frame this conclusion by providing background for the Court order and then presenting explanations why the legislature reacted to the Court warning as it did.

A Chronology of Reform

Government on the Prairie: "Tractors, Desks, and Stores"

The dominant theme of the North Dakota constitution as expressed by the state's founders in 1889 is that of government limited both by weak legal powers and by a strong popular check. Daniel Elazar, in his typology of the political cultures of the American states, labels North Dakota as "moralistic," favoring clean and limited government (Elazar 1972:96-99). The form that this "moralism" took was a very Progressive distrust of politics and politicians, and a love of direct democracy, especially when the people could check the government. Therefore, the tradition of popular referendum is quite strong. As noted below, in recent years fear of public backlash has been a wall against tax increases to pay for education reforms, even to the present day.

An examination of the formal powers of the three branches themselves further reveals this skepticism about government. The leading branch of government, the legislature, was limited to meeting for sixty working days every two years, just as the Kentucky legislature was, until the last decade. More recently, the people through referendum approved an extension to an eighty-non-consecutive-day session. Even so, nearly every interviewee related that the state legislature is still citizen-based and shows little signs of increasing professionalization, unlike Kentucky. In the words of the *Bismarck Tribune*, one of the state's leading newspapers, after the biennial session is over, "the lawmakers go back to their tractors, desks, and stores" (Gilmour 1993c).[1]

The governor fares no better under this system of limited government. Until 1964, the chief executive's term spanned only two years, less than the current four-year term. Unlike in Texas, he/she does not have a powerful lieutenant governor to deal with, but on the other hand, there are very few state offices that the governor can directly control. Following the Progressive tradition, North Dakota leads the nation in the number of independently elected state officers with ten (Council of State Governments 1995). Again, the people are trusted to select their rulers more than the corrupt politicians. Popular voice takes precedent over governing effectiveness.

Finally, the Court is also circumscribed in its authority. First, Justices are elected by the people, not appointed by the governor, for ten-year terms. A Justice commonly will resign before the end of a term, in which case the governor's interim replacement will have to immediately run in the next general election against any and all challengers on a nonpartisan ballot. Second, and more importantly, four of the five Justices of the state high court must agree before an act of the legislature can be declared unconstitutional. Again, the founders did not want unelected officers overruling popular will. This supermajority requirement is unique to North Dakota, and it had significant implications for the Court's handling of the school finance issue. All of these factors converge to form a government of substantially limited powers with a strong popular voice.

Public Education [2]

Unlike Texas and Kentucky, North Dakota has enjoyed a system of free public education since statehood in 1889. The framers of the constitution, although skeptical of government power in many respects, relaxed a bit of their suspicion when drafting the education article. It reads:

> Section 1. A high degree of intelligence, patriotism, integrity, and morality on the part of every voter in a government by the people being necessary in order to insure the continuance of that government and the prosperity and happiness of the people, the legislative assembly shall make provision for the establishment and maintenance of a system of public schools which shall be open to all children of the state of North Dakota and free from sectarian control. This legislative requirement shall be irrevocable without the consent of the United States and the people of North Dakota.

> Section 2. The legislative assembly shall provide for a uniform system of free public schools throughout the state, beginning with the primary and extending through all grades up to and including schools of higher education, except that the legislative assembly may authorize tuition, fees, and service charges to assist in the financing of public schools of higher education. (N.D. Constitution, Art. VIII, Sections 1, 2)

A reading of these provisions shows that the wording of the North Dakota education article differs slightly from that of the Texas and Kentucky constitutions in that the terms "open to all" and "uniform . . . throughout the state" appear instead of "efficient." It is unclear whether this subtle difference affected the Court's ruling.

Despite the constitutional delegation of primary responsibility for the public school system to the state, public education and its financing were almost entirely controlled by local communities for the first seventy years of statehood. The state did not assume a significant role in education funding until 1959, when the first foundation plan was adopted. The "foundation plan," a system in which students are guaranteed a "floor" or minimum amount of per-pupil spending regardless of district wealth, had been adopted by much of the rest of the country twenty to thirty years earlier in response to the Depression. The North Dakota foundation plan had a slightly different structure than that of similar plans, and featured two significant components.

First, for all districts, the state set a standard amount of state aid per pupil (originally $260) multiplied by the number of pupils in the district and distributed to each locality. This raw number was altered by two exceptions, though. On one hand, the system incorporated a "weighting factor" designed to favor "small but necessary" rural schools over larger towns, which presumably could afford more school services. This weighting factor became symbolic later in the lawsuit filed by some of the state's largest districts. On the other hand, the legislature also adjusted the base state aid payment by the so-called "mill deduct." The state set a level for the deduct—for example, twenty mills—multiplied it by the total tax base in the district, and subtracted that product from the total state aid payment. Mathematically, this favored districts with low wealth per student and high tax rates over districts with high wealth and low tax rates. For example, a twenty mill deduct proportionally affected a district taxing at thirty mills much more than a district with a rate approaching two hundred mills.

As it worked out, generally larger towns were helped because their tax base did not appear high when averaged over their greater number of students (economies of scale) and their tax rates were generally higher than in rural areas. By contrast, small towns appeared wealthier per student because of their low enrollment and generally lower tax rates. Therefore, the two adjustments in the state aid formula (the "weighting factor" and the "mill deduct") often worked at cross-purposes. These factors also became the crux of school finance politics. The second component of the 1959 foundation plan featured a mandatory countywide mill levy of 21 mills, which had an equalizing effect at least within counties. The state also agreed to ensure that no district would receive less than sixty percent of its revenues from nonlocal sources, such as the county or state.

The first foundation plan remained relatively unchanged until 1973, when all states were forced to confront the issues raised in the *Rodriguez* litigation considered by the U.S. Supreme Court. Perhaps in an attempt to forestall a lawsuit, the legislature directed a large amount of state money into the foundation plan, more than doubling the base aid payment per pupil to each district, and capped the tax rates of certain classes of districts to achieve greater parity between localities. In retrospect, the years between 1973 and 1980 may have been the best for equity advocates. This prosperity did not last, ironically, because of unintended consequences. In 1980, voters passed an initiative measure imposing a 6.5% oil extraction tax and requiring that 45% of the proceeds of the tax should be used to fund education, with the goal set of 70% state funding. The price of oil was at its peak then, and policymakers assumed that the tax revenues would be more than enough to cover the bulk of school costs. Therefore, the twenty-one mill required county levy was repealed.

Unfortunately, soon after the measure was passed the price of oil plummeted, and with it the goal of 70% state funding. Over the next few legislative sessions, lawmakers increased the base state aid payment, but the hikes could not match the loss of oil revenues after the bust. At its peak, the mill deduct could equalize at least a third of revenues, when the deduct was around twenty mills and the highest tax rate was around sixty mills. By the end of the 1980s, the costs of education had increased so much that the highest taxing district (usually Fargo) taxed over one hundred fifty mills, while the deduct remained around twenty mills. The state share of local spending, which had reached a high of over 60% at the time of the referendum, fell to around 50% by 1989 and would decrease further over time as costs increased.

Exactly who was hurt most by the failure of revenues to keep up with costs after 1980 was (and still is) a matter of great dispute. Larger districts such as Bismarck, Grand Forks, West Fargo, and Williston maintained that even though their tax rates were some of the highest in the state, their per-pupil spending amount ranked below average or near the bottom. They therefore presented a seemingly classic case of school finance inequity. No matter how high these districts taxed, they still could not raise an adequate or equal amount of funds to spend on their schools. If the state put more money into the foundation formula, or less likely, if the legislature decided to redistribute funds from "wealthier" rural districts to the cities, these districts would have greater ability to tend to their educational needs.

On the other hand, smaller rural districts argued that the larger urban districts ignored the rural funding situation. Many of these districts appeared rich because their tax base was divided over proportionately fewer students than in the urban areas. The facilities, programs, and course offerings in many of these rural schools, however, could not compare to those in the larger districts because of the lack of students. Regarding the state aid formula itself, the formula's heavy reliance on property taxes disproportionately harmed rural areas because more rural wealth was tied up in land value, not income as in the urban areas. If property were not the only criterion of wealth, many rural districts would not appear so "rich."

Second, North Dakota was (and is) experiencing a population shift from rural areas either to the "big cities" of Bismarck and Fargo or out-of-state. In fact, the state has fewer residents now than in 1930 (North Dakota State Census Data Center). The out-migration shows no signs of abating, as the number of children age 0-5 continues to decline. The effects on rural education have been significant. Many schools or districts have been forced to consolidate or cut programs (MacDonald 1994). Redistribution would be viewed by these districts as making a bad situation worse. To add more complexity, several districts do not fit into either of these categories (rural/urban). For example, districts that possess oil, gas, or coal resources are doing quite well in providing facilities and programs for their students. These districts might be tempting targets for equity advocates, but the districts already pay the state money "in lieu of" their share of property taxes. Finally, two districts, Grand Forks and Minot, house federal airbases that generate revenue for their communities, but federal law prohibits the state from taxing the bases.

This brief description illustrates the difficult position of the legislature regarding school funding. Each district in its own way could claim to be "poor" and could blame other "wealthier" districts for its problems. Lawmakers could not even rely on partisanship to make their decisions easier, as the rural/urban split internally divided both Republicans and Democrats. Redistribution did not seem at all feasible, either politically or from a policy standpoint. The only solution that would please all districts would be a significant increase in state aid, most likely from a tax increase. In 1989, Governor George Sinner, a Democrat, convinced the legislature to pass a combination of small increases in the state's major revenue sources, mostly sales and income taxes. Sinner tried to spread the pain out so no one would be too upset. Unfortunately, that strategy annoyed a broad base of voters. The tax increases were referred to the people, who promptly rejected the tax hikes by an overwhelming majority.

To add insult to injury, a tax increase specifically targeted to education was put on the ballot through initiative petition in the following year (1990), and the voters strongly turned that effort down as well. The impact these referenda had on the legislature was deep. According to one interviewee, several lawmakers were defeated for reelection because of their support of the tax increases. The legislature got the clear message that tax increases were unacceptable to the voters for any purpose. Education deserved more money, perhaps, but equity was not worth risking one's seat over.

Suing the State: "The Only Hammer We Ever Had"

By 1989, some of the state's largest districts, frustrated with the legislative deadlock underscored by the referendum defeats of that year and the following year, concluded that their best option was to pursue litigation. Following the pattern in other states, they filed a lawsuit against the state alleging violations of the state constitution. The plaintiffs were led by the Bismarck district and its superintendent, Lowell Jensen. Jensen, in consultation with the other joining superintendents, hired Calvin Rolfson, a Bismarck attorney, to represent them. The plaintiffs generally were some of the largest districts in the state, including Bismarck, Grand Forks, Dickinson, West Fargo, Grafton, Devils Lake, Mandan, Surrey, and Valley City. Notably, Fargo proper did not join, according to interviewees, because their tax base was so large (for North Dakota) that the district could not be considered "poor" under any formulation. What the plaintiff districts had in common was a relatively large school population for the available resources, driving down per-pupil spending and forcing increases in local tax rates to some of the highest levels in the state. As noted above, these districts presented the classic school finance problem.

Plaintiff districts would have to convince a court (and the politicians charged with devising a remedy) that they were being treated unfairly in a constitutional sense in comparison to the rural districts they were labeling "wealthy" for purposes of the suit. This was a difficult case to make, especially politically. This "disconnect" between the plaintiffs' view of wealth necessary to make their legal case, and the more "common sense" definition of wealth argued by the rural districts, that of course offerings, programs, facilities, and enrollment, persisted throughout the litigation. As it turned out, only one-third of the state's school districts supported the suit, while two-thirds opposed. Alternately, one might imagine a scenario in which the urban and rural districts banded together in a grand coalition to sue the state in order to force an aid increase for all. This option does not seem to have been seriously considered by the plaintiff districts, however. A few reasons can be extrapolated from the comments of interviewees. First, the interests of these districts still were so divergent that a coalition might have broken down as soon as any solution was proposed. Second, most of the rural districts could not afford to contribute any significant amount of money toward a lawsuit which they regarded as a gamble. Only Bismarck and a few other plaintiff districts had the resources to absorb the costs of an unfavorable decision. Third, the adequacy argument, although gaining popularity in court decisions around the country, still was quite speculative by comparison to the traditional rich versus poor equity arguments that would split any rural/urban alliance.

These reasons against the grand coalition idea also dampened support for the suit from the major education groups of the state, such as the North Dakota Education Association (teachers), North Dakota School Boards Association, and the North Dakota Council of School Administrators. Although these groups were generally very supportive of the possibility of obtaining more money for education as a result of the suit, their membership contained both rural and urban interests that would be at cross-purposes in the case of redistribution. Therefore, the education groups did not formally join the suit.

Turning to the suit itself, plaintiff's attorney Calvin Rolfson had two important choices to maket. First, he decided to file the suit in Burleigh County District Court in Bismarck instead of the home courts of any of the other plaintiff districts. The possibilities for a favorable hearing and convenience seem to have been the major motivations for this choice. The Burleigh County court is staffed by seven judges individually assigned at random to the cases brought before it. Each party to litigation, however, gets one "free" removal of a judge, although such a decision is relatively rare. In the case of *Bismarck School District #1 v. State* (see South Central Judicial District cite in the North Dakota cases), two changes were necessary before finding an acceptable judge. The first judge assigned to the case in June 1989 resigned in July of 1991, just as initial motions were first heard. The second judge slated was "bumped" by

Rolfson. Therefore, a third judge, William F. Hodny of Mandan, presided. Hodny, according to multiple observers, was a very meticulous, ordered, fair judge who showed strong regard for procedure. According to these same sources, he also liked to stick with a decision once he had made up his mind. If one agreed with that ruling, then one could rely on it throughout his consideration, much like Judge McCown in Austin.

The second key decision Rolfson had to make concerned the grounds for the suit. He eventually opted for two claims; first, that the state had violated the education article of the state constitution requiring a "uniform system of free public schools throughout the state (Art.VIII, Sec. 1,2)," and second, that the state had transgressed the equal protection article of the state constitution (Art.I, Sec.21, 22.) Even though the language of Article I, Sections 21 and 22, only barely resembles the federal equal protection clause of the Fourteenth Amendment, the North Dakota courts elected to read the provisions similarly (*Bismarck* 1994:255). The education clause presented the most favorable possiblities for success, though, in that most other state supreme court decisions voiding school finance systems have relied on this clause rather than equal protection (McUsic 1991).

AT TRIAL: THE HODNY DECISION

The trial opened June 16, 1992, before Hodny sitting without a jury. Both Rolfson for the plaintiffs and Laurie Loveland, the state solicitor general for the defense, focused their arguments on Article VIII, Sections 1 and 2, of the state constitution. Since there were very few precedents interpreting these provisions, both sides essentially had to create their own theories of the case. Rolfson stressed the factual finance disparities between the plaintiff districts and the rest of the state, noting the low level of spending per-pupil of the plaintiffs despite their tremendous tax effort. Little change had occurred in the system since the suit had been initially filed in 1989. The mill deduct had increased by a mill each in the 1989 and 1991 sessions, and the foundation aid payment had gone up by a small amount, but overall, the system was in status quo.

Loveland, by contrast, framed the issue in terms of structure and power. The legislature, not the courts, was charged by the constitution to construct the school system. The legislature had passed laws providing for school districts, facilities, a core curriculum, and various other necessary regulations. This structure was what the constitution required, not a chimerical goal of finance equity.

The trial itself lasted only eighteen days, but Hodny did not issue his ruling until February 1993, a month into the legislature's biennial session (the legislature meets from January to around April of odd-numbered years). The ruling, according to most interviewees, clearly focused the legislature's attention on the Burleigh County district court. Hodny declared the state's school funding system unconstitutional as violating the state education article and also the state equal protection provision. The judge justified his decision by starting with the basic premise, which was still disputed in North Dakota case law, that the state constitution created a fundamental right to an education. The combination of the education article and the equal protection provision made this right clear. Therefore, the state must meet a high burden in explaining any deviation from the standard of equality in education. Hodny ruled that "local control" was not a compelling reason for disparity in spending per child. Irrespective of local control, local wealth per student could never be an acceptable reason for inequity in provision of education. The facts clearly showed that the system provided different opportunities per child on the basis of wealth, and so the system must be declared null and void, he wrote.

Hodny then proceeded to outline the aspects of the state's financing laws that were particularly objectionable constitutionally. The overall theme of these provisions was allowance of disparity based on local wealth, including the mill deduct in the foundation formula that had failed to keep up with increases in educational costs, especially for the largest districts; the "low level of foundation educational support which fails to ensure substantial equality of resources for children in similarly situated school districts"; the "use of cost weightings (the "weighting factors") that are inaccurate and unjustifiably benefit districts with large amounts of taxable wealth"; the transportation aid program, special education fund, and facilities fund, all of which disproportionately rewarded the wealthiest districts with the resources to match state grants; and the failure of the state to reduce aid to districts that maintained huge leftover fund balances (parentheses mine) (South Central Judicial District cite: 228–29). Hodny ruled that absolute equality between districts was not necessary, but that any disparity should not be a result of differences in local wealth. To implement this decision, the judge required the state superintendent of public instruction, Dr. Wayne Sanstead, to present a plan to the 1993 Legislature that would meet the constitutional requirements as set forth in the decision.

The legislature was then required to either pass this plan or some other plan of its own device within six months that would also pass constitutional muster at the end of four years. Hodny admitted that the Supreme Court would likely revise this timetable on appeal, but he wanted the principle of deadlines in place. Finally, Hodny stated that he would retain jurisdiction for as long as necessary to meet the constitutional standard.

THE 1993 LEGISLATURE: "LET'S WAIT AND SEE"

Before turning to the immediate political reaction to Hodny's ruling voiding the state school finance system, it is useful to profile the various actors charged with implementing the court order in order to better understand their varied responses to the ruling. The policymaker first to act, Sanstead, was required to devise a plan meeting the court standards for the legislature's consideration. He was a former lawmaker and a Democrat, and currently is the longest serving state education superintendent in the nation. His position throughout the school finance debates was that education needed a significant amount of new money for all districts. Some restructuring of tax rates might be necessary in certain districts, but in general the system would work a lot better with more money in it (*Bismarck Tribune* 1993a; Crawford 1996).

The legislature that Sanstead was charged with reporting to did not share his general policy predilections. Historically, the legislature has been controlled by the Republican Party, although the state's Republicanism generally is more moderate and populist in a Progressive sense than the stereotype of the modern GOP. North Dakota Republicans on the whole do not share the emphasis on religious conservatism ascendant nationally, although they do greatly stress fiscal discipline, austerity, and limited government, as befitting the state's heritage (Gilmour 1994). In the 1993 Legislature, the Republicans controlled the Assembly by a wide margin, as was traditional. However, the Democrats had managed in the 1986 elections to capture a narrow majority in the state Senate, and had held it ever since, although they were quite fearful of losing control in the subsequent 1994 elections. These Democrats ideologically were a little more similar to those in the national party, although rural Democrats from the western part of the state could be counted on to be much more conservative. Even though, as noted above, school finance did not cleave along regular party lines, discussions

of new taxes and education as a priority tended to spur partisanship between and within the chambers.

If and when the legislature passed a school funding reform
plan, it would travel to the governor's office. The current occupant,
Republican Edward T. Schafer, was new to the job, having been
elected just three months earlier in November 1992. Schafer, like
Wallace Wilkinson in Kentucky, was a businessman with no previous political experience. He was the son of a man described by one
interviewee as "North Dakota's only philanthropist." Schafer tried
to succeed in business himself, but his fish farm went bankrupt
soon after he was elected governor, leading to a state bailout and
Democratic charges of favoritism. Schafer, also like Wilkinson (and
Bill Clements in Texas) had run on a platform of "no new taxes,"
and he clearly intended to keep that pledge. Ideologically, he was
more moderate than many legislative Republicans, but that moderation did not extend to taxes. Schafer was sympathetic to the cause
of education, but demanded that any funding increases be paid for
with program and personnel cuts elsewhere.

Given the positions of these various actors, it is not surprising
that Hodny's decision was not universally hailed in February 1993.
Two reactions stood out. First, generally policymakers were frustrated and upset by the ruling, which was largely unanticipated.
One respondent said the general mood was: "Who does he (Hodny)
think he is?" The judge was just one person dictating to a hundred-
plus-member legislative body. At least part of the resistance was
due to a feeling among the rural districts that the decision would
lead to redistribution of their resources to the large "urban" districts that had filed the suit. Paradoxically, many interviewees also
noted the legislative frustration with a perceived lack of specifics
in Hodny's ruling. If the judge was going to declare the system
unconstitutional, lawmakers wanted more guidance how to fix it.
One respondent assessed that although "there's not a person in the
state who doesn't want equity," there was a "lack of desire to take
the initiative." Hodny identified problem areas that lawmakers
were mostly already aware of, but left it to the legislature to craft
responses. One lawmaker thought Hodny should have been required
to devise an alternate system to "make his decision tougher" instead
of mere "exhortations," according to another source.

On the other hand, the second consequence of the decision was
to place the school funding issue squarely at the top of the legislative agenda. According to one legislator, Hodny "scared the pants
off people," an assessment shared by other respondents in slightly

different language. The threat was "fix it, or I'll take it over." There was a "real discussion of change" because of the suit. Another legislator reported that lawmakers took the decision "very very seriously." Aside from frustration with the content of the trial court opinion, policymakers were also unbalanced by its timing, in the middle of a typically short and chaotic legislative session. If the legislature was going to pass a new funding system, response would have to be strong and immediate. Such a response was not forthcoming. Lawmakers elected to take their time in formulating solutions to the school finance problems, typified by the Senate minority leader's public comment two weeks after the decision, "Until we get the Supreme Court's order, we need to be saying, 'No, we're not going to change'" (Smith 1993a). Many interviewees confirmed this assessment that the legislature, although quite worried, did not see the need for immediate action.

Two reasons stand out for the legislature's attitude, aside from the time pressure. First, as noted above, many lawmakers wanted to wait for the Court to rule before taking any steps that surely would be politically painful, a view encouraged by the state's legal team. Attorney General Heidi Heitkamp sent out a memo to lawmakers stating in part that it would be unrealistic to expect the Court to rule before the end of 1993, well after the legislative session. Furthermore, in a meeting with Schafer and legislative leaders, she expressed confidence that the high court would not "rubber stamp" the trial court decision (Associated Press 1993b). The constitutional requirement of a four-Justice majority (out of five) must have played a role in this opinion.

Second, the legislature took a cue from Schafer's response to Hodny's ruling. Schafer, while expressing agreement with the goals of the suit, made it clear that a tax increase was not a viable options for solving the problems. On the day of the decision, he stated: "My concern is if the court is intent on us coming up with a formula that is equitable, appropriate, and legal, we're going to have to have some time to do that. . . . We don't have a ton of money. . . . We've got to reduce (money to) this school system and give to that one" (Mensing 1993).

If redistribution would be necessary, the legislature was going to try to delay it as long as possible. To avoid the appearance of defiance of the court order, however, the House Republican leadership decided to appoint a special legislative task force to deal with the school finance problems, bypassing (and angering) the regular education committee. At first glance, this panel might remind the reader of the task force constructed in Kentucky. The differences between the two committees were significant, though, and eventually led to the repudiation of the work of the North Dakota task force.

First, the panel only included House members, meaning that neither senators nor the governor had a stake in the success of the panel. Second, leadership from the top was not as present as in Kentucky. Speaker of the House Rick Berg (R-Fargo) capably chaired the panel, but in North Dakota, the House majority leader ranks above the speaker, and majority leader Bob Martinson (R-Bismarck) did not join. As noted above, the Senate minority leader, Gary Nelson (R-Casselton), advocated waiting until a Supreme Court ruling, and the Senate majority leader, Dan Wogsland (D-Cooperstown), thought the task force was an unnecessary "knee-jerk reaction" (*Associated Press* 1993a,b). Third, there was no broader public movement for education reform (or finance reform), which was crucial in Kentucky (more on this below.)

Despite all these problems, the task force clearly took its responsibilities seriously, and was quite conscious of the Court's looming shadow. Berg at one of the early meetings framed the issues this way (as transcribed):

> Who is going to deal with the issue the best? Do we want to lose control as a legislative assembly? It's going to be a judgment call. If we feel that our best interests are going to be curbed by doing nothing, having challenged the Supreme Court, hoping the Supreme Court overturns the lower court, then we're done with this issue.
>
> The other alternative is if the Supreme Court upholds the lower court, then we will have to come back in a special session and we'll probably have a lot more correction. The third option is for the courts to simply take over everything. . . . (We have to decide) what's right in our minds as legislators for the state of North Dakota. . . . A lot of these things are right for North Dakota. . . . I'm willing to go forward with this. (No.Dak.St.Leg—Ed.Eq.Rev.Cmte 1993a)

Another notable aspect of the task force's deliberations was that some members referred to the experience of other states with school finance litigation and argued that this history showed that the legislature would have to act. One representative stated: "We have studied what they have done around the nation for years and I'm certain the supreme court will back up the judge" (ibid. 1993b). Another (incorrectly, but instructively) argued: "(I believe) that there have been cases in twenty-eight other states (and) that the case law is consistent and has never been overturned" (ibid. 1993c).

In other words, lawmakers on the task force, especially those in favor of greater equalization, were somewhat aware of the experience of other states with court-ordered reform. They felt that this constituted a persuasive argument for action. In a small way, these comments show court influence.

The task force was hampered, though, by the political deficiencies noted above, including the lack of any significant amount of new state money to put into the formula. The final recommendations of the task force, drafted into legislation as House Bill 1512, largely represented the convictions of Berg; several members of the task force would not agree to all the measures proposed (ibid. 1993b, 1993d). The bill called for increases in the mill deduct from twenty-two mills to fifty-three mills over four years. The state average mill levy was one hundred seventy-five mills by 1993, and so in some ways HB 1512 did not represent a great leap to equity for the large urban districts. The potential effects on the smaller rural districts would be enormous, though, doubling some tax rates, while increasing others by a large percentage. The exodus from the farms to the cities would accelerate.

Furthermore, the bill provided for some rural consolidations of schools, in part through the requirement that all districts provide K-12 education, instead of just K-5, for example. Consolidation is always a wrenching political issue, and times of fiscal stress exacerbate the difficulties. More than any other reason, these requirements led to the initial defeat of HB 1512 on the House floor despite the Speaker's leadership and the pressure of Hodny's decision. As a consequence, the consolidation measures were removed, resulting in a much more favorable House vote. The bill was promptly rejected by the Senate with little to no debate, however, mostly due to the negative effects of the mill deduct increases on rural districts (Gilmour 1993a, 1993b; Smith 1993b).

The plan proposed by superintendent Wayne Sanstead fared even worse with the legislature. Pursuant to the judge's order that he devise a constitutional solution, Sanstead's plan significantly restructured the school funding system, nearly doubling the foundation aid base guaranteed by the state, to over $3100 per student. The mill deduct would be abolished, and most local property taxes would vanish, while a uniform one hundred eighty mill required county levy would provide a significant equalized source of funding. Local communities could supplement the county levy up to an extra twenty-five mills. The goal expressed by the voters in the 1980 referendum of seventy percent state funding could be realized (Sanstead 1993).

The total cost of the DPI plan was $115 million, however, a huge amount by North Dakota standards. No other political leaders were willing to support Sanstead's plan because of the significant tax increase necessary to pay for it. Soon after Hodny's decision, the House and Senate majority leaders in a bipartisan statement asserted that the legislature did not need DPI to tell them what to do (Wetzel 1993a). In fact, the plan never received a vote in either chamber.

As the session drew to a close, the legislature did not want to ignore the trial court decision entirely. Even though radical (or substantial) reform had been rejected, lawmakers were willing to take smaller steps toward equity. New taxes on cigarettes and gambling, which were acceptable to Schafer, raised $23.6 million for foundation aid. The legislature raised the mill deduct two mills over two years to twenty-four mills, a slight benefit to the plantiff districts. Additionally, it reduced the "weighting factor" favoring rural districts and capped transportation payments, which disproportionately went to rural districts (Gilmour 1993c). In fact, one lawmaker argued that the changes made by the 1993 Legislature were more significant than those in 1995, although several others disagreed.

Overall, though, the reaction of the legislature to Hodny's decision was: "we'll take this seriously, but we'll also wait for the Supreme Court." One legislator put a positive spin on this response, publicly stating: "The judge's opinion was in the back of our mind, but what was in the front of our mind was a good education for all the children of North Dakota" (Smith 1993c). Another legislator summarized the session in this way: "We all stood at the cliff. We couldn't agree to hold hands as we dived into the abyss" (Wetzel 1993b). It remained for the Court to decide if the state's political leaders would have to take that plunge together.

THE SUPREME COURT

The North Dakota court system, like that of Kentucky, had recently undergone substantial restructuring, and also displayed some features unique to the state. In 1992, the state courts were unified: county judgeships were abolished and a system of district courts of general jurisdiction was created in their place. A new intermediate court of appeals heard overflow cases, but the primary appeals court in North Dakota, unlike in Texas and Kentucky, remained the state supreme court. The state supreme court is composed of five Justices, one of the smallest such bodies in the nation. Justices are elected for ten-year terms, unless one is filling out an unexpired term, in which case one must run immediately in the next general election. The Chief Justice is elected for a maximum of five years by both the Supreme Court members *and* the district judges. Supreme Court Justices must be attorneys. This requirement has been an informal bar between the Court and the legislature, since few attorneys can afford to give up their practices for a few months every two years and serve in the legislature. In other words, the career paths of Court Justices and legislators run parallel to one another, rarely intersecting. Only one Justice, Herbert Meschke, hearing the *Bismarck Public School District* (1994) case had been a lawmaker, and that service was nearly thirty years earlier.

Court elections themselves, according to all interviewees asked, are essentially contests of name recognition and experience rather than party or ideology. Lawyers pay attention, but few others do. Even within the legal profession, one does not see in North Dakota the bitter splits between plaintiffs' lawyers and business defendants present in Texas that led to multimillion dollar court campaigns. The combination of the relatively low-intensity elections and the long terms of the Justices (once one wins for the first time) insulates the Court from significant popular pressure.

This insulation, however, does not mean that the state supreme court has the freedom to become activist, even if that were its inclination. Two major structural factors limit the North Dakota Court in its jurisprudential creativity. The first is the "rule of four" votes necessary for voiding an act of the legislature. One legal source called this provision "the ultimate in legislative deference." Second, because there is no fully functional intermediate appellate court, the Court's docket is mostly composed of cases that are significant to the parties, but raise no earth-shaking constitutional questions. Family law cases, administrative revocation of driver's licenses for driving under the influence, and occasional product liability suits top the Court's agenda. It is difficult to imagine crafting an activist agenda from these cases. When I asked interviewees for their general assessments of the state supreme court's attitude toward the legislature, most reported that the Court showed great deference to lawmakers, with only a few exceptional cases to the contrary, one of which (concerning sovereign immunity) was decided after the

Bismarck case. One source close to the Court disagreed, arguing that the Court was liberal and activist, but that was not the view of the majority of lawmakers themselves. When I asked respondents for notable cases the Court had decided against the legislature's interests, most were hard-pressed to name any. The small bit of scholarly work done on the North Dakota high court reinforces this assessment (Leahy 1990).

Turning to the Justices individually, one sees a balanced and moderate court. At the center was the Chief Justice, Gerald W. VandeWalle. VandeWalle had been involved in state government for most of his adult life, most notably a twenty-year stay in the attorney general's office, where he held the education portfolio, giving him responsibility to advise the legislature about the legality of various measures concerning education. Therefore, beyond his experience in dealing with the legislature, he had become familiar with school funding issues as well. It is fair to say he knew more about the specific problems of education finance than any of his judicial colleagues. After his stint in the attorney general's office, VandeWalle moved directly onto the Court, where according to most interviewees, he was respected for his experience, fairness, and moderation.

Slightly to the ideological left of the Chief Justice were Associate Justices Beryl Levine and Herbert Meschke. Meschke's legislative service has been noted above, and Levine was the first woman ever to serve on the Court. Justice William A. Neumann was new on the Court at the time, and does not seem to have a clear ideological slant as yet, with some interviewees describing him as leaning liberal, but with others disagreeing. Justice Dale Sandstrom was the only Court member clearly to the ideological right of VandeWalle. Respondents claimed he was farther to the right than any of the other Justices were to the left. The balance of the Court clearly still remained in the center, though.

Because of the importance of the school finance issue, the Court elected to hear oral arguments in the *Bismarck* case in a rare August session. The case generated much public interest and several *amicus* briefs, from groups such as the Coal Conversion County Association, the Association of Oil and Gas Producing Counties, the North Dakota Small Organized Schools, and many others with a stake in the outcome. The *Bismarck Tribune* editorialized, "Few, if any, lawsuits in state history carry the importance of the coming state Supreme Court showdown over education finance" (Associated Press 1993c). Governor Schafer agreed, saying "There's no question that this is historic" (ibid.). The oral arguments generally plowed the same ground as in the trial court. Rolfson argued the disparities in wealth per student, while Loveland stressed the schools' compliance with basic state requirements. The Justices asked numerous questions, highlighted by Levine, who asked Rolfson whether he wanted the Court to act as a legislative appropriations committee, and worried whether "this court will be in the budget business" (*Bismarck Tribune* 1993b).

When the decision of the Court was released on January 24, 1994, it appeared that Levine's concerns were answered. She and two other Justices, Meschke and Neumann, voted to declare the state's school funding system unconstitutional under the education article of the state constitution and the state equal protection provision. In an opinion written by Neumann, these three jurists argued that education was a fundamental right in North Dakota, as provided in the education article. When analyzing the equal protection claim, therefore, one might use "strict scrutiny," but according to the three-Justice majority, since these issues were so complex and usually handled by the legislature, the Court would relax its test to "intermediate scrutiny," or whether the school funding system served an "important" governmental interest by means "substantially related" to that end. The school finance system did not even meet this reduced standard, though. "Local control" could not justify the disparities of wealth. In classic school finance fashion, these plaintiff districts taxed more to receive less. Therefore, considering the importance of an education for basic citizenship, this system could not be considered constitutionally "equal" (*Bismarck* 1994:250–63).

Sandstrom, by contrast, attacked the plaintiffs' claims, stating that they had not brought a legally cognizable case. The plaintiff districts had no standing, as they were mere creatures of the state, and any payment to them was in the form of a "gratuity" (*Bismarck* 1994:264). The taxpayer plaintiffs that had joined the suit also had no standing because they could not show specific injury. Even though there was a fundamental right to an education under the state constitution, the state was fulfilling that obligation already by creating a public school system and imposing rules and regulations upon it. No child could assert that he/she was being denied a basic education. In fact, Sandstrom noted, on national test scores of student achievement, North Dakota usually scored at or near the best in the country (a point returned to below [ibid.:270]). Therefore, there was no constitutional violation.

Because the votes of four of the five Justices were necessary to throw out the school funding system, the outcome rested on the shoulders of Chief Justice VandeWalle, a man who had spent twenty years advising the legislature on the legality of proposed education laws. His decision, for these and other reasons, was the opinion that most interviewees referred to as the "opinion of the Court" and the one to which they paid the most attention, even though it comprised less than two pages. First, the Chief Justice dispelled any doubt as to how he would vote. He faulted the large urban district plaintiffs for ignoring the counterclaims of smaller rural districts of "economies of scale" as a mitigating factor for the problems of the plaintiffs. The issues were more complex than the plaintiff districts made them appear. In other words, VandeWalle restated the common arguments concerning North Dakota school finance for the last forty years. He continued:

> Without more, I cannot conclude that the evidence supports more than a finding of inequity—an inequity which has not yet reached constitutional proportions. A comparison of the very worst with the very best of 269 school districts cannot be the basis for finding unconstitutional disparity among all districts. (ibid.:275)

VandeWalle could have concluded his ruling at this point, but he did not. Evidently, he was troubled enough by the direction of the education funding system he had observed for most of his life that he felt a further statement was necessary. The opinion proceeded:

> Despite my agreement in part with Justice Sandstrom's opinion, I write separately to emphasize the most obvious teaching of Justice Neumann's opinion, and that of the trial court, i.e. that the present system is fraught with funding inequities which I believe have not yet transgressed the rational-basis standard of review but which appear to me to be on a collision course with even that deferential standard. . . .
>
> Because the "deduct" does not approach a pragmatic "school district equalization factor" . . . it seems inevitable that the restrictions on the ability of school districts to locally raise necessary funds for districts (read for minimum curriculum), when coupled with the failure of the "deduct" to "equalize" that inability through greater State revenue for those districts having insufficient local tax resources, will eventually require a conclusion that the scheme is unconstitutional as applied to the students in those districts. Although Justice Sandstrom concludes in his opinion

that the parents and students have not, in this case, proven they have been denied a minimum curriculum taught by qualified teachers or that, by objective testing they have been denied a minimum uniform education, that proof may well be evident in the future under the present scheme. (ibid.:276)

The case was thus legally over (even the three-Justice majority overruled Hodny's retention of jurisdiction) and the state's school finance system could continue. But the Chief Justice's opinion left few observers with a sense of closure.

THE 1995 SESSION: "WE'LL GIVE YOU ONE MORE CHANCE"

The message of VandeWalle's opinion was clear to most observers: we don't want to intervene in this area if we can help it, but if you in the legislature don't do something, we'll be back. In other words, "we'll give you one more chance." This role of a state supreme court as "threat" is rarely presented as clearly. This case affords a unique opportunity to test its effectiveness. The most immediate reaction to the decision was a sense of relief that the Court was not going to take over the school system. Beyond that, attitudes varied. Some lawmakers read the decision as saying "we won" or that the system was constitutional. VandeWalle's opinion was no more than a "stern warning" or a "slap on the wrist." The threat of another lawsuit did not seem plausible to them. In the words of one such interviewee, "they shouldn't be messing in our affairs" in the first place. The Court had recognized its proper role and finally deferred. Another group of lawmakers sympathetic to the plaintiff districts interpreted the decision differently. They were much more inclined to see the "gun behind the door" in VandeWalle's opinion. In the words of one legislator, the Court had said, "we're giving you a break . . . (but it's) not going to stay that way." Another interviewee characterized VandeWalle's opinion as a "shot over the bow." This group favored immediate and strong action in the 1995 legislative session to correct the perceived faults in the system.

Therefore, it seems clear that activists on both sides of the debates were able to claim some justification for their position from the Court opinion. The message itself was clear, but its consequences were not. Therefore, the key group in deciding what the effect of the opinion would be was composed of legislators in the ideological middle. These moderate lawmakers, perhaps unsurprisingly, took a balanced approach to the Court ruling. According to one, the Court had forced the legislature to "take a broader perspective" than merely the narrow interests of one's own district. In a similar vein, according to another legislator, the Court had said "do something," had set a direction, and had mandated that "every step you take needs to go in that direction."

There was no specific timetable for reaching equity, though. In other words, the Court had required the legislature act with "all deliberate speed." Schafer in his public comments tended to agree with this last centrist view. According to the governor, "What we're trying to do is set a target out there, and start down the path to getting there (*Bismarck Tribune* 1994)." It soon became clear, however, that the governor also was not willing to break his "no new taxes" pledge to pay for education finance reform, even after the Supreme Court opinion (unlike Wallace Wilkinson in Kentucky.) He advised the legislature, "We have to do it without money attached to it. We can't solve the problem by just throwing more money at it" (Donatelle 1994).

The legislature was not scheduled to meet again until January 1995, nearly a year after the Court ruling. This delay had the potential effect of slowing down any momentum for change; to forestall this erosion, lawmakers on the education committees held a series of meetings in the interim to discuss possible solutions to the problems facing education funding. The meetings did not prove especially fruitful, however, as partisan bickering dominated. Democrats eventually forced a vote on an $80 million funding increase, which everyone knew would never be acceptable either to legislative Republicans or to the governor. Republicans, though, did not seem willing to present a plan of their own that would resolve the issues (Associated Press 1994a).

The political dynamics of the state were substantially altered by the November 1994 elections, creating more uncertainty for school finance. Like their colleagues elsewhere, North Dakota Republicans did very well at the ballot box, recapturing the state Senate. The GOP dominance in the Assembly was unchanged, meaning that the state government was unified under the Republican Party for the first time since 1981. Interviewees expressed substantially varying assessments of what the Republican takeover meant for school funding issues. Some saw it as virtually meaningless, because those questions tended to cross party lines and split urban versus rural districts instead. Others thought the GOP majority was quite important for scuttling any far-reaching reform. Blending the comments of the respondents together, while the

Republicans were not unified in their opposition to change, the 1994 elections meant that tax increases were not going to be a serious option. The party would still splinter over redistribution issues, but not over the basic question of more government spending through taxation.

Schafer, who felt a need to do something to address school funding, finally released his plan in November 1994, only two months before the legislative session was set to begin. This plan was "co-sponsored" by the Department of Public Instruction, which saw it as the best hope for more funding. Schafer asked every state agency to take a five percent cut to pay for school reform. Coupled with revenue growth, this trimming meant that over $35 million was now free for distribution to the schools, not enough for far-reaching reform, but more than a mere drop in the bucket. Schafer claimed "I think it will take two or three steps, but we can get enough funds (to reach equity)" (Associated Press 1994b). Unfortunately, the distribution mechanism of the governor's plan was quite complex. The central feature was a "guaranteed tax base" plan designed to help poorer districts that would be added on top of the existing system. Not all districts would benefit, but those with low valuations per pupil and high tax rates, such as the plaintiff districts, would do well. Furthermore, part of this plan would be paid for by indirectly taxing the funds Grand Forks and Minot received from the federal government as payments for the airbases there. The "in-lieu-of" money paid by oil and gas districts would also be redistributed, meaning that those districts would lose some funds.

The governor's plan would be relatively fiscally equalizing according to standard measures, but it faced serious public relations problems. In a statement portending badly for the plan, new Senate majority leader Nelson said, "The formula, uh, obviously, I—to be honest, I don't understand it. But if it does what the attempt is, to move us towards equity . . . and if it isn't devastating to a lot of our smaller school districts, then I think we're moving in the right direction" (Wetzel 1994). Such lukewarm support was widespread in the legislature. Although very few lawmakers strongly opposed the governor's plan, there was a feeling that, in the words of one interviewee, "the legislature is the policy-making branch" and the governor should not interfere with that authority. Adding to that view was Schafer's relative inexperience with school finance issues (he had never before held elective office) as compared with lawmakers who had spent their entire careers working with the formulas. To the extent that the governor could gain expertise through the

DPI, that was even worse from the legislative perspective because the department was not perceived as politically realistic. Therefore, the legislature was going to jealously guard its authority.

If the governor's plan ever had a chance, it was lost when a controversy erupted over the inclusion of federal impact aid to Grand Forks and Minot in the calculation of their state payments. Aside from the questionable legality of the scheme, politically these two districts were able to exert enough pressure to persuade the governor to remove that particular provision from the plan. Since the governor had shown that he could be "rolled," in the Washington term, various other interests lined up to get their piece of the available funds. The compromises necessary to satisfy these groups added yet more complexity to the governor's plan, finally dooming it. A watered-down version passed the House, but had no chance in the Senate (Smith 1995b). Even after all the changes, the Schafer plan was still more equalizing than the Senate alternative discussed below, although Bismarck, the lead plaintiff district, actually fared worse under the Schafer plan. Incongruities such as these made coalition-building nearly impossible. To sum up, Senate Education chair Layton Freborg (R-Underwood) characterized the plan as "too far, too fast, with too little" (Smith 1995a).

Freborg led the fight for the principal alternative to the governor's proposal, Senate Bill 2519, which eventually was the vehicle for the changes that became law. SB 2519 did not add any new layers to the existing system; rather, it increased various components in the formulas to provide more equity. Chief among these was the mill deduct. The mill deduct, as noted above, was intended to favor districts with high tax rates and low taxable wealth per pupil, such as the larger urban plaintiff districts. Rural districts, conversely, generally opposed raising the deduct. They appeared "wealthier" in the formula because their tax base was divided among fewer students and their tax rates were generally lower. Several interviewees related that increases in the mill deduct usually did not benefit large districts greatly, but really hurt smaller rural districts. The proof is that before the 1995 session, in the words of one interviewee, raising the deduct one mill was "like pulling teeth." It had stayed near twenty mills since its creation.

In the 1995 session, after much negotiation, a compromise was reached that would increase the deduct four mills in the first year of the next biennium and four more in the following year, from twenty-four to twenty-eight to thirty-two. Furthermore, in the following years, the deduct would automatically rise as the base foundation aid payment rose, although the deduct was also capped at twenty-five percent of the statewide average mill levy. (note: This indexing was repealed in the 1997 session.) Interviewees varied widely in their assessments of the significance of these changes, but compared to where the legislature had been, the mill deduct adjustments were noticeable. The legislature retained Schafer's allotment of $35 million new dollars for education, but redistributed it. The new money meant that the base state aid payment could increase ten percent over the previous year. The governor later claimed that the aid increase (unadjusted for inflation) was the third largest in state history, and the largest ever without a tax increase (Schafer 1996). The legislature also created a new "equity fund" somewhat similar to the governor's guaranteed tax base plan, but with much less funding (only $2.5 million.) This fund rewarded districts that were both low on property value and also low on spending per-pupil, that is, the poorest districts in the state. At the time, the chief sponsor, Rep. Jack Dalrymple (R-Casselton), justified the fund this way: "In terms of the court . . . we need to get something started in this area, even if it's only a small amount initially . . . my motivation here is that this is an area where the court criticized us specifically" (North Dakota State Legislature 1995). One more conservative interviewee described this fund as a "political ploy," but one that still afforded an opportunity to achieve more equity if the legislature was so inclined. Beyond these formula changes, the 1995 Legislature also made adjustments to the methods of funding special education and transportation, and slightly modified the "weighting factors" for rural districts, shifting funds from rural to urban districts. It is difficult to tell to what extent the Court decision motivated these changes, but they certainly moved in the Court's direction.

In the 1997 legislative session, very few changes were made either in a positive or negative direction for school finance equity. Schafer proposed another $35 million increase in education funding, with $20 million specifically devoted to equity, but the legislature ignored him (partly because Schafer gave few specifics) and put all the money into foundation aid for all districts. Of course, $35 million was still another ten percent increase in state spending, which was not insignificant. The legislature put more money into the "equity fund" for the worst-off districts, but the funding is still a drop in the bucket. Furthermore, the automatic rise in the mill deduct was repealed, although the deduct was not lowered in 1997. In the 1999 session, lawmakers again increased the amount of

state money for education, although not to the extent of the previous sessions. No fundamental changes were made, although Democrats forced a vote on an income tax increase specifically devoted to
education. The bill failed in the Republican-controlled House, however. It appears that the utility of the threat of court action is at an
end without a new lawsuit.

Perhaps ironically, prospects for a second lawsuit have dimmed
recently with the discovery that the Bismarck school district is
gaining a significant amount of new funds, not only through legislative change but even more importantly because of the decisions
of various corporations to locate in the city. The Bismarck economy
is doing so well that the district may be considered "rich" well
within the next decade. Therefore, the district likely will not provide the bulk of the funding for a second lawsuit as it did with the
first. Some of the other plaintiff districts are not enjoying nearly so
much fiscal success, but with Bismarck absent, their prospects for
litigation look bleaker.

Concerning the Court, however, the 1996 election brought some
change. In 1995, Schafer appointed Fargo attorney Mary Mering to
replace Levine, part of the unsuccessful three-Justice majority in
the *Bismarck* case. Subsequently, state agriculture commissioner
Sarah Vogel, a more liberal candidate than Mering, challenged her
in the 1996 general election for the ten-year Court term. Perhaps
referring in part to the *Bismarck* case, Vogel, in a statement that
raised eyebrows at the Court, was quoted as saying, "I think public
policy is the lure of the Court" (Cole 1996). Mering eventually prevailed, however.

HOW MUCH REFORM?: "TINKERING IN THE RIGHT DIRECTION"

When policymakers and other observers look back on the 1995
legislative session after the Court ruling, they seem unable to reach
agreement on its consequences. Approximately half of the interviewees reported substantial or some progress on school finance
equity, while the other half was more pessimistic about the legislative response. Among the half that saw little to no progress, these
comments are representative: "We just keep applying Band-Aids . . .
we haven't done anything significant." "If I were in rural North
Dakota, I'd say significant . . . (for the plaintiffs) it didn't do much."
"They do understand something has to be done, but nothing was
done . . . it was pacified . . . because of the complexity of the issues
and because of politics." "(The changes) were not improvement but

rearranging." "(They were) paper changes that didn't really equalize." Finally, one respondent characterized the system as "calcified."

The other half of interviewees, however, was much more optimistic about the adjustments in the various parts of the funding formulas made by the legislature. The theme of this group was "we're moving forward." The changes made were "not a giant step, but (they) set the direction." (We) "feel very comfortable" with the progress made. "At least we're moving," according to one respondent. "In terms of where we've been, (the reforms made were) very important . . . a good first step." Although the changes were not big, they were the "most significant in twenty years." Finally, one legislator characterized the 1995 Legislature as making adjustments that were fiscally small, but culturally "a monumental step . . . it changed the paradigms and norms." Each individual item appeared small but the combination represented a "huge philosophical shift."

Somewhere in between these assessments was a smaller third group which took a very balanced view of the legislative changes (although many of the above comments show weighing as well). The theme of this middle group was that the legislature said: "let's do as much tinkering as we need to do (and no more)." Similarly, one lawmaker reported: "there was a movement—we don't have to meet the full intent in one session—(we can do it) over a period of years." Another assessed: "Let's do what we have to because we can't afford to have courts dictating our funding system."

In part, these varying assessments appear to be an ink-blot test on the outlook of the participants themselves; they saw what they wanted to see. Ideology, although certainly playing a role, was not determinative of whether interviewees saw the changes in the funding formulas made by the 1995 Legislature as significant or not. Some liberal interviewees were relatively satisfied, while others were quite pessimistic. Some conservative interviewees reported that the legislature moved in the Court's direction, while others said the Court was ignored. In general, a liberal outlook tended to improve one's assessment of the importance of the reforms, but there was no clear pattern.

When I asked interviewees what they expected would happen in the 1997 legislative session concerning school finance, there was also a mixed response. Interestingly, although the totals were similar to the results of the question on progress in the 1995 session, the distribution of respondents was somewhat different, with some interviewees satisfied with the 1995 changes but pessimistic about the future, while others taking the opposite positions. Nearly half

of interviewees said that they doubted there would be any significant changes in 1997, and if there were, the Supreme Court decision
would not play any part in them. For example, respondents assessed
that the Court would be a "very little factor," that the legislature
has "done their thing," and that the plaintiff districts are "not
ready for another fight." To sum up, the feeling among this group
was "we've addressed this."

The other half, though, saw the Court as a continuing presence,
if more muted than in the 1995 session. Representative assessments included the claim that "there *is* a fear that if (the legislature does nothing) the Court will come back . . . it's a big issue."
"This could be a watershed year . . . the court is a presence that
won't go away." "The legislature is committed to . . . the 'tortoise'
approach . . . to keep moving in a positive way." "As long as we
keep putting money in, there is no fear . . . but if the economy goes
down, then the courts will have influence." Overall, the legislature,
will, according to this group, "(do) just enough to keep the courts off
their backs."

Given the actual results of the 1997 (and 1999) session, it appears
that the more pessimistic view was more accurate. However, the legislature still kept on putting money in, with the $35 million foun-
dation increase in 1997, even if the funds were not particularly
equalizing. In retrospect, it should not be surprising that the Court's
influence was strongest in 1995 soon after the Court decision, and
progressively weakened after that.

Due to Whom?

As in the previous two chapters, I now outline the positions of
each of the major players in the school finance debates. I assess
each set of actors' contributions to the actions taken (or not taken)
in 1995, starting with extrainstitutional influences and finishing
with institutional forces.

The Public

Very little good data exist concerning the attitudes of the populace of North Dakota concerning public school funding issues. No
statewide polls were taken during this period that dealt with these
questions. Generally, one might assume that public attitudes would
reflect the interests of one's own home districts, whether urban or

rural, and whether one's district would benefit or not from finance restructuring. If that were the case, public opinion would be mixed, as some districts would be helped and others would be hurt by greater "equalization." The only way to avoid redistribution would be through a general tax increase. The voters *had* spoken clearly on this issue, however. The tax referendum defeats of 1989 and 1990 left a strong impression in the minds of legislators and other observers that the public was in no mood for tax increases. This foreclosure of the tax option affected all legislative deliberations— the only alternative was redistribution of state funds. The legislature had some leeway from the public regarding specific solutions, though, as there was little public knowledge of the ins and outs of the various reform proposals.

The school finance issue appears to have had no impact on state elections, a potential source of public influence. No contest specifically pitted candidates with opposing viewpoints against one another. To the extent that education funding became an issue, both candidates for a legislative seat took the position that benefitted their particular district. Also, in keeping with the prohibition against judicial discussion of issues during election campaigns, no Supreme Court race became a referendum on the *Bismarck* decision. Therefore, overall, the public influenced policy deliberations by setting the general guidelines for debate (no new taxes) but left the specifics in the hands of elected and appointed officials.

THE MEDIA

Unlike in Kentucky, the North Dakota major media generally did not play an active role in pushing for reform of the state educational system. Most notably, the *Bismarck Tribune*, while sympathetic to the goals of the lawsuit, attempted to remain neutral between the various interests involved, and certainly attempted nothing like the exposés of corruption that the Louisville and Lexington papers featured on an almost daily basis. Other newspapers, such as the *Grand Forks Herald*, could be counted on to support the plaintiff large districts, but there is no evidence that their editorials had much impact on legislative deliberations.

In part, the relative media quietude reflected the fact that at least on some measures, the North Dakota school system was doing quite well. There was not the sense of crisis present in Kentucky, a state scraping the bottom of national educational quality rankings. As alluded to earlier in the chapter, on a number of national proficiency examinations, North Dakota's children scored at or near the best in the nation (*Bismarck* 1994:270). This very success, perhaps ironically, may have dampened enthusiasm for reform, even though many districts were having financial difficulties in providing that high-quality education. It is true that some policymakers were concerned about maintaining those high test rankings, but that worry did not translate into a perception of crisis necessary for fundamental reform.

INTEREST GROUPS

In a related vein, a significant limit on Court power was the lack of a broad-based grassroots movement for education reform in North Dakota similar to that which made a crucial difference in Kentucky. In Kentucky, the Court decision was indispensable for the comprehensive reform subsequently enacted, but the broad-based education movement was just as necessary to force reform as well. In North Dakota, by contrast, relatively few voices were speaking out about the need to fundamentally change the funding system. In the most immediate sense, the high "performance" of the North Dakota school system meant that the state's business community was largely uninvolved with school finance issues, unlike in Kentucky. There were no crisis events, like the inability of the Toyota plant in central Kentucky to find educated workers, that galvanized the business community into action.

Without the support of the business community, the media, and the general public, education groups were put in a very difficult position. Organizations such as the North Dakota Education Association, North Dakota Council of School Administrators, North Dakota School Boards Association, could not argue for redistribution for "equity," because they would be hurting a large portion of their own membership. On the other hand, the strategy they were forced to pursue, lobbying for more money for the system as a whole, appeared self-serving without the support of outside actors or the Court. The legislature could safely ignore these demands, which for the most part, they did. A grand coalition for change could not be assembled.

THE GOVERNOR AND EXECUTIVE BRANCH

Another notable contrast between the North Dakota and Kentucky experiences was the differing roles of the governors, even though these men shared somewhat similar backgrounds. Both Wilkinson and Schafer came to the governor's office from private business, and neither had held elective office before. Even though Wilkinson was a Democrat and Schafer a Republican, both ran on a platform of fiscal austerity and "no new taxes," although both were relatively sympathetic to the cause of education. Both enjoyed legislative majorities of their party in both houses of the state legislature.

One significant difference between these two governors was their personal style of working with their legislatures, however. Schafer was the more amiable and consensus-oriented of the two. Interviewees found his ideology difficult to pin down, but most expressed personal regard for him, even if some respondents discounted his substantive knowledge of some of the issues. By contrast, Wilkinson and the Kentucky legislature were in "open political warfare," in the governor's words. The governor saw the legislature as greedy power barons, while the legislature saw the governor as an ignorant would-be tyrant (only a small exaggeration.)

When Schafer proposed a relatively modest, but still significant $35 million increase in education funding along with some redistribution, though, the legislature took the money but completely restructured its allocation in the state aid formulas. The Schafer plan itself barely got a vote. In Kentucky, the legislature enacted many of the education reform proposals Wilkinson had suggested, even if he would not necessarily have approved of the entire package from the outset. As noted in chapter 4, the entire Kentucky public school system was revamped. How can one explain these seemingly counter-intuitive outcomes? I would argue that the political context was different in Kentucky and North Dakota in two significant ways. First, there was not the outside pressure for reform in North Dakota that there was in Kentucky, as discussed in the previous section. Second, the Supreme Court decision was much more forceful in Kentucky than in North Dakota, a point returned to below. Therefore, one cannot explain these varied results merely by assessing the positions of the legislative and executive branches.

Before leaving the executive branch, one should briefly mention the role of the state department of public instruction (DPI). Even though the state superintendent was the actor first charged with responding to the trial court decision, his influence over the legislature was minimal because of conflicting agendas. Sanstead wanted a significant boost in overall education spending, while the GOP-led legislature was not willing to consider the new taxes necessary to pay for such an increase. In effect, the DPI was reduced to another interest group like the NDEA or NDSBA protecting the interests of all its members, wishing to anger none by proposing redistribution of existing resources. The DPI was useful, however, in providing school funding data to legislators.

THE LEGISLATURE

Since I have already discussed the steps taken to deal with the school funding problem in the 1995 Legislature, the significance of those changes, and the legislature's relationship with the governor, it remains to consider the interaction between lawmakers and the Court, discussed in this and the following section. Several interviewees posited that the Court ruling in *Bismarck* had some influence on the legislature's handling of the school finance issue in the 1995 legislative session and possibly beyond, although the extent of that influence is disputed. This section will present a more systematic analysis of the Court's impact on the legislative policy-making process.

One fundamental point that emerged from the interviews was that nearly all state policymakers concerned in any way with education paid attention to the Court ruling and took it seriously. Virtually no interviewee reported any "disconnect" or lack of respect of the Court by the legislature or other leaders. It is clear that the Court decision was carefully analyzed by those policymakers most directly affected by the decision and that those less directly concerned at least got a strong summary of the Court's decision. Lack of communication or respect was not an issue, which is an important point given other recent scholarship, which posits courts as disconnected from the political branches (Rosenberg 1991).

When I asked policymakers whether they thought the Court gained or lost any power or prestige with the legislature because of *Bismarck*, most either reported "no change" or a slightly positive impact. Only two respondents said that the Court might have lost prestige with the legislature, and neither were lawmakers. For those who said that the Court's overall relations with the legislature were unaffected, the general feeling was "they're doing their job." As one interviewee said, if not, "what can you do?" Any court-legislative effect was "a wash" because "we didn't disagree with making changes." VandeWalle's opinion was "well-written" and provided "an appropriate list of suggestions." Those respondents who argued that the Court gained in prestige claimed that "the legislature understands the judicial role and power a little better." Most importantly, the Court gained in the eyes of the legislature because "(the Court) recognized the legislative problems . . . instead of shoving them down their throats." The legislature was "somewhat thankful" that the Court issued a "moderate" decision and gave the legislature "one more chance." Therefore, the Court was respected as having legitimate authority in this area.

Beyond mere communication, there is the question of whether the legislature actually acted on the Court's opinion after comprehending it. Did the Court persuade the legislature to take actions that it would not have otherwise? The answer appears to be "yes." Even though interviewees nearly equally divided as to whether the changes made in the 1995 legislative session were significant, most interviewees reported that the legislature made at least some modifications directly as a response to the Court decision. Chief among these changes were the increases in the mill deduct (and its indexing to foundation aid) and the creation of the equity fund. Sample comments from interviewees on this question of Court influence included: "(the changes) never would have happened without the Court . . . there was never agreement on how to change." "(Without the Court,) why go through the hassle?" "(The Court) softened us up a little to see the view of the plaintiffs." "The deduct went up because (we) didn't want to revisit the courts." "Without the court case, the level of funding would be substantially less . . . the mill deduct was definitely because of the Court."

It should be noted that even some of those interviewees who were rather skeptical about the significance of the changes made by the 1995 Legislature still acknowledged judicial influence. One lawmaker characterized the reforms as "minor," but without the Court "even minor reform would not have happened." Similarly, another interviewee said that the changes "will never be enough," but they were "much more than without the Court." Furthermore, the few interviewees who saw little to no influence often were not arguing that the Court would not have had influence if the decision had been different (a point returned to below), but rather that legislators had looked at the decision and said "we won." It had little influence for these few policymakers, but mostly because they did not see the Court as requiring them to do anything. Only a couple of interviewees said that the changes in the 1995 session would have happened with or without the Court, and even these assessments were guarded.

Another way to approach the question of Court influence is through the hypothetical question posed to policymakers of what the legislature would have done if in fact the Court *had* gotten the four votes to declare the funding system unconstitutional. Would the political response have been different? If so, then there was a potential for effectiveness, even if the Court chose in *Bismarck* not to exercise it. When interviewees were asked this hypothetical question of "what if?", a clear majority, after noting that the initial response would be "chaos," in the words of one interviewee, reported that the legislature would have taken stronger action if the Court had voided the school funding system. Respondents split on whether the changes would have been only somewhat stronger or a great deal stronger, but the overall theme, that the Court would have made a difference, was clear. Only one interviewee disagreed, saying that the legislative response would have been much the same even if the Court had voided the system. This respondent was a leading legislator, and so this opinion has to be taken more seriously, but other powerful sources disagreed with this judgment.

The specific remedies that the legislature would have chosen were not clear. Some interviewees assessed that the Court could have forced the legislature into a tax increase, because redistribution or consolidation were so politically unpalatable. Lawmakers then would try to use the court decision as a shield (as in Kentucky) and argue to their constituents that "the Court made us do it." Other respondents strongly disagreed, arguing that even the Court could not have forced a tax increase, given North Dakotans' deep distrust of tax hikes. Yet, these interviewees said that the legislature still would have been forced to act. Options would have included: much greater increases in the mill deduct, reexamination of the measure of district wealth with changes in the formula from property value to income tax base, or more redistribution of state aid. A few interviewees even claimed that "restructuring" somewhat similar to that in Kentucky would have taken place, although the extent of the reforms would not be as far-reaching.

Even the assessments of respondents who were slightly less sanguine about the prospects for change even if the Court had declared the system unconstitutional were notable. A few of this group claimed that the legislative response would have depended on how the Court decision was written. They doubted radical change would take place, but mostly because they did not think the Court, due to its history and personnel, would order such an upheaval, even if it did void the school funding system. To extrapolate, they posited a direct proportionality between the strength of the wording of the Court decision and the political response. One interviewee quite concerned about protecting legislative prerogatives agreed with this sliding scale of court impact. The 1995 Legislature did more than it would have done if there had been no court case, but it would have gone even further if the result had been different. How much more change would have occurred would depend upon the wording of the Court opinion.

Overall, the consensus response was that the legislature would have been forced to act. "We wouldn't have had any choice," according to two separate interviewees. "The choice would have been taken away from us," said a third. "There would have been justification (for further reform)," according to another respondent. There would have been a "brick over the Assembly," as reported by another source. "(You) can't ignore them . . . (because of) the separation of powers," argued another policymaker. Underlying these comments is a view of the legislature as a reactive body that needed an external force like the Court to push it into action. One interviewee stated that the legislature needed "a shot of courage" to act. Without the Court, reported another, "there is a fair amount of (legislative) inertia." "(The legislature) wouldn't have done anything otherwise," said a third. One highly placed interviewee took pains to stress that this "inertia" did not reflect legislative lassitude, but rather was a result of the crowded calendar of a body that could only meet for a few months every two years. Given scarce time resources, policy issues did not receive significant legislative attention without a serious push. The Court, though, was one of those external forces that could raise an issue like school finance to the top of the legislative agenda.

"THE LURE OF THE COURT":
THE COURT'S ROLE IN THE POLICY PROCESS

The above comments show that the Court had a significant amount of potential influence with the political branches charged with responding to its decisions. The question then becomes, "why did policymakers take the Court so seriously?" Why did they report that the Court at least hypothetically could have forced the legislature into quite politically unpopular actions? What were the sources of Court power? Of course, one cannot identify a single factor that by itself persuaded or was capable of persuading a one-hundred-fifty member legislature (and a governor) to act. To repeat a phrase from the Kentucky chapter, "multiple forces converged." In part, the Court seemed to have influence because its members, especially the Chief Justice, were well-liked and respected by the legislature. Lawmakers trusted the Court not to send them off in a wild goose chase for equity. Traditional respect for the separation of powers, also present in the interviews, dovetails with this view of the Court's influence as stemming from prestige.

On a more pragmatic level, several interviewees might have reported Court influence because they were sympathetic with the goals of the plaintiff lawsuit. As in Texas, there was a built-in constituency in the North Dakota legislature and in the larger policy community for significant reform in the funding system, and that hope for change might have colored their views of court influence. The results of the interviews, however, do not necessarily support subject bias. As noted earlier, when asked how much progress the 1995 Legislature had made, liberal and conservative interviewees internally split. On the specific question of Court influence in 1995, both liberal *and* conservative interviewees noted changes that were made specifically in response to the Court. The hypothetical question about "what if the Court *had* voided the system?" shows the most evidence of ideological bias, in that liberal interviewees generally thought there would be more change than conservative respondents, but even here, the conservative view may have been colored by those subjects' perceptions that the Court decision would be weaker than the liberal respondents hypothesized, and even the conservatives generally thought that a decision of unconstitutionality would make some difference beyond what the legislature actually did in 1995.

Therefore, respect for the Court, concern for the separation of powers, and general ideological support for reform were some reasons why the North Dakota Court was or could have been effective. These factors were also present to a greater or lesser extent in Texas and Kentucky as well. This section, however, will highlight another source of Court power that was not present to any significant extent in the other two states: immediate experience with another institutional reform case. (note: in Texas, federal judges had ordered significant changes in various policy areas controlled by the legislature such as the state prison and mental health systems, but interviewees there reported that those cases had no impact on the state's handling of the school funding issue.)

In 1982, in response to a lawsuit brought by a group entitled the Association for Retarded Citizens (ARC), a federal district judge, Bruce Van Sickle, ordered the state legislature to make significant changes in the state's mental health facilities, chiefly in the main state hospital in Grafton. Van Sickle specified a long list of criteria the state would have to meet to comply with his order. The legislature, led by House majority leader Earl Strinden, strongly resisted the judge's order, initially complaining about violations of the separation of powers and judicial overreaching. Most interviewees who were involved in state government during the lawsuit admitted that the system needed to change, but many resented the manner in which Van Sickle ordered the legislature to act. Ultimately, the suit dragged on for many years, finally coming to a close in 1996, fourteen years after the initial decision, at a tremendous cost to the state (Condon 1996). It is therefore unsurprising that when Hodny issued his decision at the trial court level, newspaper stories reporting the ruling immediately drew comparisons between the school finance litigation and the "ARC" lawsuit (*Wood* 1993; *Bismarck Tribune* 1993a). These comparisons continued as the case was being heard by the Supreme Court (Associated Press 1993).

Since the legislature had this previous and ongoing experience with comprehensive court orders, did it affect lawmakers' response to the Court's school finance ruling? When asked, a narrow majority of interviewees reported that the ARC suit did have some impact, although a substantial number argued that the other suit did not make much difference in the legislature's handling of the school funding issue. This result is not strictly statistically significant, but at least by comparison to the other two states in this study, many more interviewees in North Dakota were willing to say that previous court rulings had some influence on legislative policymaking. For those respondents who reported that the ARC suit helped persuade the legislature to act on school finance, sample comments included: "The legislature was very aware of the amount of money for (the ARC suit)." The suit was "fresh in everyone's mind." It "put the fear into them." The message was: "having courts dictate is not good government." When asked whether the fact that the ARC orders came from a federal judge versus the school finance decision by the state supreme court, most of these interviewees downplayed any federal/state differences. One respondent said "a court is a court." Others doubted that the legislature would make that type of differentiation, although a few policymakers said that a federal judge might be more resented.

On the other side, the interviewees who disagreed that the ARC suit affected the legislative response to the school funding decision stressed the difference in the substantive issues or highlighted the distinction between federal and state courts. Some

respondents noted that the state had almost completely ignored
the mental health system before the ARC suit, while by contrast,
the legislature was quite aware of school funding problems, even
though lawmakers had been unable to produce solutions. Additionally, the state-federal distinction played a role in that policymakers
noted the relative historical passivity of the state supreme court,
its nature as an elective body, and its plural membership compared
to a single federal judge. For all these reasons, these respondents
did not make a link between the two lawsuits.

The fact, however, that a majority of respondents did see some
linkage leads one to conclude that scholars examining the sources
of judicial power should not ignore the role of previous court orders,
even if issued by different courts, on political responses to judicial
decisions. The North Dakota experience with mental health and
school finance argues for such consideration, combined with tests
of other potential sources of court power also found in North
Dakota such as ideological agreement with the results of the court
verdict, generalized respect for the Court, and concern for the principle of separation of powers.

SUMMING UP

This chapter opened by asking the question: How effective can
courts be when "threatening" policy-making bodies without taking
specific action? Michael McCann's *Rights at Work* (1994) explores
this issue of threatened court action, but in his work, the "threat-
eners" are usually movement activists, not the justices themselves.
Therefore, the experience of the North Dakota Supreme Court with
school finance reform in the *Bismarck* case affords a rare opportunity to examine the possibilities for courts themselves taking on
this "gun behind the door" role. The evidence gathered from this
case study suggests that courts choosing to "threaten" rather than
act possess several potential strengths, but also suffer from significant weaknesses. As the reader has probably noticed by this point,
a lot of the arguments presented in this chapter have a dual quality to them, an "on the one hand, on the other hand"-edness. This
ambiguous nature started at the top, from the Supreme Court decision itself upholding the system while threatening a different
result.

First, concerning the strengths, a "threatening" court can usually count on support from a significant faction in the legislature
and the policymaking community. This faction will constantly remind

wavering legislators of the court's warning, thereby keeping the pressure on to take action. Second, the court itself will often enjoy some respect or prestige with the legislature. Dovetailing with this attitude is a concern for the separation of powers, which most lawmakers take seriously. Therefore, the legislature will try to take steps in the direction of a threatened court order, if the measures proposed are not too politically damaging or harmful from a policy perspective. Third, as McCann found, a threatened court decision can be effective because of legislative fear of expensive and time-consuming litigation that ultimately can lead to a loss of control by policymakers. The ARC suit is a fine example of this motivation to avoid conflict. In other words, a threatened court order can be successful if the legislature believes that the threat is serious and can be backed up by real injuries if not complied with.

On the other hand, the power of a "threatening" court is also limited in significant ways, as the North Dakota experience shows. First, this type of court decision may not give policymakers the guidance necessary to deal with very complex policy issues. In North Dakota, legislators faced a choice of quite unpalatable options, which was not made easier by a Supreme Court opinion saying "do something, or we'll come back." Although the Chief Justice hinted at some areas for the legislature to examine, the opinion did not give lawmakers specific advice as to how to resolve the difficulties (and might have been resisted if that were tried by the Court). If there were easy political solutions to the problems of public school funding, the legislature would have found them long before the lawsuit.

Second, a "threatening" court opinion will not be as effective as it potentially could be if there is not external support in the policy community for change in the preferred direction of the court. As in Kentucky, even when the court goes far beyond mere "threatening" and acts, issuing a comprehensive order, an outside coalition of interests may be necessary to produce significant change. In North Dakota, such a movement was not in place and so the Court's threat fell on deafer ears.

Third, and finally, there is no substitute for the real thing. The Court upheld the school funding system as constitutional, however strongly the Chief Justice threatened otherwise. Therefore, lawmakers could legitimately claim victory as an excuse not to act.

I will claim in the concluding chapter that there is a kind of action-reaction dynamic to legislative responses to court decisions. In this case, if the Court opinion had gone further in requiring the legislature to act, it is likely that the legislative response would have been stronger (a claim borne out by the interviews). Since the Court was not willing to invest a large amount of judicial prestige and resources on the school funding issue, however, the legislature was not about to exceed the minimum necessary to comply, especially since any change would be difficult. In the words of one interviewee, the legislature wanted to "do just enough to get the Court off their backs." Overall, therefore, taking into account all of these strengths and weaknesses, this chapter reaffirms the general argument that courts can persuade the political branches to act on certain issues, and under certain conditions. Even given the limits discussed above, a strong majority of interviewees reported that the Court either convinced the legislature to go farther in school finance reform than it would have otherwise, or that the Court could have forced change if it had been so inclined. As compared with the high courts of Texas and Kentucky, the North Dakota Supreme Court wanted less and therefore got less. Yet that does not mean that it was not successful.

CHAPTER **6**

~

State Supreme Courts and the Different Paths to Public School Finance Equity Reform

The evidence from the case studies suggests that in all three states, the state supreme court had some influence on the policy process. Therefore, one may ask, in what way? Was the Court's power consistent over time, or did it vary according to the stage in the process? What kind of influence did the Court have, and how strong was it? Was the Court able to dictate specific legislation, or was its effect quite generalized and diffuse? Could the Court produce sweeping changes, or merely incremental reform? What were the relative contributions of the courts and other environmental forces in producing change? What were the sources and limits of Court power?

A Chronology of Court Influence: Agenda Setting to Post-Implementation

Agenda-Setting

If a court is to influence policy, it must be able to place an issue on the agenda of the political branches. In all three states, regardless of which role the Court took, there is strong evidence that the Court succeeded in moving school finance equity reform to the top of the legislative priority list. This is an impressive achievement considering that all three state legislatures meet only once every two years, excluding special sessions, with the Kentucky and North Dakota legislative sessions especially brief (sixty and eighty days, respectively.) In these cases, agenda space was particularly constrained.

In Texas, low-wealth plaintiff districts centered around San
Antonio brought a suit charging that the inequities in public school
finance between rich and poor areas of the state violated the state
constitutional requirement that the state's public school system be
"efficient." The Texas Supreme Court[1] in 1989 unanimously agreed,
declaring the system to be unconstitutional in the case of *Edgewood
I.S.D. v. Kirby* (Cases Cited: Texas 1989). School finance reform dominated the state policy agenda (although not the election agenda) for
the next six years. The state's major newspapers, the *Dallas
Morning News* and the *Houston Chronicle*, consistently ran stories
and editorialized about the legislature's attempts to create a school
funding system acceptable to the state supreme court. The battles
over redistribution of funds even attracted the attention of national
newspapers such as the *New York Times* (New York Times 1992).

Over the next six years, the Court and legislature entered into
a dialogue over the outlines of a new funding system. The legislature first merely put more money into the existing system, but was
rebuffed by the court. The Court then gave a list of suggestions as
to what might be constitutional. The legislature then selected an
option that it thought would probably pass muster under the
Court's own guidelines, but the Court rejected that solution as well,
arguing that it had not "preapproved" any plan. Finally, the legislature enacted a strongly redistributive plan, which the Court finally
narrowly upheld in 1995 (Cases Cited: Texas 1995).

It is clear that policymakers in Texas made an enormous effort
to resolve the school finance issue. The *five* special sessions necessary to produce the first attempt at reform, Senate Bill 1, show
how seriously the legislature and governor took the issue, although
they did not agree on a solution. Subsequent to Senate Bill 1, every
time the Court voided the school funding system on constitutional
grounds, the legislature quickly responded with another attempt to
satisfy the Court. Twice, the threat by the trial judge to appoint a
special master to redistribute school funds more equitably helped
convince the legislature to act, also showing judicial agenda-setting
power.

The constant skirmishes over school finance became an increasingly partisan issue over time, and probably drove at least two education committee chairs into retirement. One was quoted as complaining that she had spent six years as the chair of the school
finance committee instead of her formal title as education committee chair (Dubose 1993). This example illustrates the power of the
Court to put an issue on the top of the legislative agenda, even when

lawmakers would rather move on to other policy questions. It is extremely unlikely that the Texas legislature would have spent a full six years dealing with education finance and producing a system that no one is truly happy with if the Court had not intervened.

In Kentucky, litigation began with a suit filed by school superintendents mostly from relatively poor eastern Kentucky. They also cited the state constitutional requirement of "efficiency" of the state public schools, to gain more funding for their districts. Education reform was already a staple of policy discussion, with the state's major newspapers, the *Louisville Courier-Journal* and the *Lexington Herald-Leader*, plus various interest groups, focusing on the issue. The movement for reforming the state's public school system, one of the worst in the nation at the time, only reached a critical stage after the Supreme Court's decision in 1989 declaring the entire state public school system to be unconstitutional, however (Cases Cited: Kentucky 1989). The Court articulated a list of characteristics of a new school system to be built from the ground up, and also promulgated a set of ability standards that children graduating from the new school system would have to meet. This court order went far beyond any other decision in this area across the nation before or since. Subsequently, the newspapers ran stories and editorials concerning the issues nearly every day.

One might expect a legislature to resist such a broad exercise of judicial authority. Yet, the state's political leaders, a few of whom had close ties to the Chief Justice who wrote the Court opinion, decided to take the opportunity to meet and exceed the Court's requirements. Even though the grassroots movement for education reform had been building for years, it took the Court decision to liberate policymakers by giving them political leverage to finally deal with the issue and make the changes that various interests were advocating. As a direct response to the Court's order, the legislature and the governor created a joint task force to reconstruct the public schools in three areas: curriculum, governance, and finance. The task force hired outside consultants to inform them of the latest innovations in educational theory, incorporated these into a bill called the Kentucky Education Reform Act (KERA), and passed the bill along with over one billion dollars of new taxes to pay for it. Education reform occupied the vast majority of legislative resources during the 1990 regular session, and remains at or near the top of the legislative agenda to this day. Now, despite resistance to some aspects of KERA, the Kentucky public school system is regarded as one of the nation's leaders in education reform (Jennings 1990; Appelbome 1996).

The third case study, in North Dakota, presents a different pattern. In North Dakota in 1989, some of the state's largest school districts, spearheaded by the state capital district of Bismarck, filed suit against the state for violating the state constitutional requirement that the public school finance system be "uniform." These plaintiff districts were frustrated by a legislative impasse between themselves and smaller rural districts. Both sides considered themselves "poor" for various reasons. New taxes were not an option, as the voters, in the strong North Dakota tradition of popular referendum, had strongly rejected any revenue increases.

The North Dakota Supreme Court was able to force consideration of the school finance issue, even without declaring the funding system unconstitutional. Before the Court's decision, the *Bismarck Tribune* reported: "Few, if any, lawsuits in state history carry the importance of the coming state supreme court showdown over education finance. But whatever the outcome, change is on the horizon for North Dakota's schools" (Associated Press 1993). The Court in 1994 voted three to two in favor of the plaintiff districts' claims of unconstitutionality (Cases Cited: North Dakota 1994). In North Dakota, however, the votes of four of the five Justices are needed to void an act of the state legislature. The potential fourth vote, the Chief Justice, voted to uphold the system but strongly warned the legislature that if changes were not made in the funding formulas, the result would be different next time. Therefore, the Court was taking on the role of "threat."

Policymakers themselves reported that the legislature and governor followed the court proceedings quite closely, starting with the trial court decision declaring the school funding system in violation of the constitutional provision of educational "uniformity," and continuing until the Supreme Court's ruling was handed down. After the decision was issued, a majority of interviewees asserted that the Chief Justice's opinion was taken "very very seriously," in the words of one respondent. Some policymakers did not think that the Court's opinion influenced the legislature to take significant action. Many of these interviewees, however, thought that a major reason for that perceived lack of influence was the fact that the Court upheld the constitutionality of the school funding system. In other words, the state "won." If the result had been different, according to nearly every one of these respondents, the legislature would have taken stronger steps to deal with the issue. Even more legislative time and energy would have been devoted to producing a solution acceptable to the Court. According to more than one interviewee, "we would have had no choice."

Subsequent to the Court threat, school finance moved to the head of the 1995 legislative agenda. One leading North Dakota political analyst commented afterwards that "As expected, school finance hung over the entire session like an unlined dark cloud" (Omdahl 1995). $35 million that could have been used for other state priorities were devoted specifically to school finance. The aid formulas were also slightly adjusted to favor the larger plaintiff districts over smaller rural districts. The policymakers I interviewed disagreed over the significance of these changes, with some claiming real progress and others saying that the reforms were mere "tinkering." Most were willing to give the Court credit for producing some change, however. A clear majority also thought that if the Court decision would have been stronger, the legislative response would have been more forceful as well (a point returned to below.) Therefore, the Court was at least moderately successful as a "threat." Judicial agenda-setting power was present, even though the Court did not rule squarely in favor of reform.

It should be noted concerning this discussion of agenda-setting that education issues regularly occupy a significant place on the calendars of state legislatures, regardless of court orders. Other priorities voice strong claims as well, however, such as crime and punishment, welfare, health care, transportation, and the environment. Given the extremely limited legislative sessions, it is quite significant that the three courts were all able to force the issue of school finance equity to the top of the policymaking agendas, showing the potential power of judicial agenda-setting.

Legislative Compliance: How Much, How Far?

Consideration does not always lead to action, though. How successful were these courts in persuading their legislatures not just to deliberate, but to act? The evidence suggests that, although external environmental factors are very important for explaing the degree of reform achieved, courts can be independently effective in producing results from the political branches, a point more fully elaborated in the later section concerning the sources and limits of judicial power. Judicial "role" is key for understanding the differences in legislative compliance from state to state.

In Texas, the state supreme court assumed a "negotiator" role with the political branches, issuing multiple serial decisions, which hinted at possible solutions to the school finance crisis while not mandating particular outcomes. The Court consistently set deadlines for policymakers to meet in constructing a new funding system, however. The legislature and governor responded to each decision by passing reform laws, three in total. In the words of one participant, the process was accomplished "serially and rapidly" instead of featuring one dramatic push. In each stage in the process, there is evidence that the Texas policymakers took the Court's opinions quite seriously, and consulted them for specific constitutional guidance. After *Edgewood* I, a relatively general decision, the legislature[2] wrongly thought that more money in the system would be enough to satisfy the Court. Subsequent to *Edgewood* II (Cases Cited: Texas 1991), however, hearings were held and legal experts were brought in to interpret the Court's opinion and discuss the possible court responses to a number of alternative plans. In other words, the Court's decision helped structure debate. The legislature did not necessarily follow this advice, but it certainly was aware of the potential problem areas in their preferred solution, the County Education Districts. Similarly, legislative leaders specifically lobbied the Court in their *amicus* brief on the motion for rehearing, subsequently labeled *Edgewood* IIA (Cases Cited: Texas 1991), for more guidance on two particularly thorny legal issues.

When the Court voided the County Education Districts in *Edgewood* III (Cases Cited: Texas 1992), lawmakers expressed great frustration, in part because they thought they had been responsive to the Court's prior opinions. Therefore, when devising what became the final solution, the so-called multiple-choice plan, the legislature was extremely sensitive to any issues of inequity that might incur yet another unfavorable Court decision. In fact, one plan was specifically rejected because it exempted seven districts out of a thousand from equalization. The final plan is one of the most redistributive in the nation, setting an absolute cap on district wealth per student and giving districts "options" for reducing their tax base wealth to meet state standards.

The result of the Court-legislature interaction was a school funding system that gradually became more equitable in each stage in the process. Overall, according to the trial court opinion in the last *Edgewood* trial, the tax base ratio of the richest to poorest district in the state was 700:1 in 1989, before the first Court decision. In 1994, it was 1.16:1. Perhaps a more representative measure of change over the same time period was that the poorest quartile of districts gained sixty-six percent in state aid while the richest quartile lost fifteen percent. The bottom half of districts in terms of wealth gained $1.9 billion in state aid, while the top half only received $491 million more in state assistance. Furthermore, aside from the very wealthiest districts, very few districts lost money through the *Edgewood* process. In total, state aid increased thirty percent from 1989 to 1994 (Cases Cited: Texas 1994).

The Texas experience shows that state supreme courts can successfully "negotiate" with the political branches. In fact, one leading school finance expert reports that Texas now boasts one of the most equitable funding systems in the nation (Picus 1995). In this situation, incrementalism may have pushed the process further than any single comprehensive decision ever could have. This was true for a variety of reasons, including the persistence of plaintiff groups for both rich and poor districts that would not give up lobbying the Court, and the willingness of both the Supreme Court and the trial court to set deadlines and threaten action if these were not met.

It is true that the courts did not always produce clear guidelines for policymakers, and that the Justices themselves may not have been pleased with the final result (which was probably more redistributive than many of the Republican members would have desired). It is also true that the give-and-take negotiation between the Court and legislature frustrated policymakers so much that a constitutional amendment weakening court jurisdiction on school finance issues was proposed and received a substantial number of votes. An examination of the process as a whole, though, shows that policymakers not only listened to the Court and considered school finance equity as an agenda item, but acted forcefully to comply with the Court decisions. One leading legislator observed: "Let's do exactly what the Court wants and see how they like it."

In Kentucky, the Court's role as a "path-breaker" produced a different dynamic from the incremental results of the Texas Court, but also led to compliance with the Court's goals (and beyond). As noted above, the Kentucky Supreme Court did not just void the school funding mechanism, but the entire state system of public education. Lawmakers had to rebuild from the ground up. The Court helped set guidelines for the new system by promulgating lists of characteristics that the new system should feature, and abilities that graduates of the public schools should possess.

From the interview data with policymakers, it appears that the primary contribution of the Court decision was to change perceptions of what education reform could be accomplished. The Court gave the legislature an excuse, in other words, to make changes that some leading lawmakers had wanted to implement for a long time but could not because of the political constraints against raising taxes. Even so, many of the ideas that the legislative-gubernatorial task force enacted into law did not come either from the Court or the task force members themselves, but from various interest groups or the outside consultants that the task force brought in to aid in devising the new system.

Therefore, the impact of the Court decision in Kentucky was different from that in Texas, in that lawmakers in Kentucky did not closely study every detail of the Court opinion. In fact, one prominent lawmaker admitted that at no time in the task force deliberations did the question: "Will this satisfy the Court?" ever arise, although this assessment may be an exaggeration. One cannot conclude that the Court decision had no influence, however. It made a difference because of the tone of the opinion, and because of the Court's willingness to be a "path-breaker," regardless of the specifics. Giving the legislature and governor a shock was what was needed, not a precise blueprint for action. As the same leading legislator put it, "the Court opened up a window the legislature had never seen before."

As a result of the Court's opening that window, the legislature and governor passed a reform law that is now seen as one of the leading education innovations in the nation. The state's education curriculum, governance, and finance were all overhauled, with over $1 billion in new taxes appropriated to pay for the reforms (and other projects as well). Specifically concerning the original issue of the lawsuit, finance equity has greatly improved since the suit was filed in 1989. In Kentucky, "adequacy" of funds was as great an issue as distribution. Under KERA, combined state and local aid to districts has risen forty percent from 1989 to 1994, and the equity gap, according to one state agency report, has closed fifty-two percent since KERA was enacted (Office of Education Accountability 1995). Data such as these bolster the argument that the "path-breaking" of the Court did not just lead to agenda consideration, but to action by the political branches.

As opposed to the relatively active roles played by the Texas and Kentucky courts, the North Dakota Supreme Court held back from full participation in the policymaking process concerning school finance equity, preferring to take on the part of "threat." In 1994, the state high court narrowly upheld the constitutionality of the funding system. Although a majority of the five Justices voted to invalidate the system, the four-vote supermajority required to strike down an act of the legislature permitted the system to survive. However, the Chief Justice's deciding vote in favor of the system was tempered by an opinion strongly hinting that if the legislature did not make changes, the result might be different the next time.

If the Texas legislature became immersed in the details of its Court's opinions, while the Kentucky legislature was relatively unconcerned with each sentence and paragraph, the North Dakota legislature took a relatively moderate approach to consideration of the Court's opinion threatening to declare the school funding system unconstitutional. From the interview data, it appears that the leading lawmakers, especially those on the education committees, paid close attention to the Court's opinion and were aware of all the concerns the Court raised. As noted below, the legislature even made some changes in the funding formulas specifically in response to the court's suggestions.

A significant percentage of lawmakers read the Court's opinion closely enough to see that the legislature "won" and that the system was upheld. This verdict somewhat blunted the force of the Chief Justice's language threatening a different result if changes were not made. Thus for many, the Court decision was not seen as a real threat. Still, one should not minimize the influence of the Court decision on the changes that the legislature and governor made (see North Dakota Legislative Council 1995 for a good summary of these changes). A clear majority of interviewees reported that certain adjustments to the funding formulas were direct results of the Court decision. For example, the so-called mill deduct, which somewhat equalized funds between high-tax and low-tax districts, was significantly increased compared with any previous hikes and was indexed to rises in overall state aid for the first time.

A $2.5 million "equity fund" was created to benefit the poorest districts in the state. Even though this amount is a "drop in the bucket," the fund was created due to the Court. Its chief legislative sponsor argued during the session that: "In terms of the Court . . . we need to get something started in this area, even if it's only a small amount initially . . . my motivation here is that this is an area where the Court criticized us specifically" (House Appropriations Committee 1995).

Furthermore, the $35 million in new state aid to education should not be minimized. This increase was the third largest in state history and the largest ever without a tax increase. Therefore, one can say that the Court's role as "threat" was certainly successful in agenda-setting, and beyond mere deliberation, was at least mildly successful in persuading the political branches to take specific action in response to judicial concerns.

Overall, the evidence from these three case studies shows that each of these Courts either was effective in producing significant policy change in the desired direction of their opinions, as in Texas and Kentucky, or could have been effective if more forceful, as in the case of North Dakota. Reform in Texas produced one of the most equitable finance systems in the nation. The Kentucky Court catalyzed a reform movement, which led to comprehensive reform of curriculum, governance, and finance, and one of the most innovative state school systems nationwide. The North Dakota Court at a minimum set the policy agenda for the legislature, and also produced some pro-equity changes that would not have happened otherwise.

One can discern a notable pattern in the results presented here. Legislative and executive compliance with these Court decisions seems to be based on an action-reaction dynamic. In other words, the stronger the language of the Court opinion and the more persistent the Court in keeping pressure on the political branches for a solution, the stronger the policy response as a result. The Kentucky decision was the most far-reaching in language, and also produced the most comprehensive reform. The Texas decisions started out at a more general level, and initially produced more stopgap change. But as the Texas Court persisted, the legislative responses became more compliant and progressively more redistributive. In North Dakota, the Court's weak position led to the least reform of any of these three states. Policymakers reported, though, that if the North Dakota Court *had* voided the system, the legislature and governor would have been forced into stronger action. I will return to this action-reaction dynamic later in the chapter.

POSTDECISION COURT INFLUENCE

The final step in the chronology of court influence is the question of whether courts can exert influence even after compliance has been reached with their decisions. The evidence suggests that the answer is a qualified yes. In each state, the high court still is a presence in school finance politics, but in a much more limited role than during the active period immediately following the Court decision. Furthermore, the ongoing influence of the Court is as much a function of the legislative perception of the willingness and ability of the litigants to file suit again as it is a political judgment concerning the preferences of the justices themselves.

In Texas, most interviewees did not think that the Court would be willing to revisit the school finance issue anytime soon, in large part because of the bruising battles and four Court decisions necessary to achieve the present system. Lawmakers did slightly adjust the funding formulas in favor of equity in the 1995 legislative session as insurance against the Court's return. The legislature also put $170 million into capital facilities funding, an issue highlighted by the trial court and to a lesser extent, the state supreme court in its last opinion. One lawmaker reported that "the moment of crisis is past . . . we're not looking back." At the same time, another interviewee assessed that the overall mood is, "if you've got the money, put it into education." The 1999 Legislature did just that, using a state surplus to both cut taxes and boost education spending, including more facilities money for the poorest districts. Furthermore, there seems to be a tacit agreement among Texas policymakers not to make any changes that would substantially decrease equity, for fear of Court return (Carr and Fuhrman 1999).

In Kentucky, the Court's ongoing influence is probably less than in Texas, but in large part that is due to the perception that policymakers enacted a law in 1990 (KERA) that not only met but far exceeded the Court's goals. At the same time, though, when the governor proposed a mandatory across-the-board pay increase for teachers that might adversely affect equity between districts, the state senate majority leader argued that if the bill were passed, the Court would return to take over education policymaking again. The bill did not pass, and thus, the threat of the Court remains a presence, albeit mainly at the rhetorical level.

Similarly, in North Dakota, the Court's opinion in 1994 may still be exerting some pressure on the legislature, mostly through the rhetoric of supporters of greater equalization warning of the potential legal consequences if the legislature does not take further action. At least some policymakers reported in the interviews that they expected the legislature to continue to proceed, if slowly, on the path to greater equalization, in part out of ideological interest but also in order to ensure that the Court does not return to the issue in a more serious way than it did in the first *Bismarck* case. On the other hand, several interviewees discounted the possibility of a new lawsuit being filed in the near future because of limited resources on the part of the plaintiffs and because the lead plaintiff district, Bismarck, is rapidly becoming a "rich" district itself.

Overall, these state supreme courts have retained continuing influence in the policy arena after the initial compliance period is present, but at a much lower level. One would expect this influence to gradually decrease over time, although as noted above, the threat of another lawsuit was successfully invoked in Kentucky six years after the initial court ruling. In general, across the three states, lawmakers do not feel the need to take significant continuing affirmative steps to meet Court demands. In the words of one interviewee, "they've done their thing, we did our thing." In all three states, though, any policy proposals that are perceived as retreating from the Court order are viewed with great suspicion. Outright subversion is not regarded as plausible. Aside from the rhetorical benefits to supporters of equalization in using the Court as an ongoing threat, this "cementing" of reform is the major contribution of Court involvement after the initial period of compliance.

Sources and Limits of Judicial Power

We can now turn to the implications for judicial impact theory more broadly. I argue above that the courts in this study possessed and exerted influence on the political branches throughout the policy-making process and beyond. These courts were more or less effective in achieving their goals, in part depending upon their chosen role in the process. An action-reaction dynamic was present, with courts issuing broader opinions with more persistence producing more change from legislatures than courts that did not.

These results seem to contradict Gerald Rosenberg's claim in the influential book *The Hollow Hope* that courts are rarely, if ever, effective in producing significant social change (Rosenberg 1991). In *The Hollow Hope*, Rosenberg asked scholars of judicial politics to focus on the question of the potential effectiveness of court orders in producing social reform. Using case studies of *Brown v. Board of Education*, *Roe v. Wade*, and other landmark U.S. Supreme Court decisions, Rosenberg argued that even high-visibility court orders are ignored by politicians until convenient to implement. These decisions are ineffective in producing the significant social change that the litigants and their interest-group sponsors seek. Court power is thus a "myth" or a "hollow hope."

Rosenberg's methodological approach and substantive conclusions are much disputed (McCann 1992; Bohte et al. 1995). His underlying question, however, informs the central issue of this project: What are the sources and limits of judicial power in setting the agendas of the legislative and executive branches, and thus setting the stage for responsive change? Later in this chapter, I note in more detail the broader differences between this work and

Rosenberg's. For the moment, though, in fairness to Rosenberg, one should note and fully examine his own conditions for court success as applied to these three case studies.

This project is primarily concerned with court decisions for which the legislative and executive branches have essentially sole implementation responsibility, unlike other cases where either compliance also depends upon local actors such as school board officials (for example, *Brown v. Board of Education*) or police officers (for example, *Miranda v. Arizona,*) or the decision is relatively self-enforcing (for example, *Roe v. Wade* making certain abortions legal). In other words, in the school finance cases, implementation by outside actors was necessary, but the legislative and executive branches were the only outside actors directly involved in compliance with the court orders.

None of Rosenberg's case studies (*Brown, Roe, Baker v. Carr*) deal with the specific issue of a supreme court order to a coordinate political branch—that is, a legislature or chief executive. It is difficult to imagine, though, that his findings would have been significantly different if he had applied his list of conditions for court success to U.S. Supreme Court relations with Congress or the President. Although the literature is mixed (Casper 1976; Adamany 1973), a number of studies beginning with Dahl (1957) downplay the independent effectiveness of the U.S. Supreme Court in persuading Congress to act (Ulmer and Canon 1976; Marshall 1989). Therefore, since Rosenberg would likely claim that courts are no better at convincing their constitutionally coordinate branches to act, it is fair to test his hypothesis based on the evidence from these case studies.

We should begin with a discussion of the general willingness of the state "political" branches to enact school finance equity reform. According to Rosenberg, courts can only be effective if the legislature and executive already support the desired changes. Courts then ride the winds of change that are already blowing. How well does this model fit the evidence presented here? These case studies offer some support for Rosenberg's arguments. In all three states, there were a significant number of legislators, some executive branch officials, and one or two governors who already supported the goal of school finance equalization and were willing to take steps to make it happen. These policymakers formed a core of support for the court decisions requiring greater equity, and their presence was certainly necessary for any "success" the courts achieved.

It is not likely that the changes in school funding that occurred would have been made without judicial involvement, however. In none of these states did the faction supporting greater equalization command a majority or near majority in their state legislatures. For example, in Texas, only about one-third of lawmakers could be classified as "liberal" or representing predominantly Hispanic districts that were prime beneficiaries of greater finance equity. Another one-third of the legislature was conservative and Republican. The key, therefore, became persuasion of the one-third of moderate lawmakers who, although primarily Democrats, had not been willing to "bite the bullet" in making significant changes to the school funding system. In all three states, this kind of division was present to a greater or lesser extent. Therefore, an external force such as the Court was needed to produce reform. In all three states, policymakers reported that a significant proportion of the changes that were made, whether great or small, were directly or indirectly due to the influence of the Court. This is the single most important finding of this study. In Texas, for example, a lawmaker stated: "The Court gets most of the credit . . . otherwise, members would have just voted their districts." In Kentucky, one respondent assessed, the theme was "the Court justified the action . . . the courts made us do it." In North Dakota, even though the changes will "never be enough," according to one interviewee, they were "much more than without the Court."

The question then becomes, what persuaded lawmakers to take the steps outlined previously to achieve at least some equity? Why were these three state supreme courts effective? Rosenberg still potentially could argue that his model incorporates these findings. Rosenberg believes that courts can succeed in producing significant social change, but only if a lengthy and stringent set of standards are met, many of which need to be present for a court to be successful (Rosenberg 1991:36). Therefore, one should ask, were these conditions relevant to the effectiveness of the three courts examined here? This evidence shows that some of Rosenberg's guides were present, others were not, and there was at least one potential court strength that he does not mention in *The Hollow Hope*. I will now turn to a point-by-point discussion of the conditions for court success.[3]

Legislative-Executive Relations

Since Rosenberg claims that active support by the legislative and executive branches is necessary for court effectiveness, one might begin by assuming that the legislatures and governors in these three case study states must have had good working relations. When the courts handed down their decisions voiding the school finance system, the two branches must have fully cooperated in designing solutions. The evidence from these case studies does not support this hypothesis, however, lending greater weight to the argument that the courts made an independent contribution to the policy process.

The Kentucky experience is the most notable in this regard. The relationship between the legislature and newly elected Governor Wallace Wilkinson, a businessman with no previous political experience, was contentious from the start and only worsened over time. Wilkinson felt that the legislature had grown too powerful, and meant to reclaim some traditional gubernatorial prerogatives. The legislature strongly resisted any erosion of its newly won authority. This institutional conflict affected debates concerning every state issue, including school finance. After Wilkinson's term ended,[4] the state Senate majority leader said, "Relations between the two branches hit an all-time low as far as I can remember, so low that I doubt we'll see it again in the foreseeable future" (Loftus 1990).

At the same time, however, these same political leaders passed one of the most important laws in twentieth-century Kentucky history. The legislature and governor were able to set aside their differences and work together to pass a comprehensive restructuring of the state school system. As noted later in the chapter, the broader interest group movement and media support for change can explain this result to an extent, but one should not slight the Court's role in breaking through this institutional deadlock.

In Texas, relations between the state legislature and the two governors who served during the *Edgewood* litigation varied, but in neither case could be considered positive and cooperative. First, the Democratic legislature and "no new taxes" Republican governor William Clements were quite rocky, due to the legislature's desire to raise taxes to pay for education finance equity and the governor's insistence that no new funds were needed. Without the Court threat to appoint a special master to redraw district boundaries, it is quite possible that nothing would have been accomplished.

Second, Democratic governor Ann Richards enjoyed a less contentious working relationship with the legislature than Clements, but at the same time, the legislature ignored the few school funding solutions that Richards promulgated. Her role was not as a participant, but as a public supporter of greater equity. The weak institutional position of the Texas governor, whose only real policy-shaping tool is the veto, no doubt contributed to Richards's passive participation.

On the other hand, the Texas lieutenant governor wields significant institutional power due to his/her role as presiding officer of the state Senate, with the ability to appoint committee chairs and set the floor schedule. Lieutenant Governors Bill Hobby and Bob Bullock both supported school finance reform, with Bullock especially forceful in moving the process toward resolution. Bullock was key to the degree of equity of the legislation that the Court finally upheld in 1995. This is not to say that the Court had no role, however. Without the Court's constant pressure, it is quite possible that Bullock would not have continued to design politically unpopular school funding formulas.

In North Dakota, by contrast, relations between the legislature, traditionally controlled by Republicans, and Republican governor Edward Schafer, were relatively amicable. The interviewees that I spoke with generally expressed personal regard for the governor, although many questioned his political experience, as Schafer, like Wilkinson in Kentucky, had never held political office before. Even with the advantage of good relations between the legislature and executive, though, unlike in the other two case study states, the North Dakota political system produced the least school finance reform. Schafer proposed legislation that would have made strides toward equity, but the legislature substituted its own program, which was relatively less equalizing, although still an improvement over the previous system.

Therefore, what can one conclude concerning the importance of the legislative-executive relationship for court success? It would be a mistake to say that good relations between the legislature and governor are detrimental to the construction of public policy, or even that they make no difference. All else being equal, supporters of reform would rather have both branches committed to working together in support of their cause. The evidence from these case studies, however, shows that contrary to Rosenberg's thesis, a good institutional relationship is not always necessary for court effectiveness. A well-crafted and well-timed court decision can channel institutional rivalry in productive directions, as politicians compete with each other to either claim credit or avoid blame for reform. In other words, courts can succeed by catalyzing consensus between the legislative and executive branches where little existed before.

"Ample Legal Precedent"

Rosenberg argues that a court can only be effective when there is "ample legal precedent" for the reforms that the court mandates.

In other words, politicians are more likely to accept a court decision that seems to follow from previous decisions or clear constitutional language. However intuitive this point might be, the evidence from these three case studies does not support this condition. Regarding clear constitutional language, arguably, one does not find it in the case of public school finance equity. The constitutional provisions at issue in these three cases (and indeed, in most similar cases across the country) are relatively vague, stating at best that the legislature (not the Court) has a duty to create a state system of free public schools that is "efficient," "thorough and efficient," "uniform" or "open to all" (Thro 1989). Given the language of these provisions, one could defensibly read them to require funding equity between districts, but one could also make a plausible case for an opposite conclusion. Furthermore, in none of the three states were there previous court decisions that came close to requiring the same level of equity that the Texas and Kentucky Courts did, and the North Dakota Court almost did. For example, in Texas, conservatives complained quite bitterly (and correctly) that for over one hundred years of state history the constitutional provision on education had never been read to require the standard of equity mandated in *Edgewood*. Kentucky history was no different.

One could attempt to save the argument by claiming that "ample legal precedent" did not have to come from the implementers' own state, but from other states. It could be argued that the broader nationwide school finance reform movement convinced policymakers that change was appropriate and inevitable. This argument possesses some plausibility, in that many states across the country made school funding reforms after the *Serrano* case in California drew national attention to the issue, even when no case was filed (Fuhrman 1980).

As applied to the specifics of these three states, though, this argument is supported by only limited evidence. When I asked policymakers about the experience of other states, a fair number could name a few other states that had had to deal with court orders on this issue. When I asked them whether this experience led them to view their state's responsibilities differently, though, most said that the other states' battles had little effect, because the issues were so different (at least according to them.) There was little specific influence of legal precedent in the legislative arenas. (It is still possible, however, that the experience of other states influenced the *courts* in their consideration of the school finance equity issue.) In fact, the legislature that made the most changes in response to the Court decision, Kentucky, chronologically was the first of the states to resolve the issue. On the other hand, North Dakota, the last Court of the three to rule, produced the least reform from the legislature, even with the Texas and Kentucky precedents already in place. Therefore, the condition of "ample legal precedent" does not seem to apply to this evidence.

Before leaving this question, though, one piece of evidence should be highlighted as a potential source of court power that at least tangentially connects with the condition of "ample legal precedent." In North Dakota, a suit had been filed in federal court, twelve years before the *Bismarck* case, regarding living conditions in the state mental hospital. A federal district judge ruled that the state was not living up to minimum standards in housing those patients the hospital was charged with serving, and promulgated a long list of conditions that the state had to meet in reforming the hospital. The state resisted, led by the legislature, and the end result was a suit that lasted fourteen years at a tremendous cost to the state (Condon 1996). When the state trial court in North Dakota declared the school funding system unconstitutional, the media immediately made the connection to the so-called ARC (Association for Retarded Citizens) lawsuit (Wood 1993; *Bismarck Tribune* 1993; Associated Press 1993).

When I asked state policymakers about any possible carryover effects from that suit to school finance, around half of the interviewees reported that the previous case, even though it was in federal court and concerned a different issue, had some effect on the legislature in that lawmakers did not want to repeat the battles again. It may be stretching the definition of "ample legal precedent" to note this factor here, but it shows the potential importance of previous court decisions, even those issued by other courts on other issues, as a potential source of judicial strength and effectiveness.

"Costs are Imposed to Induce Compliance"

Rosenberg claimed in *The Hollow Hope* that courts can also be effective when they can impose costs on the political branches. In this section, instead of the term "costs," I use the term "sanctions" to refer not just to monetary punishments, but also court threats to take specific actions that policymakers would strongly disfavor, such as judicial redrawing of school district boundaries or a court order closing all public schools in the state. Fear of this judicial retribution motivates the legislature and executive to act. Overall, one sees some support for this thesis, but certainly not in all three states.

The experience of the Texas Supreme Court (and Travis County Circuit Court) is the best case for the argument that the threat of sanctions by courts can be effective. At numerous points in the process, an approaching Court deadline helped convince lawmakers to act, at least to keep the "dialogue" between the political branches and the courts going. First, lawmakers finally reached agreement with Clements on the first reform plan after the trial judge threatened to appoint a special master, a known liberal, to redistribute state aid funds on his own. After the Court voided this equalization effort, it set a firm deadline after which it would enjoin all state funds to Texas public schools, essentially shutting the schools down. The legislature subsequently passed another attempt at reform. The Court again declared the school funding system to be unconstitutional, and set yet another deadline, this time eighteen months away in order to give the legislature more time to consider options. After a proposed constitutional amendment that would have resolved the issue was defeated by the voters, the legislature finally passed a plan acceptable to the Court, only days before the judicial deadline was set to expire.

When I asked policymakers how seriously they took the Court threat to close the schools down, answers varied, although almost no one wanted to take the chance the Court would follow through on its threat. Incidentally, they all did think that if the choice were up to the trial court judge, he definitely would have issued the injunction closing the schools. The threat of school closure was especially fearsome to interviewees. When asked who the general public would blame for the crisis, most respondents named the legislature as the institution bearing the political heat, because the legislature was closest to the people. Justices in Texas are also elected, but most interviewees said that voters paid less attention to their election races. In other words, the legislature had much more to lose than the Court if the schools were shut down. Perhaps the Court would not have ultimately taken that step, but legislators definitely did not want to take the chance. As one lawmaker said at the time, "we want to surrender, we just don't know where to turn ourselves in."

Therefore, the threatened imposition of sanctions, or "costs," by the Court was effective in keeping the process of reform moving, thereby adding support to Rosenberg's argument. In the other two case studies, though, the courts did not employ a sanction strategy, and policymakers generally did not believe sanctions were a possibility. For example, in Kentucky, most interviewees did not even consider the possibility of noncompliance, although not all thought the reforms would go as far as they eventually did. The broader movement for school reform in the state, coupled with the sweeping nature of the Court decision, essentially ruled out nonresponse as an option. Therefore, there was no worry about Court-imposed punishments (although there was a lot of concern over "voter-imposed punishments"—that is, election losses.) In North Dakota, fear of Court sanctions was also not an issue, although for different reasons than in Kentucky. At the most basic level, the Court could not "punish" the legislature and executive, because in fact the Court declared the school funding system constitutional. There was no wrong to redress, in other words. This again shows the limitations of the North Dakota court's role as a "threat." The best that the Court could do was to threaten to void the system in the future, but the legislature could delay worrying about potential sanctions until that time. As I argued earlier in the chapter, the legislature still took some steps in the direction of the court's opinion. One could also make a claim that the North Dakota experience with the ARC mental health lawsuit should count as a potential "cost to induce compliance" in that lawmakers feared similar negative consequences if they did not take action. If North Dakota lawmakers acted, however, it was not necessarily because of fear of Court-imposed costs.

"The Court Made Me Do It": Court Decisions as Excuses

Another of Rosenberg's conditions concerned whether "administrators and officials crucial for implementation are willing to act and see court orders as a tool for leveraging additional resources or hiding behind" (Rosenberg 1991:36). In the three case studies of this project, the "administrators" and "implementers" were legislators and executive branch officials. There is support for this condition, but only in one state. In Kentucky, ability to use the Court as a "shield" was crucial, in keeping with Rosenberg's condition of implementers hiding behind court decisions to take actions they wanted to anyway. Chief plaintiff litigator Bert Combs said that the Court decision was a means to persuade the "limber twigs" in the legislature that it was politically safe to support education reform (Combs 1991). Several interviewees supported this assertion, arguing that the court decision "allowed leaders to say to followers, 'We have to do this.'" As one legislator put it, "there was a freedom of the moment . . . the Court did us a favor by giving us political cover."

In Texas and North Dakota, though, using the Court as a "shield" to hide behind was not a major motivation for lawmakers to act.

When asked about that possibility, most interviewees dismissed it, saying that the public would blame the lawmakers anyway for any negative consequences, such as school shutdown or loss of funds. Responsibility could not be shifted. The Kentucky experience, though, shows that it is possible for the Court to wittingly or unwittingly play this role of political "shield" for the political branches.

Public Support

In *The Hollow Hope* Rosenberg argued that courts have a greater chance of success when the public is either supportive of the judicial declaration at issue or at least is not strongly opposed to the court ruling. Here, I will break down the condition of "public support" into two categories: first, attitudes of the public at large and, second, attitudes of policy activists, as the two were often different and contain varied lessons for study of court effectiveness.

THE GENERAL PUBLIC

First, concerning the views of the public regarding school finance reform in each of these three states, Rosenberg's hypothesis is largely supported. The Kentucky Court enjoyed the greatest amount of popular approval for its decision, at least as far as one can measure; there are little reliable data on this point. The broader movement for school reform initiated by various interest groups and sustained by the state's major newspapers apparently persuaded a significant portion of the state's population that school reform was necessary, even if new taxes would be imposed to pay for it (Kaukas 1990). The public supported school reform to the largest extent of any of the case studies, and the Court was also the most successful.

In Texas, the populace, at least according to interviewees, seemed to favor the Court's initial rulings in *Edgewood*. The principle that "everyone should get an equal education" resonated with the average Texan. As the litigation wore on and the solutions to the equity problems became more redistributive, however, public support fell off sharply. In fact, in the only instance where the public was directly asked for its views on school finance equity, a proposed constitutional amendment was defeated by a 2:1 margin in a statewide referendum. Ironically, though, largely because of the continued pressure of the Court, the legislature subsequently passed a reform law even more complex and redistributive than the solution the voters had just strongly rejected. Therefore, one should not unduly emphasize the role of popular influence on this issue.

In North Dakota, it is unclear what the state's population as a whole felt, if anything, about school finance equity between the larger districts of the state and the smaller rural schools. No good data exist. We do know, or at least strongly suspect, though, that the voting population was not willing to pay for increased equity through higher taxes. Statewide tax referenda were defeated in 1989 and 1990, with the latter proposed tax increase specifically devoted to education. Interviewees reported that these rejections had a significant impact on the North Dakota legislature's readiness to increase taxes to achieve more funding equality between districts. New taxes were not an option. This constraint in turn limited the legislature's potential response to the Court's "threat," although at least some respondents claimed that if the Court had actually declared the funding system unconstitutional, new taxes would have been strongly considered.

Overall, the evidence presented here seems to back Rosenberg's condition of public support as an important condition for court success, if not a necessary prerequisite (see Texas.) One should also keep in mind, however, that even if the general public evinces either a supportive or a negative attitude toward public school finance reform, that view is typically quite general and diffuse. To wit, the public usually is uninformed concerning specific state school funding mechanisms, unsurprisingly. This lack of knowledge leaves quite a bit of policy leeway for legislatures and courts to operate within.

Furthermore, judicial elections do not seem to be a significant limit on the flexiblity of courts to act in this area. In all three states, Supreme Court Justices had to run in contested elections, although the procedures and term lengths varied from state to state. State judicial ethics codes barred candidates from discussing specific issues during the election campaigns, however, increasing the difficulty of a challenger gaining political support due to opposition to the Court's school finance rulings. When I asked interviewees about any electoral impact of school finance on Court races, most respondents did not find any, except in Texas, where a few Justices lost some votes in wealthier areas whose schools had lost money due to *Edgewood*, but not enough votes to decide a close race. Again, popular influence was present, but limited.

In other words, so long as the general constraints imposed by the public are not violated ("no new taxes") courts can still be quite successful in persuading policymakers to act. For example, taxes were not raised to pay for either of the last two significantly redistributive school funding equity plans in Texas. Therefore, one should not be too hasty in minimizing the potential for court effectiveness, even when the judiciary faces a generally hostile public.

INTEREST GROUPS

One might expect elected politicians to pay attention to the wishes of the general public concerning compliance with court decisions. The views of relevant interests involved also might carry considerable weight with lawmakers, depending upon the interest and the issue. Therefore, one should ask, was interest group or other outside support, or at least lack of opposition, a necessary condition for judicial effectiveness? As with support from the population at large, the evidence from these three case studies shows that the reaction of outside actors may be a significant factor in determining the extent of reform, but certainly is not the only influence. Courts and politicians themselves possess a fair amount of power independent of the interests.

In Kentucky, it is virtually undisputed that the broader movement for school reform in the state led by elite groups such as the Prichard Committee for Academic Excellence and various other business and education groups, with the strong support of the state's leading newspapers in Louisville and Lexington, set the stage for far-reaching education reform. This well-organized and well-funded movement had been pressuring the state legislature and executive branch for nearly a decade before the Court decision declaring the Kentucky public education system unconstitutional. After the decision, these groups were ready to step in and give the legislative-executive task force their prescriptions for rebuilding the system, although the politicians themselves tried to block interest group access to the task force deliberations.

Even though the broader education reform movement was necessary for fundamental reform along the Court outlines, according to these same policymakers, it took the Court decision to "shock" the system into change. The broader reform movement had not been successful until after the Court ruling. The Court's unique contributions were to focus the politicians' complete attention on the school system and to give them enough leeway by the sweeping nature of the Court opinion to implement the changes they desired and then blame any negative consequences on the Court. No other actor or set of actors could have played that role. Therefore, in

Kentucky, we see strong interest group influence, but also an independent judicial contribution to policymaking.

In North Dakota, the interest group dynamic was different. Unlike in Kentucky, there was no great clamor for comprehensive education reform. One of the chief reasons for this quiescence was that, at least measured by standardized tests, the school system was one of the best in the nation (Cases Cited: North Dakota 1994: 270). Some interviewees thought that given the state's relatively small and homogenous population, the outcomes should be even better, but overall, the schools were not in crisis. The consequence of the lack of a broader reform movement for the court-legislative dynamic was that when the Court merely "threatened" reform rather than declaring the school funding system unconstitutional, lawmakers felt less pressure to act. Given the relatively high student performance, perhaps "tinkering" instead of far-reaching change has its benefits (although financially strapped districts would beg to disagree). Regardless of the normative question, however, it is clear that the absence of a large reform coalition severely dampened the impact of the Court's "threat." At the same time, the legislature did make some changes that many interviewees found significant, and would have made even more reforms if the Court had taken the leap to void the funding system on constitutional grounds. Therefore, we see again the importance of the positions of outside actors *and* the Court as key elements in the political response to judicial declarations.

The Texas case study presents a different court-legislature-interest group relationship than the other states. In Texas, broader education reform issues were being considered around the same time as school finance equity reform, but separately, on parallel tracks. In fact, fundamental nonfiscal changes were enacted in 1984[5] and 1995, framing the ten-year time period of *Edgewood*. However, discussion of school finance reform was never coupled with curriculum or governance reform. The effect of this division was that the state's major business and education interests were not as involved in the debates over fiscal equity between districts as they were in the other issues, such as local district power, textbook selection, teacher merit pay. This is not to say that the legislature was not lobbied concerning finance reform issues, but that the pressure came from smaller, less organized interests within each member's district. Therefore, legislators had more freedom to decide whether to merely vote their district's interests or whether to back an unpopular Court-ordered solution. Many moderate leadership

Democrats had relatively safe seats, and so compliance with the Court was a little easier for them than if large interests had opposed reform more strongly.

Even if there was no broader movement for school finance equity in Texas, one should not ignore the role of a few interests in particular in sparking reform. These were the interest groups involved in filing the lawsuits that kept Court attention (and there-fore, legislative attention) focused on school finance. The Mexican-American Legal Defense and Education Fund (MALDEF) supplied the lead attorney, Albert Kauffman, plus financial support. The Equity Center, working closely with MALDEF, provided necessary school finance expertise and analysis. These groups did not give up after the first (and second, and third) attempts of the legislature to enact school funding reform. Their persistence was a major reason for the degree of equity the Texas system possesses today. On the other side of the issue, wealthier districts, led by the Dallas and Houston suburbs, also helped prolong the lawsuit, perhaps to their regret, by legally challenging the more redistributive solutions attempted by the legislature. Therefore, interest group influence was present, but channeled through the judiciary much more than through the legislative or executive branches. These groups had never been truly taken seriously by the legislature before the suit.

The picture sketched by these three case studies is complex, featuring varying degrees of both judicial involvement and interest group influence. Overall, the most reasonable conclusion one can draw is that the presence or absence of broad interest group move-ments can either strengthen or weaken the effectiveness of court orders, but that the courts themselves can exert a powerful independ-ent influence on those movements and groups—as well as directly on the legislature and governor, if they choose to do so. Rosenberg seems to claim that the larger political environment is nearly wholly determinative of court success, while the evidence here sug-gests that although the broader configuration of interests is quite prominent in influencing the political response to a judicial decla-ration, the courts are not nearly as powerless as Rosenberg sees them. Both courts and interests are important influences, not merely one or the other.

Judicial Prestige and the Separation of Powers

Thus far this section has only considered conditions for judicial effectiveness that Gerald Rosenberg mentioned explicitly or implicitly in *The Hollow Hope*. The evidence from the case studies reveals another factor that should also be discussed as partly determinative of court success, however. One can discern in Rosenberg's model a view of court-legislative relations as quite mechanistic, based on narrow cost-benefit analysis, at least on the part of the legislature and executive. Compliance with court decisions seems just a matter of minimizing political costs or gaining desired benefits through using the court as a "shield," for example. As we have seen, the evidence from these case studies strongly supports certain elements of this view.

Missing from this account, however, is the more fluid concept of judicial "prestige," and also the respect political officials possess for the principle of separated powers implicit in both the federal and state systems of government.[6] Throughout this chapter I have argued that legislators and executive branch officials took the rulings of their state supreme courts very seriously. There was no "disconnect," as Rosenberg seems to claim, between the branches. The more mechanistic factors can partly explain the attention paid to the courts, but not completely. I shall now therefore turn to a discussion of judicial prestige and separation of powers, highlighting the role of the Chief Justice of each Court as an important conduit between the court and the political branches.

The Kentucky experience provides a good example of this type of interbranch interaction. Chief Justice Robert Stephens was clearly the political leader of the Kentucky Supreme Court, as he was the only Justice with substantial experience in public life. Stephens also had formed strong friendships with some of the more powerful leaders in the legislature, especially the Senate. This interbranch connection may well have paved the way for the legislative acceptance of a decision as far-reaching as *Rose*. When I asked interviewees whether the state supreme court had gained or lost any prestige or respect with the legislature because of the school finance issue, most respondents said that there was no change in attitudes. This was true even though the Court had ordered the legislature to completely reconstruct an institution over which the legislature was thought to have a fair amount of control and primary responsibility.

The reasons for this lack of backlash were many, but the effect was, in the words of one legislative source, "it got to be a friendly alliance . . . (the Court and the legislature) were in this together." A lawmaker stated: "thank heavens we had the Court." The freedom that the Court gave the legislature to restructure the school system and raise the taxes to pay for it may have a great deal to do with the relative sanguinity with which the legislature viewed the Court. The good relations Stephens had built over time with the legislature, though, aided by some previous decisions protecting legislative prerogatives, definitely smoothed the way.

In North Dakota, Chief Justice Gerald W. VandeWalle did not possess the close personal ties with legislative leaders that Stephens did, but he did enjoy a great deal of legislative respect. Before becoming Chief Justice, VandeWalle had spent twenty years in the state attorney general's office advising legislators on the constitutionality of proposed laws dealing with education. Therefore, he knew how to deal with the popular branch of government, especially concerning an issue such as school finance equity. VandeWalle was praised for his intellect, honesty, and moderation by nearly every interviewee, and his opinion threatening to void the school funding system if changes were not made was taken much more seriously because his name was on it. When North Dakota policymakers were asked whether the Court had gained or lost any prestige with the legislature because of its school finance ruling, which some perceived as wishy-washy, one might expect some resentment; in fact, the opposite was the case. Most interviewees said the Court had not lost any respect in the legislature, and some said the Court actually gained, because, according to one source, "(the Court) recognized the legislative problems . . . instead of shoving them down their throats," which a direct order would have done. Overall, the legislative attitude was: "they're doing their job." If not, "what can you do?"

The Texas experience is different in that there was a fair amount of conflict between the branches during the debates over school finance reform. The "negotiator" role of the Court frustrated many political leaders, some of whom felt that the Court was "jerking them around" without a clear plan or goal. Some, although by no means all, of the blame fairly or unfairly centered on Chief Justice Thomas R. Phillips, a relatively young Chief Justice who had not had time to build up a good working relationship with the Texas legislature. Phillips himself had not served in the legislature previously, although many of his judicial colleagues had. It is unclear how the presence of former legislators on the Court affected the interbranch relations. The conflict reached the point where a constitutional amendment weakening court jurisdiction over school finance issues was proposed in the House and received a substantial number of Republican votes. Later news articles reported various legislative slights at the Court and especially Phillips, including the cancellation of the biennial State of the Judiciary speech to the legislature (Elliott 1993). On the other hand, one lawmaker reported, "nobody ever went anyway." Therefore, one should ask, how serious was the rift between the Court and legislature?

Regardless of the short-term sniping, a clear majority of interviewees reported either "no change" or actual improvement in judicial-legislative relations because of *Edgewood*. Although several respondents disagreed, some sources argued that the Court gained respect in legislative eyes because it showed that it could stand its ground in the face of tremendous political pressure. More plausible, though, is the claim that the legislature did not seriously retaliate against the Court because of generalized respect for the separation of powers. Interviewees said, for example, that "legislators expect this out of courts." "I'm not sure the legislature respected the Court to begin with—they have their branch and we have ours," claimed another. To summarize, Senate Education Committee chairman Bill Ratliff, a Republican himself, publicly responded to Republican legislative attempts to weaken the Court's jurisdiction by retorting, "I suppose I'm corny. I believe in the American system of separation of powers" (Rugeley 1993a).

In each of these states, narrow cost-benefit calculations surely played a large role in determining the extent of legislative compliance with the rulings of the state supreme courts. As this section has attempted to demonstrate, however, personality and principle have to be factored into the equation as well. The role of personality and leadership is especially notable considering that in all three states, at the elite level, everyone seemed to know everyone else. Friendship and rivalry influenced action, as alliances were made and broken. Concerning principle, one should not underestimate the extent to which politicians take seriously ideas such as the separation of powers, interbranch independence, and comity. Perhaps this is just because they need someone else to blame when things go wrong. Regardless, this respect for principle was present to a greater or lesser extent in all three states.

THE POLITICS OF RIGHTS: THE UTILITY OF LEGAL ACTION

Finally, one last point should be mentioned. Two of the major studies in the field of court effectiveness, Gerald Rosenberg's *The Hollow Hope* (1991) and Michael McCann's *Rights at Work* (1994) on gender pay equity, are concerned not only with the conditions for court success but also with the relative utility of social reform litigation for the movement activists themselves. Rosenberg believes that the promise of litigation is a chimera and only diverts resources more efficiently used in grassroots mobilization. McCann, on the other hand, argues that legal action itself may be a tool for political organization and that activists are not excessively optimistic, just realistic, about what courts can accomplish.

The evidence from this project leans toward McCann's more optimistic viewpoint, supplemented by Stuart Scheingold's analysis in *The Politics of Rights* (1974). Scheingold argued that judicial rights declarations were like "bargaining chips" for movement activists in mobilization: potentially valuable, but only if used in the correct way, that is, in conjunction with serious political organizing and lobbying. In these three case studies, one can see why this is so. As noted in the section on courts and interest groups, strong judicial decisions coupled with a broad-based movement produced the most change the fastest, as in Kentucky.

In all three states, though, the plaintiff litigators realized benefits from legal action. In Texas, the repeated litigation compensated for the lack of a comprehensive reform coalition and was responsible for much of the progress toward equity that the Texas legislature made. In Kentucky, the plaintiff school districts succeeded beyond their hopes in increasing the amount of funds available to their schools. In fact, these districts may have produced more "significant social reform" than they wanted to, given the various accountability and governance reforms, such as a ban on nepotism in district hiring, a major source of patronage in many of these districts.

In North Dakota, the picture is more complex, but still exhibits some benefits of legal action. As noted earlier in the chapter, most interviewees reported that several specific changes mostly attributable to the courts were made in the 1995-1997 funding formulas. The Bismarck school district, the lead plaintiff, seems especially pleased with the results. Of course, Bismarck is also becoming a "rich" district, and some of the other plaintiff districts may not be so sanguine about the possibilities for legal action. In North Dakota there was little grassroots organization for change, however, and that may have contributed to the limits on reform as much as any litigation failures.

When I interviewed various persons affiliated or strongly connected in some way with the plaintiff groups, almost none of them expressed reservations about their decisions to sue the state. Most felt that it was the only way to get the process moving in their preferred direction. Most were also conscious of the limits of legal change, especially after the active period immediately following the suit. They realized that it was then time to return to grassroots organization. As the trial judge in the Texas case admonished the plaintiffs at the end of the laborious *Edgewood* case, "So what you all really need to do is work it all out in the Legislature and not come back, all right?" (*Austin American-Statesman* 1995) If one keeps in mind the caveats expressed by Scheingold (and Rosenberg) about the need for political mobilization as complementary to legal action, the evidence from this project shows that going to court to accomplish significant social reform does not have to be a "hollow hope."

Judicial Power: Where Are We, And Where Do We Go From Here?

The preceding discussion of the sources and limits of judicial power as seen through the framework of Gerald Rosenberg's *The Hollow Hope* shows that the interbranch relationships between the judiciary and the legislative and executive branches are guided by a multitude of factors. Motivations for action are complex and fluid, and a strategy that may work well for a court in one situation may not be effective in the next. Rosenberg's list of conditions, while usefully identifying several key guideposts for assessing court effectiveness, should not be taken as necessary or even sufficient for successful judicial action in all cases.

At this point it is fair to note some of the differences between this work and Rosenberg's, as these may partially explain our different research outcomes. First, this project has only examined one issue, public school finance equity reform, which Rosenberg does not discuss in *The Hollow Hope* for obvious reasons, as it is not a federal concern. It is quite possible that court involvement in school funding reform might be more successful than judicial action concerning other issues that do not receive as much media attention (Smith 1994). On the other hand, the deeply political nature of the problems, the additional funding usually required to solve them, and the overall complexity of the issue lead one to believe that dealing with school finance equity is not an "easy call" for the courts, either.

Second, this project centers on state supreme courts, not the U.S. Supreme Court. Although scholarly interest in state courts is growing (Brennan 1977; Tarr and Porter 1988; Songer 1995), these tribunals still suffer the reputation as less competent and less politically insulated than their federal brethren, because of their popular election in most states (Neuborne 1977). One might imagine, therefore, that if, as Rosenberg claims, the U.S. Supreme Court cannot get its decisions enforced, state supreme courts would have an even more difficult struggle and would be less effective. The evidence presented here suggests the opposite result, however.

When I asked interviewees whether they perceived any differences between compliance with federal court orders and rulings from the state supreme court, responses were mixed. Several respondents claimed that the level of government (state or federal) made no difference, that "a court is a court." Others, though, noted a greater level of fear of federal courts, which is not surprising, especially in Texas, where the state prison system and mental health facilities were subjects of federal court supervision for an extended period of time. Similarly, in North Dakota, a lengthy and costly federal suit over conditions in the state mental hospital was just ending at the time of the school finance litigation.

One could argue that greater fear of the federal courts led to greater compliance with federal court orders than those of the state supreme court. Yet, interviewees, especially legislators, were also generally more frustrated with the "outsider" federal courts than with the state supreme courts, although in Texas it was a close race. This frustration might also lead to greater noncompliance, especially in a complex policy area difficult for judges to monitor. Interviewees generally expressed greater trust in the state supreme court, partly due to its structure as a collective body, not an individual federal judge who could be more easily faulted for ideological bias. (Note: the failure of Alabama politicians to act could be partially attributed to the lack of a collective Supreme Court decision on the merits, instead of the ruling of a single trial judge.) This trust also resulted from the state court's nature as an elected body. The Justices had to gain the approval of many of the same voters that the legislators and governors did. This helped reassure the politicians that the state Justices were not going to issue rulings far out of touch from political reality, which the politicians would then have to implement. One should not underestimate the importance of interbranch trust concerning sensitive political issues such as public school finance equity.

The evidence from these case studies suggests that state supreme courts are less isolated from the legislature and executive branches than the federal courts are from Congress and the President. Perhaps this is the reason why the "disconnect" that

Rosenberg hints at between the judiciary and the political branches was barely present, if at all, in these three states. These branches were intimately intermixed in each other's business. Paradoxically, these close connections actually seemed to help the state courts bridge the gap between decision and implementation, between right and remedy. An article by George D. Brown notes the mutually supportive relationships between the state courts and state legislatures and executives, at least regarding the issue of court-ordered school finance reform.

> An alternative analysis is that state courts, unconstrained by Article III of the United States Constitution, are developing their own approaches to a particularly complex form of institutional litigation. What the cases represent is not so much a judicial "resolution" of a problem, but rather one step in an ongoing approach to a multi-dimensional social question. The state courts engage in a dialogue about that question with the political branches almost to the point where they become partners in crafting a solution. That solution does not come from the court nor is it imposed by the court. Judicial decisions resemble a set of guidelines for the next, legislative step in the process rather than judgments designed to affect the rights and duties of a particular set of litigants. The judicial decree is not, as in the federal norm, the "centerpiece" dictating who shall do what. The court does declare a duty, but its order is essentially advice on how to perform that duty. These binding advisory opinions are quite different from the manner in which Article III courts handle reform litigation. This does not mean that the state approach is inferior (Brown 1994).

Future research on judicial effectiveness in producing significant social reform should take note of this potential difference between federal and state court intervention in complex public policy litigation. Rosenberg himself has said that the theories advanced in *The Hollow Hope* should be tested by studies moving outward and downward, so to speak, to comparative work and also state-level analysis. The work so far, to which this project is only one contribution, suggests a plausible theory in need of some refinement and refocus (Reed 1995). Future research hopefully will provide this sharpening of view.

Future researchers will find a public school finance landscape which is complex and rapidly changing. For example, currently the Ohio legislature and governor are preparing to respond to a second court declaration of unconstitutionality, and cases are working their way up the judicial ladders of Florida, New Mexico, and New York. These courts may express worries about becoming entangled in policy matters that they feel are best left to legislators and executives. Some may even cite the cases in New Jersey and Texas as examples to avoid (Illinois 1996; Rhode Island 1995). Yet, one can argue that both courts eventually persuaded their legislatures to make significant progress toward the goals that the courts set (see chapters 2 and 3). Courts may have to be persistent, issuing multiple decisions (see Arizona, New Hampshire, and Vermont in chapter 2), but the end result generally is a move toward compliance.

To expect comprehensive reform immediately after a court decision may be unrealistic (although see Kentucky), but if one views the court's goals as less fixed, one can be optimistic concerning judicial effectiveness in participating in the school funding debates. Granted, legislatures and executives often try to do the minimum possible, but the judicial ruling seems to raise that minimum. Furthermore, legislatures sometimes go beyond "buying off" the poorest districts and take the politically difficult decision of capping or redistributing the wealth of the richest districts in the state (see Texas, Vermont, Wyoming, and Kansas). If court decisions were so useless, so "hollow" to plaintiff school districts, it seems unlikely that equity and adequacy suits would be so pervasive and persistent. This study shows that, at least from the plaintiffs' perspective, hopes are not unfounded.

Some academic work on this issue seems consistent with Rosenberg in arguing that multiple sets of actors must work together for significant reform to be achieved (Augenblick 1998; Carr and Fuhrman 1999). There must be a strong catalyst for action, such as a court decision. The political leadership must be supportive and stable. A reform coalition of outside groups, possibly including the media, must persuade both the general public and legislature that reform is not only possible, but necessary. Issues of race and class must be minimized.[7] I do not disagree with the conclusion that reform can only come from a combination of forces, of which the courts are only one. However, I am more optimistic than these authors about the possibility of this coalition forming, as either happened or could have happened in each of the three case studies.

The lesson of this project is not that these courts always will succeed or fail if they decide to declare their states' finance structures unconstitutional, but that courts are generally more effective when they invest more of their own political capital in a decision, in terms of forcefulness of the decision language and willingness to set clear and firm deadlines for legislative compliance. The lack of such a decision on the merits by the Alabama high court (as opposed to a procedural ruling) weakened the force of the mandate to comply. The North Dakota Court took a small risk, and enjoyed a relatively small return. Both the Texas and Kentucky Courts took substantial gambles with their own prestige, however, and over the long run, it appears that both emerged relatively unscathed and successful in persuading their legislatures to make substantial reforms.

This work should help settle the question of *whether* courts make a contribution in this area. I have also developed some hypotheses as to *how*, *when*, and *why* courts matter. Further research will test these views.

Cases Cited

Federal Courts

Alden v. Maine, 119 S.Ct. 2240 (1999).
Baker v. Carr, 369 U.S. 186 (1962).
Board of Education of Oklahoma City v. Dowell, 498 U.S. 237 (1991).
Brown v. Board of Education (I), 347 U.S. 483 (1954).
Brown v. Board of Education (II), 349 U.S. 294 (1955).
Carolene Products Co., U.S. v., 304 U.S. 144 (1938).
Douglas v. California, 372 U.S. 353 (1963).
Estelle v. Justice, 426 U.S. 925 (1976).
Freeman v. Pitts, 503 U.S. 467 (1992).
Goldberg v. Kelly, 397 U.S. 254 (1970).
Griffin v. Illinois, 351 U.S. 12 (1956).
Harper v. Virginia State Board of Elections, 383 U.S. 663 (1966).
In re Clements, 881 F.2d 145 (5th Cir. 1989).
McInnis v. Shapiro, 293 F.Supp. 327, *aff'd sub nom McInnis v. Oglivie*, 394 U.S. 322 (1969).
Michigan v. Long, 463 U.S. 1032 (1983).
Miranda v. Arizona, 384 U.S. 436 (1966).
Missouri v. Jenkins, 495 U.S. 33 (1990).
Missouri v. Jenkins, 115 S. Ct. 2573 (1995).
Printz v. U.S., 521 U.S. 898 (1997).
Reynolds v. Sims, 377 U.S. 533 (1964).
Roe v. Wade, 410 U.S. 113 (1973).
San Antonio I.S.D. v. Rodriguez, 411 U.S. 1 (1973).
Skinner v. Oklahoma, 316 U.S. 535 (1944).
Swann v. Charlotte-Mecklenburg Board of Education, 402 U.S. 1 (1971).
U.S. v. Fordice, 505 U.S. 717 (1992).
Wyatt v. Stickney, 334 F.Supp. 1341 (M.D. Ala. 1971).

State Courts

Alabama:
Ex parte James, 713 So.2d 869 (1997).
Opinion of the Justices, 624 So.2d 107 (1993).
Alabama Coalition for Equity v. Hunt, 624 So.2d 110 (Montgomery Co. Circuit Ct 1993).
Alaska:
Matanuska-Susitna Borough School District et al. v. State, 931 P.2d 391 (1997).
Arizona:
Hull v. Albrecht, 960 P.2d 634 (1998).
Hull v. Albrecht, 950 P.2d 1141 (1997).
Roosevelt Elementary School District #66 v. Bishop, 877 P.2d 806 (1994).
Shofstall v. Hollins, 515 P.2d 590 (1973).
Arkansas:
Dupree v. Alma School District #30 of Crawford County, 651 S.W.2d 90 (1983).
California:
Serrano v. Priest (II), 557 P.2d 929 (1977).
Serrano v. Priest (I), 487 P.2d 1241 (1971).
Colorado:
Lujan v. Colorado State Board of Educ., 649 P.2d 1005 (1982).
Connecticut:
Sheff v. O'Neill, 678 A.2d 1267 (1996).
Horton v. Meskill, 486 A.2d 1099 (1985).
Horton v. Meskill (I), 376 A.2d 359 (1977).
Florida:
Coalition for Adequacy and Fairness in School Funding v. Chiles, 680 So.2d 400 (1996).
Georgia:
McDaniel v. Thomas, 285 S.E. 2d 156 (1981).
Idaho:
Idaho Schools for Equal Educ. Opportunity v. Evans, 850 P.2d 724 (1993).
Thompson v. Engelking, 537 P.2d 635 (1975).
Illinois:
Committee for Educational Rights v. Edgar, 672 N.E.2d 1178 (1996).
Blase v. State, 302 N.E. 2d 46 (1973).
McInnis v. Shapiro, 293 F.Supp. 327, aff'd sub nom *McInnis v. Oglivie*, 394 U.S. 322 (1969).
Kansas:
Unified School District No. 229 v. State, 885 P.2d 1170 (1994).
Knowles v. St. Board of Educ., 547 P.2d 699 (1976).
Caldwell v. Kansas, Civil No. 50616 (Kan. Dis. Ct., 8/30/72).

Kentucky:
> *Kentucky Department of Education v. Risner* et al., 913 S.W. 2d 327 (1996).
>
> *Jones v. Board of Trustees of Kentucky Retirement Systems*, 910 S.W.2d 710 (1995).
>
> *Kraus v. Kentucky State Senate*, 872 S.W.2d 433 (1994).
>
> *Chapman v. Gorman*, 839 S.W.2d 232 (1992).
>
> *Philpot v. Patton*, 837 S.W.2d 491 (1992).
>
> *State Board of Elementary and Secondary Education v. Howard*, 834 S.W.2d 657 (1992).
>
> *Rose v. Council for Better Education*, 790 S.W. 2d 186 (1989).
>
> *Council for Better Education v. Collins*, No.85-CI-1759 (Franklin County Circuit Court, Kentucky, October 14, 1988) .
>
> *Holsclaw v. Stephens*, 507 S.W.2d 462 (1973).
>
> *Russman v. Luckett*, 391 S.W.2d 694 (1965).
>
> *Matthews v. Allen*, 360 S.W.2d 135 (1962).

Louisiana:
> *La. Assn. of Educators v. Edwards*, 521 S.2d 390 (1988).

Maryland:
> *Hornbeck v. Somerset County*, 458 A.2d 758 (1983).

Massachusetts:
> *McDuffy v. Sec. of the Exec. Office of Educ.*, 615 N.E. 2d 516 (1993).

Michigan:
> *Milliken v. Green*, 212 N.W. 2d 711 (1973) vacating
>
> *Milliken v. Green*, 389 Mich.1, 203 N.W.2nd 457 (1972).

Minnesota:
> *Skeen v. State*, 505 N.W. 2d 299 (1993).
>
> *Van Dusartz v. Hatfield*, 334 F.Supp. 870 (D. Minn. 1971).

Missouri:
> *Akin v. Director of Revenue*, 934 S.W.2d 235 (1996).

Montana:
> *Helena Sch. Dist. v. State*, 769 P.2d 684 (1989).

Nebraska:
> *Gould v. Orr*, 506 N.W. 2d 349 (1993).

New Hampshire:
> *Opinion of the Justices*, 725 A.2d 1082 (1999).
>
> *Claremont Sch. Dist. v. Governor*, 725 A.2d 648 (1998).
>
> *Opinion of the Justices*, 712 A.2d 1080 (1998).
>
> *Claremont Sch. Dist. v. Governor*, 703 A.2d 1353 (1997).
>
> *Claremont Sch. Dist. v. Governor*, 635 A.2d 1375 (1993).
>
> *Jesseman v. State,* No. 83–371 (N.H. February 13, 1984)

New Jersey:
> *Abbott by Abbott v. Burke*, 710 A.2d 450 (1998).
>
> *Abbott by Abbott v. Burke*, 693 A.2d 417 (1997).
>
> *Abbott by Abbott v. Burke*, 643 A.2d 575 (1994).

Abbott v. Burke, 575 A.2d 359 (1990).
Robinson v. Cahill (V), 355 A.2d 129 (1976).
Robinson v. Cahill (IV), 339 A.2d 193 or 351 A.2d 713 (1975).
Robinson v. Cahill(III), 335 A.2d 6 (1975).
Robinson v. Cahill (II), 306 A.2d 65 (1973).
Robinson v. Cahill (I), 303 A.2d 273 (1973).
Robinson v. Cahill, N.J. Super. 223, 286 A.2nd 187 (1972).
New York:
    Reform Educational Financing Inequalitites Today (R.E.F.I.T.) v. Cuomo
        655 N.E. 2d 647 (1995).
    Board of Educ., Levittown v. Nyquist, 439 N.E. 2d 359 (1982).
North Carolina:
    Leandro v. State, 488 S.E.2d 249 (1997).
    Britt v. N.Car. Board of Educ., 357 S.E. 2d 432 (1987).
North Dakota:
    Bismarck Public Sch. Dist. #1 v. State, 511 N.W.2d 247 (1994).
    Bismarck Public Sch. Dist. #1 v. State, South Central Judicial District,
        Civil No. 41554.
Ohio:
    DeRolph v. State II, 728 N.E.2d 933 (2000).
    DeRolph v. State (IA-motion for reconsideration and clarification), 678
        N.E.2d 886 (1997).
    DeRolph v. State I, 677 N.E.2d 733 (1997).
    Board of Educ. v. Walter, 390 N.E.2d 813 (1979).
Oklahoma:
    Fair School Finance Council v. State, 746 P.2d 1135 (1987).
Oregon:
    Coalition for Equitable School Funding v. State, 811 P.2d 116 (1991).
    Olsen v. State, 554 P.2d 139 (1976).
Pennsylvania:
    Danson v. Casey, 399 A.2d 360 (1979).
Rhode Island:
    City of Pawtucket v. Sundlun, 662 A.2d 40 (1995).
South Carolina:
    Richland County v. Campbell, 364 S.E.2d 470 (1988).
Tennessee:
    Tennessee Small School Systems v. McWherter, 851 S.W. 2d 139 (1993).
    State v. Meador, 284 S.W. 890, 891 (Tenn.1926).
Texas:
    Edgewood I.S.D. v. Meno (IV), 893 S.W. 2d 450 (1995).
    Edgewood I.S.D. v. Meno (IV), trial opinion No. 362516-B, delivered
        1/26/94 (250th Judicial District, Travis County, Texas) at 64-65.
    Carrolton-Farmers Branch I.S.D. v. Edgewood I.S.D. (III), 826 S.W. 2d
        489 (1992).
    Edgewood I.S.D. v. Kirby (II), 804 S.W. 2d 491 (1991).

Edgewood I.S.D. v. Kirby (I), 777 S.W. 2d 391 (1989).

Edgewood I.S.D. v. Kirby, 761 S.W.2d 859 (Tex.Ct.App. 1988).

Edgewood I.S.D. v. Kirby, No. 362,516 (250th Dist.Ct., Travis County, Texas, June 1st, 1987).

San Antonio I.S.D. v. Rodriguez, 411 U.S. 1 (1973).

Rodriguez v. San Antonio Independent School District, 337 F.Supp. 280 (W.D. Tex. 1971).

Mumme v. Marrs, 120 Tex. 383, 40 S.W.2d 31 (1931).

Love v. City of Dallas, 120 Tex. 351, 40 S.W.2d 20 (1931).

Vermont:

Anderson v. State, 723 A.2d 1147 (1998).

Brigham v. State, 692 A.2d 384 (1997).

Virginia:

Scott v. Commonwealth, 443 S.E.2d 138 (1994).

Washington:

Seattle Sch. Dist. v. State, 585 P.2d 71 (1978).

Northshore Sch. Dist. #417 v. Kinnear, 530 P.2d 178 (1974).

West Virginia:

St. ex rel Boards of Educ. v. Chafin, 376 S.E.2d 113 (1988)-*Pauley* impact

St. ex rel Bd. of Educ. v. Manchin, 366 S.E. 2d 743 (1988).

Pauley v. Gainer, 353 S.E.2d 318 (1986).

Pauley v. Bailey, 324 S.E.2d 128 (1982).

Pauley v. Kelly, 255 S.E. 2d 859 (1979).

Wisconsin:

Vincent v. Voight, 614 N.W. 2d 388 (2000).

Kukor v. Grover, 436 N.W. 2d 568 (1989).

Wyoming:

Campbell County School Dist. v. Ohman, 907 P.2d 1238 (1995).

Washakie County Sch. Dist. #1 v. Herschler, 606 P.2d 310 (1980).

No supreme court decisions in: Delaware, Hawaii, Indiana, Iowa, Maine, Mississippi, Nevada, New Mexico, South Dakota, Utah.

◇

Texas Interview Questions

Note for all interview question lists:

Not all questions were asked of all interviewees due to time constraints. As the interviews were semistructured, the order of the questions varied somewhat from interview to interview. Furthermore, follow-up questions are not all noted here. However, this is the basic template of questions that I took to every interview.

Interview Questions (Non-Judges)

Were you surprised by the state supreme court's ruling in *Edgewood* I?
—how did those around you react?
What did you think the Court's message was in its decision?
—was the decision clear?
How much of an effort do you think the Legislature made to comply with the court decision, and why?
—how costly was it politically to comply with the Court's decision(s)?
What did you think the public reaction was to *Edgewood*?
—did public opinion play a role in the debates?
—what is your impression of the public's knowledge/feelings about the state supreme court?
What interest groups had the most influence in the *Edgewood* debates?
—why not others?
What was a typical day like during the special sessions on school finance?
—what did you do, and who did you talk with?
Were you surprised by the Court's ruling in *Edgewood* II striking down Senate Bill 1?
—what did you think the court wanted?
—how much of an effort did the Legislature make to comply?
What did you think would happen if the Court was not satisfied?
—did you take the school closure threat seriously? Why/why not?
What effect did the opinion on the motion for rehearing (*Edgewood* IIA) have on the debate?
—Did you take the Court's ruling less seriously because it was no longer unanimous?

247

When the court issued its opinion in *Edgewood* III striking down the County Education Districts, what was the reaction in the Legislature?
  —were you surprised?
How much of an effort was made to comply with *Edgewood* III?
  —did you think the multiple-choice plan satisfied the court's concerns?
Were you surprised that the Court finally upheld the system in *Edgewood* IV?
Some observers, including dissenting members of the Court, felt that the Court changed positions over the course of the six years of *Edgewood*. Did you think the Court took a clear position throughout?
  —if so, what was it?
  —if not, what were the changes, and how do you account for them?
Should the Court have been more specific in its decisions about what it wanted, as in Kentucky, where the state supreme court voided the entire school system, not just the finance mechanism, and defined a long list of goals and standards for the new system to meet? Should the court have been that specific? Would that have helped?
What would have been the reaction if the court in Texas had laid down a list of guidelines?
Did you ever think that passing the Culberson amendment to remove the courts from the process entirely was a viable option, and why/why not?
How do you think the Legislature's previous experience having to deal with court orders concerning the prison system, mental health system, etc. affected the response to the *Edgewood* decision?
  —did it make the Leg. more or less likely to comply, or did it make any difference?
Since we've been talking about the dialogue between the Legislature and the Court in this case, I wanted to ask you: What does the Legislature generally do when it wants to let the Court know it is pleased, displeased, or just confused by its rulings? How do you let the Court know?
Would the Leg.'s reaction be communicated informally to the Justices? For instance, do you know any of the Justices personally, and do Justices ever informally consult with members about issues, such as judicial reforms?
Occasionally, news articles would say that the Legislature was worried because "sources on the Court" told members that the Court was about to strike down the system again. What kind of "sources" would these be?
Some observers have said that the *Edgewood* case went a long way toward "politicizing" the Court. Do you agree?
  —do you think the Court kept within its constitutional boundaries in this case?
  —if so, what would have been too much?
  —if not, in what way?
Do you think the Court gained/lost any power or prestige because of its school finance decision(s)?

—Was there a backlash against the Court in the Legislature?

Finally, how equal would you say the school finance system is today?

—how much credit/blame does the Court deserve for that?

—did the Court's involvement help speed the process along, did it delay reform, or did it not have much effect either way?

—would the Legislature have changed the system without court involvement?

—why didn't just the threat of court action work, as it did in Massachusetts and Idaho?

Now that the case is over, do you feel that the Legislature has to be very careful in monitoring the educational equity issue because the Court might return, or do you think the Court will now give the Legislature some latitude?

Do you anticipate having to deal with the school finance issue again?

Now, what questions should I have asked in order to find out what really happened? What did I miss?

Interview Questions (Judges)

How do you see your job as a Justice on the Supreme Court?

—what is your role in state government?

What would you say the similarities and differences are between your job as a Justice and the job of a legislator?

—(for the former legislators) Do you think your experience in the Legislature has helped you as a Justice, and if so, how?

—(for non-legislators) Do the justices who have served in the legislature ever share their experiences there with you, and does that help you sometimes in making decisions involving the Legislature?

How does election change your job, if at all?

How much do you think the general public knows about the state Supreme Court?

Is their attitude generally favorable or unfavorable?

Do you think the *Edgewood* case altered either their knowledge about or evaluation of the Court?

How do you explain the unanimity of *Edgewood* I?

What message was the Court trying to send, and do you think the Legislature received it?

—was it clear and specific enough?

Some observers have said that the Court went too far in *Edgewood* II in trying to achieve equality. Do you agree?

Whose decision was it to issue the opinion on the motion for rehearing in *Edgewood* II (A)?

—why did it address the local enrichment issue?

What was the effect on the Legislature of *Edgewood* II (A) in your judgment?

—did the Legislature get the wrong message?

How do you explain why the Legislature passed SB 351 with the constitutional flaws found in *Edgewood* III?

What message was the Court sending in *Edgewood* III, and was it clear and specific enough?

Who drew the *Edgewood* IV opinion assignment, and did that assignment hold?

In general, do you think the Court was sending a clear and consistent message to the Legislature?

How seriously do you think the Legislature took the threat of school closure?

What do you think the political and public reaction would have been to school closure?

—who would be blamed?

Do you think there was any resentment in the Legislature against the Court because of *Edgewood*?

—did you lose any influence, prestige, or goodwill?

Just generally, when the Legislature wants to send you a message, either positive, negative, or just that they're confused about a decision, how do they do that?

—do you ever interact with members on a social basis?

—do you ever consult with them on an individual basis?

Some observers have said that the *Edgewood* case went a long way toward "politicizing" the Court. Do you agree?

What do you think the proper role of the state supreme court is in state government?

—do you think the Court overstepped its boundaries in this case?

—if so, how?

—if not, what would have been too far?

In Kentucky the Supreme Court voided the entire school system, not just the finance mechanism, and promulgated a long list of goals and standards for the new system to meet. Why didn't the same thing happen in Texas, and what would have been the reaction if it had?

How equal would you say the finance system is today after *Edgewood*?

How do you explain the long delay in getting to this point?

Do you think the Legislature's response to your decision in *Edgewood* was affected by previous court orders on prison overcrowding and mental health facilities, and if so, how?

—did it make them more or less willing to comply?

In general, do you think the Court helped speed the reform process along, contributed to the delay, or neither?

—could the Court have handled the situation better, and if so, how?

Do you think the Legislature would have acted without court pressure?

Do you expect to have to deal with this issue again sometime in the future?

Is there anything else that I should be asking about, but haven't?

APPENDIX **2**

~

Kentucky Interview Questions

Interview Questions (Non-Judges)

Were you surprised when you first heard of the superintendents' suit against the state?

—how did those around you react?

—did you think that the Senate bill to deny standing to the districts was a good idea?

Did you think that the suit would be successful?

Did you think the school funding system was constitutional?

What effect did Judge Corns's decision have on the policy debates?

—what message was sent, and did the Legislature listen?

Were you surprised that the Supreme Court upheld Judge Corns?

Had the Kentucky Supreme Court ever made a decision as far-reaching in your memory?

—did that lack of experience with the Court make the Leg. more or less likely to comply, or did it make any difference?

—did you have experience with far-reaching federal court orders, and what were the similarities/differences?

What did you think the Court's message was in its decision?

—was the decision clear?

—was it specific—did you know what the Legislature had to do to respond?

Did you think the Court had exceeded its proper role in state government?

—what is the Court's proper role?

—if exceeded, why?

—if didn't exceed, what would have been too much?

After the decision was handed down, how much effort was made to deal with the specifics of the Court decision?

—was satisfaction of the Court's guidelines an important consideration, or did the Legislature strike out on its own in restructuring the system?

—did you look at the experience of other states with court-ordered reform at all?

251

Why was a task force appointed instead of using the regular legislative process?

Why do you think the Legislature made such an effort to comply with the court decision?

What did you think would happen if the Court was not satisfied?

—did you take the school closure threat seriously? Why/why not?

—Did you take the Court's ruling less seriously because it was not unanimous?

What interest groups had the most influence in the KERA debates?

—why not others?

What did you think the public reaction was to *Rose*?

—did public opinion play a role in the debates?

—what is your impression of the public's knowledge/feelings about the state supreme court?

Was there any voter backlash against either the Court or the Legislature because of KERA, and if so, how large was it?

Do you think the Court gained/lost any power or prestige with the Legislature because of its school finance decision(s)?

—Was there a backlash against the Court in the Legislature?

Since we've been talking about the dialogue between the Legislature and the Court in this case, I wanted to ask you: What does the Legislature generally do when it wants to let the Court know it is pleased, displeased, or just confused by its rulings? How do you let the Court know?

Would the Leg.'s reaction be communicated informally to the Justices? For instance, do you know any of the Justices personally, and do Justices ever informally consult with members about issues, such as judicial reforms?

Occasionally, news articles would say that the Legislature was worried because "sources on the Court" told members that the Court was about to strike down the system again. What kind of "sources" would these be?

Since KERA's passage, how much progress do you think Kentucky has made on the reform effort?

—how equal would you say the school finance system is today?

—how much credit/blame does the Court deserve for that?

—did the Court's involvement help speed the process along, did it delay reform, or did it not have much effect either way?

—would the Legislature have changed the system without court involvement?

—why didn't just the threat of court action work, as it did in Massachusetts and Idaho?

Has the system been consistently funded?

—how high a priority is funding of KERA for you and the Legislature?

—how much of implementation has been driven by fear of another Court decision?

Do you think the Court has taken a clear position on KERA since it was passed?

—if so, what is it?

—if not, what are the changes, and how do you account for them?

—do you think that new personnel on the Court will affect the Court's position on compliance?

Do you feel that the Legislature has to be very careful in monitoring the educational equity issue because the Court might return, or do you think the Court will now give the Legislature some latitude?

Do you anticipate having to deal with the school finance issue again?

Now, what questions should I have asked in order to find out what really happened? What did I miss?

Interview Questions (Judges)

Why did you first decide to run for the Kentucky Supreme Court?

—was there something specific that you wanted to accomplish?

How do you see your job as a Justice on the Supreme Court?

—what is your role in state government?

What would you say the similarities and differences are between your job as a Justice and the job of a legislator?

How many current or former Justices have served in the Legislature in your memory?

—has that experience (or lack thereof) affected the Court's relations with the Legislature?

How does election change your job, if at all?

How much do you think the general public knows about the state Supreme Court?

Is their attitude generally favorable or unfavorable?

Do you think the *Rose* case altered either their knowledge about or evaluation of the Court?

Why did the Supreme Court take the Rose case directly from the trial court?

How was the opinion assignment determined?

How important was unanimity in this case (as in Texas, where lots of compromise produced a unanimous opinion?)

To what extent did you look at the experience of other states which had undergone court-ordered school finance reform? What messages (if any) did you draw from those other cases?

In Texas the state supreme court's opinion striking down the system only dealt with the finance aspect and did not contain the type of prescriptions and goals that the Kentucky opinion did. Why did the Court decide not to move in that direction, and what would have been the reaction if it had?

Some observers have said that the Court stepped over its judicial boundaries in *Rose* in trying to achieve an "efficient" system. How would you respond to that?

—what would have been too much?

What goals were you trying to achieve in the opinion? What message was the Court trying to send, and do you think the Legislature received it?

—was it clear and specific enough?

Why did the court decide to supplement its opinion in response to the request from the legislative leaders?

> —were you concerned the Legislature would get the wrong message?
>
> —why supplement here and not in the legislative redistricting case?
>
> —is this a proper role for the Court?

What was the effect on the Legislature of the supplementary opinion in your judgment?

> —did the Legislature get the right message?

How seriously do you think the Legislature took the threat of school closure?

What do you think the political and public reaction would have been to school closure?

> —who would be blamed?

Do you think there was any resentment in the Legislature against the Court because of *Rose*?

> —did you lose any influence, prestige, or goodwill?

Just generally, when the Legislature wants to send you a message, either positive, negative, or just that they're confused about a decision, how do they do that?

> —do you ever interact with members on a social basis?
>
> —do you ever consult with them on an individual basis?

What effect do you think the later decisions concerning specific aspects of KERA, such as the teacher political participation ban and the nepotism ban have had on the school reform process?

> —Given the personnel changes on the Court, how strong is the commitment today to school reform on the Court?

How equal would you say the finance system is today after *Rose*?

In general, do you think the Court helped speed the reform process along, contributed to the delay, or neither?

> —could the Court have handled the situation better, and if so, how?

Do you think the Legislature would have acted without court pressure?

Has the Kentucky Legislature had to deal with court orders this broad and important in the past on other issues? How do you think that experience affected their response to the *Rose* decision?

Where does the *Rose* decision fit in the history of the Kentucky Supreme Court?

Do you expect to have to deal with this issue again sometime in the future?

Is there anything else that I should be asking about, but haven't?

APPENDIX 3

~

North Dakota Interview Questions

Interview Questions (Non-Judges)

Were you surprised when you first heard of the superintendents' suit against the state?

What was the school funding system like before the suit?

—did you think that there was a problem there that the Legislature had to address?

Did you think that the suit would be successful?

What effect did Judge Hodny's decision have on the policy debates?

—what message was sent, and did the Legislature listen?

—what did you think would happen if the Legislature did not comply with the order?

Did you think that the Supreme Court would uphold his ruling?

What message did the Supreme Court decision send to the Legislature, if any?

—was there a clear message?

—how closely did you examine the opinions?

Did Chief Justice VandeWalle's opinion influence debate over school funding issues?

—did you think his opinion was a proper use of the judicial role, and why/why not?

Did you feel like the Legislature had to respond in some way to the court decision in the 1995 session?

What has the state's economy been like in the last few years? Has the Legislature had to deal with severe budget constraints, or not?

Have interest groups played a role in school funding debates, and if so, which have had the most influence?

—why not others?

What did you think the public reaction was to both the court decision and the school funding issue generally?

—did public opinion play a role in the debates?

—what is your impression of the public's knowledge/feelings about the state supreme court?

What was the Governor's role in responding to the Court's decision?
—what kind of working relationship do the Legislature and the Governor have?

How much "progress" on funding issues did the Legislature make in the 1995 session after the Court ruling?
—how equal is the funding system today?
—how much credit/blame does the Court deserve for that?
—did the Court's involvement help speed the process along, did it delay reform, or did it not have much effect either way?
—would the Legislature have made the changes it did without court involvement?

Hypothetically, what do you think would have happened if the Supreme Court had followed the reasoning of the three-justice majority and declared the funding system unconstitutional? What would the Legislature have done?
—if acted, why so? fear of court sanctions? right thing to do?
—if not, why not?

How involved has the North Dakota Supreme Court been in policy-making issues in your experience?
—has the Legislature had to respond to court orders, either state or federal, on other issues, and what were the similarities/differences with school funding?
—has that other experience influenced how the Legislature dealt with the school finance issue, or has it made no difference?
—did you look at the experience of other states with court-ordered school finance reform at all?

Was there any voter backlash against the Legislature because of school funding issues from Judge Hodny's decision to the present, and if so, how large was it?

Do you think the Court gained/lost any power or prestige with the Legislature because of its school finance decision(s)?
—was there a backlash against the Court in the Legislature?

Since we've been talking about the dialogue between the Legislature and the Court in this case, I wanted to ask you: What does the Legislature generally do when it wants to let the Court know it is pleased, displeased, or just confused by its rulings? How do you let the Court know?

Would the Leg.'s reaction be communicated informally to the Justices? For instance, do you know any of the Justices personally, and do Justices ever informally consult with members about issues, such as judicial reforms?

Looking to the future in the 1997 session and beyond:
—how high a priority is education funding and equity for you and the Legislature compared with other state issues?

Has the Supreme Court given any further indications of its attitude toward school funding issues since the ruling?
—do you anticipate another lawsuit filed by either poorer or richer districts?

Do you feel that the Legislature has to be very careful in monitoring the educational equity issue because the Court might return, or do you think the Court will now give the Legislature some latitude?

Now, what questions should I have asked in order to find out what really happened? What did I miss?

Interview Questions (Judges)

Why did you first decide to run for the North Dakota Supreme Court?

—was there something specific that you wanted to accomplish?

How do you see your job as a Justice on the Supreme Court?

—what is your role in state government?

What would you say the similarities and differences are between your job as a Justice and the job of a legislator?

How many current or former Justices have served in the Legislature in your memory?

—has that experience (or lack thereof) affected the Court's relations with the Legislature?

How does election change your job, if at all?

How much do you think the general public knows about the state Supreme Court?

—Is their attitude generally favorable or unfavorable?

Do you think the *Bismarck* case altered either their knowledge about or evaluation of the Court?

To what extent did you look at the experience of other states which had undergone court-ordered school finance reform? What messages (if any) did you draw from those other cases?

Did the Court ever consider issues of adequacy and educational outcomes as well as finance equity?

—why did the Court decide not to move in that direction, and what would have been the reaction if it had?

Were you concerned about overstepping judicial boundaries in the *Bismarck* case in trying to achieve an "uniform" system? Where do you think those boundaries are?

—what would have been too much?

What goals were you trying to achieve in the opinion? What message was the Court trying to send, and do you think the Legislature received it?

—was it clear and specific enough?

What was the effect on the Legislature of the dissenting opinion of the Chief Justice in your judgment?

—did the Legislature get the right message?

Hypothetically, what do you think the Legislature would have done if you had voided the system?

What sanctions could you use to force compliance, if any?

What do you think the political and public reaction would have been to school closure?

—who would be blamed?

Do you think there was any resentment in the Legislature against the Court because of *Bismarck*?

—did you lose any influence, prestige, or goodwill?

Just generally, when the Legislature wants to send you a message, either positive, negative, or just that they're confused about a decision, how do they do that?

—do you ever interact with members on a social basis?

—do you ever consult with them on an individual basis?

How equal would you say the finance system is today after *Bismarck*?

In general, do you think the Court helped speed the reform process along, contributed to the delay, or neither?

—could the Court have handled the situation better, and if so, how?

Do you think the Legislature would have acted without court pressure?

Has the North Dakota Legislature had to deal with court orders this broad and important in the past on other issues? How do you think that experience affected their response to the *Bismarck* decision?

Where does the *Bismarck* decision fit in the history of the North Dakota Supreme Court?

Do you expect to have to deal with this issue again sometime in the future?

Is there anything else that I should be asking about, but haven't?

Notes

Chapter 1

1. Relatively relaxed rules of standing to sue in state courts have aided this trend, including school finance litigation (Hershkoff 1998).

2. To the extent that Horowitz's study was replicated at the state level, the conclusions were just as negative for judicial efficacy. The most notable article in that regard was Bert Neuborne's "The Myth of Parity" (1980). Neuborne argues that state courts have less resources—political, financial, and institutional, to enforce their decisions than their federal counterparts.

3. Here McCann refers to "affiliates of the left-oriented Critical Legal Studies movement as well as to many liberal-left social scientists specializing in studies of reform litigation impact" (McCann 1994:2). These scholars generally view rights discourse as a cruel snare. According to this group, law and rights are concepts generated by the ruling elite to give the oppressed the illusion of power and autonomy, when in fact legal forms are malleable only to the will of the governing class.

Chapter 2

1. The term "wave" comes from Thro (1990).

2. Coons et al. (1970) never actually used the term "fiscal neutrality" in *Private Wealth and Public Education* (although see pp.346–50; 425–26), but the term came to be associated with their approach.

3. For full citations for this and all following school finance cases, see the Table of Cases following the bibliography.

4. Recently, some commentators have described a "fourth wave" of cases linking claims of education finance inequality with racial segregation (McMillan 1998). The leading case is *Sheff v. O'Neill* (1996), in which the Connecticut Supreme Court declared that the system of public education had violated the desegregation clause in the state consitution. A similar lawsuit was eventually settled in Minnesota (O'Connor 2000).

259

Chapter 3

1. The following discussion is taken in part from Hobby and Walker (1991).

2. By most accounts, this was a friendly suit.

3. Since the case never went to trial, there is no citation.

4. 1984 Tex. Sess. Law Serv. 28 (Vernon).

5. 1990 Tex. Sess. Law Serv. 1 (Vernon).

6. The original name at the Texas Education Agency, which helped develop this plan, for these districts was Regional Education Districts, or REDs. This name was dropped for obvious reasons.

7. The massive revision of the education code passed in the 1995 session was a direct result of Ratliff taking the entire thousand-page code with him home every night and making notes while paging through it on his laptop computer (Walt 1995).

8. This was the same electorate that overwhelmingly sent Republican Kay Bailey Hutchison to the U.S. Senate to replace Lloyd Bentsen.

9. When Clements was discovered to have made untrue statements about his involvement in a football scandal at Southern Methodist University, his response reportedly was "I didn't have my hand on the Bible at the time."

10. One legislator told a joke that reflects the underlying legislative attitude toward the federal courts: "Question: What is the difference between a federal judge and God? Answer: God doesn't think he's a federal judge."

11. Phillips had been appointed a year earlier by Governor Clements to replace Chief Justice John Hill Jr., but was forced to immediately run for reelection in 1988.

Chapter 4

1. In fairness, low assessments were a more significant problem in the poorer districts in eastern Kentucky than in the rest of the state, although no district was completely innocent (Wolfson 1989).

2. This movement gained momentum in 1983 with the publication of the U.S. Department of Education report entitled *A Nation at Risk* (National Commission on Excellence in Education 1983). This report highlighted numerous deficiencies in school systems nationwide in preparing students for their later lives and sparked numerous news articles with such titles as "Why Johnny Can't Read."

3. Except for two bipartisan coalitions, Republicans have never controlled either chamber in the state legislature in the twentieth century, and have only won the governorship under extraordinary circumstances (Garrett 1995a).

4. Combs also had the legal assistance of attorneys Debra Dawahare and Theodore Lavit, both of Wyatt, Tarrant, and Combs.

5. According to one Court source, Stephens decided to write the opinion because of the importance of the case.

6. There were Republican legislators who could fit into each of these three factions as well, although the bulk would be classified in the status quo group.

Chapter 5

1. In fact, I experienced some initial difficulty locating interviewees due to the short wheat harvest season in May.

2. A good source for North Dakota school finance history is provided by a document entitled "Education Finance—Background Memorandum," prepared by the North Dakota Legislative Council staff for the Education Finance Committee every two years.

Chapter 6

1. Texas has two state high courts, one for civil cases and another for criminal appeals.

2. When I say "the legislature," I mean primarily the legislative leadership in both chambers plus influential members of the education committees. Not every lawmaker followed the *Edgewood* proceedings closely. However, according to the evidence from my research, since the Texas legislature remains strongly elite-dominated, the leadership is an acceptable substitute for the body as a whole.

3. Two of Rosenberg's conditions do not apply to this particular issue, "positive incentives are offered to induce compliance" and "court decisions allow for market implementation" (p. 36.)

4. Kentucky governors were constitutionally limited to a single four-year term until after Wilkinson left office, timing which was not coincidental.

5. Some readers might recall House Bill 72, passed in 1984 under the leadership of Texas billionaire H. Ross Perot. One of its most controversial provisions was the so-called no-pass, no-play rule concerning the proper relationship between academics and extracurricular activities, such as high school football.

6. The principle of the separation of powers is explicit in some state constitutions.

7. It is undoubtedly true that racial divisions can slow or stall progress toward equity, as seems to have happened in New Jersey and Alabama, for example. However, as outlined in chapter 3, Texas was able to overcome racial divisions between whites and Hispanics while making reforms. For further discussion of this issue, see Ryan (1999).

Bibliography

Adamany, David. "Legitimacy, Realigning Elections, and the Supreme Court," *Wisconsin Law Review* 790 (Sept.1973).

Alexander, Kern with John Brock, Larry Forgy, James Melton, and Sylvia Watson (members of the Select Committee to Judge Ray Corns, Franklin Circuit Court, Kentucky, September 15, 1988). "Constitutional Intent: 'System,' 'Common,' and 'Efficient' As Terms Of Art (Report by the Select Committee)," reprinted in 18 *Journal of Education Finance* 142 (1989).

Anthony, Gregory P. and G. Alan Hickrod, "Toward a State School Finance Report Card: A Research Note," 18 *Journal of Education Finance* 281 (1993).

Appelbome, Peter. "Revamped Kentucky Schools Are A Study In Pros and Cons." *New York Times* 4/1/96:1.

Aronow, Geoffrey F. "The Special Master in School Desegregation Cases: The Evolution of Roles in the Reformation of Public Institutions through Litigation," 7 *Hastings Const. L.Q.* 739 (1980).

Associated Press. "School Reforms Satisfy Group That Sued," *Louisville Courier-Journal* 4/9/90:2B.

————. "Legislators Grapple with School Finance," *Dickinson Press* 2/10/93 (1993a).

————. "Some Pressure Off Legislature," *Jamestown Sun* 2/27/93 (1993b).

————. "School Lawsuit Showdown Nears," *Bismarck Tribune* 8/8/93:2C (1993c).

————. "Demos Back Bill Raising Education Funds," *Bismarck Tribune* 10/7/94:6A (1994a).

————. "Schafer Outlines Legislative Goals," *Bismarck Tribune* 11/3/94:2C (1994b).

————. "State Supreme Court Upholds Transitional Funding Formula For Wealthy Schools," Associated Press State and Local Wire 7/23/99.

Augenblick, John. "The Role of State Legislatures in School Finance Reform: Looking Backward and Looking Ahead" in Marilyn J. Gittell (ed.),

Strategies for School Equity: Creating Productive Schools in a Just Society. New Haven, CT: Yale University Press, 1998.

Austin American-Statesman (staff and wire). "Judge to Districts: Take Fight to Capitol," 3/14/95:B3.

Banks, Jonathan. "State Constitutional Analyses of Public School Finance Cases: Myth or Methodology?" 45 *Vand.L.R.* 129 (1991.)

Barone, Michael and Grant Ujifusa. *The Almanac of American Politics*. Washington, D.C.: Barone and Co., 1992.

Becker, Theodore L. and Malcolm M. Feeley, eds. *The Impact of Supreme Court Decisions*. 2nd ed. New York: Oxford University Press, 1973.

Benson, Charles S. "Definitions of Equity . . . in Texas, New Jersey, and Kentucky," 28 *Harv. J.on Leg.* 401 (1991.)

Berger, Peter L. and Thomas Luckman. *The Social Construction of Reality*. New York: Anchor, 1966.

Berger, Raoul. *Government by Judiciary*. Cambridge, MA: Harvard University Press, 1977.

Bismarck Tribune. Editorial. "Sanstead Plan Too Rich for North Dakota's Blood," *Bismarck Tribune* 3/19/93:4A (1993a).

———. Editorial. "Getting Right to the Point," *Bismarck Tribune* 8/16/93: 4A (1993b).

———. Editorial. "Without More Money, School Reform Is Dead," *Bismarck Tribune* 9/30/94:4A.

Bleiberg, Larry. "Ruling May Bring Pressure to Merge the Independents," *Louisville Courier-Journal* 6/9/89:1A.

Bodie, Rick. "Kentucky Schools a Model for States," *Orlando Sentinel* 1/17/94:A5.

Bohte, John, Roy B. Flemming, and B. Dan Wood, "The Supreme Court, The Media, and Legal Change: A Reassessment of Rosenberg's *Hollow Hope*." Paper presented at the Annual Meeting of the American Political Science Association, Chicago, 1995.

Borges, Walter. "Justice Hightower Changes Horses; Democrat, GOP Trio Form Solid Bloc, Study Finds," *Texas Lawyer* 12/16/91:1.

Borges, Walter, and Robert Elder, Jr. "High Court Majority Goes up for Grabs," *Texas Lawyer* 1/11/88:1.

Bork, Robert H. *The Tempting of America*. New York: Simon and Schuster, 1990.

Brennan, William J. "For 'Loose' Construction." Address to the Text and Teaching Symposium, Georgetown University, October 12, 1985, Washington, D.C. Reprinted in Peter Woll, *American Government: Readings and Cases*. 11th ed. New York: HarperCollins, 1993.

———. "State Constitutions and Individual Rights," 90 *Harvard Law Review* 489 (1977).

Brooks, A. Phillips. "Attorney Urging an End to School Finance Lawsuit," *Austin-American Statesman* 6/5/99:B3.

Brown, George. "Binding Advisory Opinions: A Federal Courts Perspective on the State School Finance Decisions," 35 *B.C. L.R.* 543 (1994.)

Bundt, Julie. "Equity and Comparative State Responses to Education Finance Reform." Paper presented at the 1995 Annual Meeting of the American Political Science Association, Chicago.

Cambron-McCabe, Nelda and Allan Odden, eds. *The Changing Politics of School Financing*. Cambridge: Ballinger, 1982.

Camp, William and David Thompson. "School Finance Litigation: Legal Issues and Politics of Reform," 14 *J. of Ed. Fin.* 221 (1988).

Carr, Melissa C. and Susan H. Fuhrman. "The Politics of School Finance in the 1990s" in National Research Council, *Equity and Adequacy in Education Finance: Issues and Perspectives*. Helen F. Ladd, Rosemary Chalk, and Janet S. Hansen, eds. Washington, D.C.: National Academy Press, 1999.

Casper, Jonathan. "The Supreme Court and National Policy-Making," 70 *American Political Science Review* 50 (1976).

Champagne, Anthony. "Judicial Reform in Texas," 72 *Judicature* 146 (1988).

Chayes, Abram. "The Role of the Judge in Public Law Litigation," 89 *Harvard L.R.* 1281 (1976).

Clausing, Jeri. "Texas House Debates $450 Million Equalization Plan," UPI 4/9/90 (1990a).

———. "Conference Committee Agrees to Compromise $555 Million Education Bill," UPI 4/22/90 (1990b).

———. "Kilgarlin Appointed Master in School Case," UPI 5/9/90 (1990c).

———. "House Passes Budget Cutting Bill; Gears Up For Tax Fight," UPI 5/10/90 (1990d).

———. "House Falls Short of Override, Ends Special Session," UPI 5/29/90 (1990e).

———. "Clements Agrees to Tax Hike to Fund Schools, Human Services," UPI 6/1/90 (1990f).

Cole, Janell. "Vogel Running for High Court," *Bismarck Tribune* 4/13/96:1A.

Coleman, James S. Foreword to Coons, Clune, and Sugarman, *Private Wealth and Public Education*. Cambridge, Mass.: Belknap, 1970. p.vii.

Combs, Bert. "Creative Constitutional Law: The Kentucky School Reform Law," 28 *Harvard Journal on Legislation* 367 (1991).

Commercial Appeal (Memphis, TN). Editorial. "Teacher Pay: It's not Best Measure of School Aid Fairness," 6/18/98.

Commonwealth of Kentucky, Franklin Circuit Court, Civil Action No. 85-CI-1759, Brief for Defendants.

Condon, Patrick. "Decision Ends 16-Year Battle," *The Forum* (Fargo) 5/21/96:1A.

Coons, John, William Clune, and Stephen Sugarman. *Private Wealth and Public Education*. Cambridge, Mass.: Belknap, 1970, p.vii.

Council of State Governments. *The Book of the States 1994–1995*. Chicago: Council of State Governments and American Legislators, 1995.

Corcoran, Thomas and Nathan Scovronick. "More Than Equal: New Jersey's Quality Education Act" in Marilyn J. Gittell (ed.), *Strategies* for *School Equity: Creating Productive Schools in a Just Society.* New Haven, CT: Yale University Press, 1998.

Cortez, Albert. "Power and Perseverance: Organizing for Change in Texas" in Marilyn J. Gittell (ed.), *Strategies for School Equity: Creating Productive Schools in a Just Society.* New Haven, CT: Yale University Press, 1998.

Craddick, Tom. "Sky Isn't Falling, So Reject School Amendment," *Houston Chronicle* 2/23/93:A17.

Crawford, Ellen. "Sanstead Makes Bid for Fourth Term," *The Forum* (Fargo) 2/20/96:B1.

Cropper, Carol Marie. "Kentucky to Appeal School-Finance Ruling," *Louisville Courier-Journal* 6/3/88:1A (1988a).

———. "Funds. Judge Also Tells 5-Member Committee to Suggest Ways to Eliminate Waste," *Louisville Courier-Journal* 6/8/88:1B (1988b).

———. "Legislators Will Get Early Start on Schools," *Louisville Courier-Journal* 6/15/88:1A (1988c).

———. "Combs Asks Support From Prichard Panel in Light of School Suit," *Louisville Courier-Journal* 7/18/88:1B (1988d).

———. "Judge Orders State to Find More Money for Schools," *Louisville Courier-Journal* 10/15/88:1A (1988c).

Cross, Al. "Deals, Ideals Help Reforms Gain Passage," *Louisville Courier-Journal* 3/22/90:1A (1990a).

———. "Session's Legacy Will Be a Stronger Legislature," *Louisville Courier-Journal* 4/15/90:1D (1990b).

———. "Conference Features Kentuckians, School Reform," *Louisville Courier-Journal* 7/25/90:1B (1990c).

———. "School-Reform Law Draws Attention at Conference," *Louisville Courier-Journal* 8/6/90:1B (1990d).

———. "Ads Inflate Credit Due Wilkinson for Reforms," *Louisville Courier-Journal* 2/5/91:1A (1991a).

———. "The Wilkinson Years; Amid Tumult, Controversy, and Ill Will, Real Progress," *Louisville Courier-Journal* 12/8/91:1D (1991b).

———. "Bruce Regains Chair of Banking, Insurance," *Louisville Courier-Journal* 2/4/96:2B.

Cross, Al, and Tom Loftus. *Louisville Courier-Journal* 3/11/90:1A.

Cuellar, Henry. "Considerations in Drafting a Constitutional School Finance Plan: A Legislator's Perspective," 19 *Thurgood Marshall Law Review* 83 (1993).

Dahl, Robert A. *Who Governs?* New Haven: Yale University Press, 1961.

———. "Decision Making in a Democracy: The Supreme Court as a National Policy Maker," 6 *Journal of Public Law* 279 (1957).

Dallas Morning News. "Q and A on Senate School Finance Plan," *Dallas Morning News* 5/14/93:24A (1993a).

———. "School Finance: Senate Plan is Acceptable Short-Term Measure," *Dallas Morning News* 5/14/93:28A (1993b).

————. "Parker Considering Retiring from Senate," *Dallas Morning News* 7/30/93:34A (1993c).

————. Editorial. "School Finance: Texas Supreme Court Shirked its Duties," *Dallas Morning News* 2/1/95:14A.

Darling, Martha. "Necessary but Not Sufficient: Moving from School Finance Reform to Education Reform in Washington State" in Marilyn J. Gittell (ed.), *Strategies for School Equity: Creating Productive Schools in a Just Society*. New Haven, CT: Yale University Press, 1998.

Davis, Alice. "Education Reform: Are Kentucky's Schools Getting Better?" *Cincinnati Enquirer* 6/4/95: Editorial D01.

Dayton, John. "The Judicial-Political Dialogue: A Comment on Jaffe and Kersche's 'Guaranteeing a State Right to a Quality Education.'" 22 *J. of Law and Educ.* 323 (1993).

Dickinson Press. 2/10/93.

Dinan, John. "Can State Courts Produce Social Reform? School Finance Equalization in Kentucky, Texas and New Jersey," 24 *Southeastern Political Review* 432 (1996).

DiStaso, John. "Senate, House Leaders Work On *Claremont*," *The Union-Leader* (Manchester, NH) 7/20/99: C3.

Dittrick, Paula. "Clements: School Funding Is Biggest Issue Facing Texans," UPI 4/18/88.

Diver, Colin. "The Judge as Political Powerbroker: Superintending Structural Change in Public Institutions," 65 *Virginia L.R.* 43 (1979).

Dolbeare, Kenneth and Phillip Hammond. *The School Prayer Decisions: From Court Policy to Local Practice*. Chicago: University of Chicago Press, 1971.

Donahue, Terry. "Conference Committee Passes Bill," UPI 3/21/91.

Donatelle, Kristine. "Brainstorms, Partisan Sniping Engross Politicians," *Bismarck Tribune* 3/20/94:1D.

Dove, Ronald. "Acorns in a Mountain Pool: The Role of Litigation, Law, and Lawyers in Kentucky Education Reform," 17 *J. of Ed. Fin.* 83 (1991).

Dubose, Louis. "Interview with Ernestine Glossbrenner." *Texas Observer* 1/15/93:5.

Elazar, Daniel. *American Federalism: A View from the States*. Thomas Crowell: New York, 1972.

Ellers, Fran. "Two Judicial Races not Expected to Cause Major Shift on State Supreme Court," *Louisville Courier-Journal* 11/2/90:4B (1990a).

————. "Election '90 Wrapup; GOP Gains In Legislature Attributed To Fund Raising," *Louisville Courier-Journal* 11/8/90:1B (1990b).

Elliott, Janet. "At the Capitol, Court Wore a Dunce's Cap: Hamstrung by *Edgewood* Backlash," *Texas Lawyer* 6/7/93:1.

Elmore, Richard F. and Milbrey Wallin McLaughlin. *Reform and Retrenchment: The Politics of California School Finance Reform*. Cambridge: Ballinger, 1982.

Enrich, Peter. "Leaving Equality Behind: New Directions in School Finance Reform," 48 *Vand. L.Rev.* 101 (1995).

Evans, William N., Sheila E. Murray, and Robert M. Schwab. "The Impact of Court-Mandated School Finance Reform" in National Research Council, *Equity and Adequacy in Education Finance: Issues and Perspectives.* Helen F. Ladd, Rosemary Chalk, and Janet S. Hansen, eds. Washington, D.C.: National Academy Press, 1999.

————. "Schoolhouses, Courthouses, and Statehouses after *Serrano*," 16 *Journal of Policy Analysis and Management* 1: 10-31 (1997).

Executive Editor, "The Kentucky Case Introduction," 15 *Journal of Education Finance* 134 (1989).

Fair, Daryl R. "Prison Reform by the Courts." pp.149-159 in *Governing Through Courts.* Eds. Richard A.L. Gambitta, Marilyn L. May, and James C. Foster. Beverly Hills: Sage, 1981.

Feeley, Malcolm M. "Hollow Hopes, Flypapers, and Metaphors," 17 *Law and Social Inquiry* 745 (1992).

Feeley, Malcolm M. and Edward Rubin. *Judicial Policymaking and the Modern State.* New York: Cambridge, 1998.

Fiss, Owen M. "The Supreme Court, 1978 Term- Foreword: The Forms of Justice," 93 *Harvard L.R.* 1 (1979).

Forgy, Larry. "A School-Reform Dissent," *Louisville Courier-Journal* 4/19/90: 7A (Forum).

Fuller, Lon L. "The Forms and Limits of Adjudication," 92 *Harvard L.R.* 353 (1978.)

Fuhrman, Susan. "State-Level Politics and School Financing," in Cambron-McCabe and Odden, eds. *The Changing Politics of School Financing.* Cambridge: Ballinger, 1982.

————. "School Finance Reform in the 1980's," *Education Leadership* (Nov. 1980) 122.

————. *State Education Politics: The Case of School Finance Reform.* 1979.

Gale, Diana. "The Politics of School Finance Reform in Washington State, 1975-1979." diss.-U.Wash. AAC 8121196 (1981.)

Garrett, Robert. "Will Kentucky Seize the Moment? Earlier Efforts at Reform Have Come Up Short," *Louisville Courier-Journal* 6/8/89:1A (1989a).

————. "The Once-Lowly Legislature has Arrived," *Louisville Courier-Journal* 6/9/89:1A (1989b).

————. "Patronage, Politics Thwart Attempts to Improve Schools," *Louisville Courier-Journal* 9/3/89:1A (1989c).

————. "The Speaker: Shrewd, Deft, Ambitious," *Louisville Courier-Journal* 11/13/92:1A.

————. "Kentucky May Become True 2-Party State," *Louisville Courier-Journal* 11/9/94:1A.

————. "Happy Days Are Here-But Only for the GOP," *Louisville Courier-Journal* 5/7/95:1D (1995a).

————. "The Race for Governor; Forgy: A Lifetime in Politics," *Louisville Courier-Journal* 10/29/95:1D (1995b).

————. "Democrat Adopted GOP Tactics," *Louisville Courier-Journal* 11/8/95:1A (1995c).

————. "Don't Let Window Slam Shut on Public Schools," *Louisville Courier-Journal* 2/18/96:1D (Forum).

Gernant, Eric. "From *Robinson v. Cahill* to *Abbott v. Burke*: New Jersey Attempts School Finance Reform." diss-Fordham DAI-A 52/07, p. 2408, Jan.1992.

Gilmour, Deneen. "School Equity Effort Rejected," *Bismarck Tribune* 4/1/93: 1B (1993a).

————. "House Passes School Equity," *Bismarck Tribune* 4/9/93:1B (1993b).

————. "It's Over! Session Ends," *Bismarck Tribune* 4/25/93 (1993c).

————. "Senate Republicans Reward Freshmen," *Bismarck Tribune* 12/9/94: 6C.

Gittell, Marilyn J. (ed.). *Strategies for School Equity: Creating Productive Schools in a Just Society*. New Haven, CT: Yale University Press, 1998.

Glick, Henry R. *Supreme Courts in State Politics*. New York: Basic Books, 1971.

Goertz, Margaret E. "Steady Work: The Courts and School Finance Reform in New Jersey" in Marilyn J. Gittell(ed.), *Strategies for School Equity: Creating Productive Schools in a Just Society*. New Haven, CT: Yale University Press, 1998.

Goertz, M. E. and Janet Hannigan. "Delivering a 'Thorough and Efficient' Education in New Jersey: The Impact of an Expanded Arena of Policy Making," 4 *J.of Ed.Fin.* 46 (1978).

Goetz, Stephen and David Debertin. "Rural Areas and Educational Reform in Kentucky: An Early Assessment of Revenue Equalization," 18 *Journal of Education Finance* 163 (1992).

Greenhouse, Linda. "Justices Limit Brady Gun Law as Intrusion on States' Rights," *New York Times* 6/28/97:A1.

Grossman, Joel B. "Beyond the Willowbrook Wars: The Courts and Institutional Reform Cases," *American Bar Foundation Research Journal* 249 (1987).

Grubb, W. Norton. "The First Round of Legislative Reforms in the Post-*Serrano* World", *Law and Contemporary Problems* 38 (1974).

Hamilton, Alexander and James Madison and John Jay. *The Federalist Papers*. New York: Mentor, 1961.

Hanushek, Eric. "The Impact of Differential Expenditures on School Performance," 18 *Educational Researcher* 45 (1989).

————. "When School Finance 'Reform' May Not Be Good Policy," 28 *Harvard Journal on Legislation* 423 (1991).

Harp, Lonnie. "The Plot Thickens," *Education Week* 5/18/94 13:34:20.

————. "Texas Senate Backs Massive Rewrite of School Laws," *Education Week* 4/5/95: 14:28:19.

————. "Landmark Education Ruling Turns 10," *Louisville Courier-Journal* 6/9/99:1B.

Harrison, Russell S. and G. Alan Tarr. "School Finance and Inequality in New Jersey." Paper delivered at the 1995 Annual Meeting of the American Political Science Association, Chicago.

Heise, Michael. "The Effect of Constitutional Litigation on Education Finance: More Preliminary Analyses and Modeling," 21 *J. of Ed. Fin.* 195 (1995).

Hershkoff, Helen. "School Finance Reform and the Alabama Experience" in Marilyn J. Gittell (ed.), *Strategies for School Equity: Creating Productive Schools in a Just Society*. New Haven, CT: Yale University Press, 1998.

Hickrod, G. Alan et al. "The Effect of Constitutional Litigation on Education Finance: A Preliminary Analysis," 18 *J. of Ed. Fin.* 180 (1992).

Hobby, William and Billy Walker, "Legislative Reform of the Texas Public School Finance System, 1973-1991," 28 *Harv. J.on Leg.* 379 (1991).

Hobby, William and Mark Yudof, "Texas Got Itself into this School Finance Mess, How's it Going to Get Out?" *Houston Chronicle* 12/15/91: Outlook 5.

Hochschild, Jennifer L. *The New American Dilemma*. New Haven: Yale University Press, 1984.

Holland, Holly. "Kentucky Educational Reforms Show Successes and Pitfalls," *Baltimore Sun* 1/8/95: Tabloid 8.

Horowitz, Donald. *The Courts and Social Policy*. Washington, D.C.: Brookings, 1977.

House Appropriations Committee (North Dakota Legislature). Education and Environment Subcommittee. Minutes of hearing on Senate Bill 2519, 3/28/95.

Houston Chronicle. Editorial. "Catch-22: Resolve School Financing Via the Constitution," *Houston Chronicle* 1/31/92.

Howington, Patrick. "Schools, The Curriculum has More Holes than a Golf Course," *Louisville Courier-Journal* 11/28/89:1A (1989a).

———. "Governor Has Led Effort," *Louisville Courier-Journal* 12/18/89:1A (1989b).

Howington, Patrick and Judy Bryant. "Election '90; Senior Lawmakers Blame Ouster On Tide of 'Vote Ins Out,'" *Louisville Courier-Journal* 11/7/90:1B.

Howington, Patrick and Michael Jennings. "Tax, School Bill Passes After Emotional Plea," *Louisville Courier-Journal* 3/30/90:1A.

Howington, Patrick, Michael Jennings, and Richard Wilson. "The Kentucky Legislature: House Passes Reform Bill After Heated Debate," *Louisville Courier-Journal* 3/22/90:1A.

Hubsch, A.W. "The Emerging Right to Education Under State Constitutional Law," 65 (4) *Temple Law Review* 1325–1348 (1992).

Jacob, Herbert. "The Elusive Shadow of the Law," 26 *Law and Soc. Rev.* 565 (1992).

Jaffe, Mark and Kenneth Kersche. "Guaranteeing a State Right to Quality Education: The Judicial-Political Dialogue in New Jersey." 20 *J. of Law and Educ.* 271 (1991).

Jamestown Sun. 2/27/93.

Jennings, Michael. "School Panel's First Meeting Yields Little," *Louisville Courier-Journal* 7/13/89:1A (1989a).

———. "Other States and 'Vision' May Help Panel Define Adequacy," *Louisville Courier-Journal* 8/20/89:1A (1989b).

———. "Curriculum Panel Wants the Lead in School Reform," *Louisville Courier-Journal* 8/22/89:1A (1989c).

———. "Group Says Schools Need a 'Court of Appeals'," *Louisville Courier-Journal* 9/24/89:1B (1989d).

———. "Legislators Say They Can't Change Course on School Reform," *Louisville Courier-Journal* 12/11/89:1B (1989e).

———. "Sight of Its Goals; Difficulties, Risks Separate Vision from Reality," *Louisville Courier-Journal* 1/29/90:1A (1990a).

———. "Critics Chisel at Education Plan as Reform Shifts into High Gear," *Louisville Courier-Journal* 2/22/90:1B (1990b).

———. *Louisville Courier-Journal* 4/12/90:1A (1990c).

———. "School Reform Left Lawmakers Bloody but Victorious," *Louisville Courier-Journal* 4/15/90:1A (1990d).

———. "Reform Plan Seen as National Model, Gets Wide Support," *Louisville Courier-Journal* 5/6/90:1A (1990e).

———. "Law Shuffles Districts' Revenue, Figures Show," *Louisville Courier-Journal* 9/13/90:1A (1990f).

———. "Wealthier Districts Quietly Press State for More Money," *Louisville Courier-Journal* 4/30/92:1A (1992a).

———. "Democratic Foes Turn School Reform, Incumbency Against Noe in Primary," *Louisville Courier-Journal* 5/17/92:1B (1992b).

Jennings, Michael and Patrick Howington. "School-Reform Bill Gets Senate Approval," *Louisville Courier-Journal* 3/29/90:1A.

Jennings, Michael and Andrew Wolfson. "Election '92; Kentucky Senate; Incumbent Legislators Make It a Clean Sweep," *Louisville Courier-Journal* 11/4/92:1B.

Johnson, Bob. *Louisville Courier-Journal* 3/5/89:1A.

Johnson, Charles A. and Bradley C. Canon. *Judicial Policies: Implementation and Impact.* Washington, D.C.: Congressional Quarterly Press, 1985.

Johnson, Frank M. "The Constitution and the Federal District Judge," 54 *Tex. L.R.* 903 (1976).

Johnston, Jocelyn M. "Changing State-Local Fiscal Relations, School Finance, and Kansas: The Price of Equity," Paper presented at the 1995 Annual Meeting of the American Political Science Association, Chicago.

Kaukas, Dick. "Bluegrass State Poll: Education Outranks Jobs as State's Main Problem," *Louisville Courier-Journal* 12/2/90:1B.

Keesler, William. "Contrasting Views, Personalities Mark Supreme Court Race," *Louisville Courier-Journal* 10/31/88:1A.

Keeton, Laura and Cindy Rugeley. "Schools' Funding Fray Heats up; Both Sides Use Fear as a Weapon," *Houston Chronicle* 4/15/93:A17.

Kingdon, John W. *Agendas, Alternatives, and Public Policies*. Boston: Little, Brown, 1984.

Kraemer, Richard H. and Charldean Newell. *Texas Politics*. St. Paul: West Publishing Co., 2nd ed. 1984: 199.

Lane, Christopher. "Measuring the Equity of Education Funding in New Jersey Under the Quality Education Act." diss.-Columbia University Teachers College, DAI-A 54/12 p. 4357 (1994.)

Langford, Mark. "Mattox, Richards Offer Education Funding Plans," UPI 1/11/90 (1990a).

———. "Legislative Leaders Question Viability of Governor's Education Plan," UPI 5/3/90 (1990b).

———. "Statewide Property Tax Seen as Best Solution to School Funding Crisis," UPI 1/24/91 (1991a).

———. "Trial Begins in Wealthy Districts' Challenge of School Finance Law," UPI 6/17/91 (1991b).

———. "'Taxed-Off' Texans Toss Tea Bags in Revolt Against New Taxes," UPI 7/22/91 (1991c).

———. "Judge Upholds 'Robin Hood' Plan for County Tax Districts for Schools," UPI 8/7/91 (1991d).

———. "Senate Overwhelmingly Adopts Ratliff School Finance Bill," UPI 5/12/93 (1993a).

———. "Conference Committee Approves School Finance Bill," UPI 5/25/93 (1993b).

Lawson, Gil. "Combs Ousts Stephenson from State's High Court," *Louisville Courier-Journal* 11/9/88:1B.

Leahy, James E. "The Constitution is What the Judges Say It Is," 65 *North Dakota Law Review* 491 (1990).

Lehne, Richard. *The Quest for Justice*. New York: Longman, Inc. 1978.

Lewis, Anthony. "Justices on a Mission," *New York Times* 6/30/97:A11, 1997.

Lexington Herald-Leader. "Cheating Our Children," special series originally running from November 12 to December 15, 1988, and reprinted in January of 1990.

Loftus, Tom. "Wallace Wilkinson; Shifting Gears on Taxes Raises Some Questions," Louisville Courier-Journal 12/6/89:1A.

———. "Wilkinson's in Love, But the Question Is, 'With Whom?'" Louisville Courier-Journal 2/4/90:1D (1990a).

———. "Wilkinson's Tax Plan—In Praise of All of It," *Louisville Courier-Journal* 2/18/90:1D (Forum) (1990b).

———. "Education, Taxes Dominated, Stranding Some Other Issues," *Louisville Courier-Journal* 4/15/90:1A (1990c).

———. "State Orders Counties to Raise Tax Assessments," *Louisville Courier-Journal* 9/23/94:3B.

———. "John 'Eck' Rose: He Gained Unrivaled Power as Legislature Asserted Itself" *Louisville Courier-Journal* 4/23/95:1D.

———. "Forgy Denies Charge by Patton that He Wants KERA Ended," *Louisville Courier-Journal* 10/31/95:3B.

———. "Courts Won't Like Raises For All Teachers, Rose Warns," *Louisville Courier-Journal* 2/3/96:8A (1996a).

———. "Legislative Pay Raised; Panel Drops Raises For Teachers But Adds Funds For Schools," *Louisville Courier-Journal* 3/21/96:1A (1996b).

———. "GOP To Gain State Senate Majority," *Louisville Courier-Journal* 8/23/99:1A.

——— and Michael Jennings. "Panel Passes Tax Bill But Alters It, Breaking Leaders' Pact With Governor," *Louisville Courier-Journal* 3/20/90:1A.

——— and Richard Wilson. "Tax Increase Only Shows Scattered Impact," *Lousiville Courier-Journal* 11/7/90:1B.

Louisville Courier-Journal. Editorial. "For The History Books," *Louisville Courier-Journal* 4/1/90:2D (Forum).

———. Editorial. "Defending KERA," *Louisville Courier-Journal* 10/31/95:8A.

———. "Sliding Backward," *Louisville Courier-Journal* 1/28/96:2D (Forum).

MacDonald, John. "Rural N.D. Schools Dropping in Population Fast," *Bismarck Tribune* 2/13/94:2D.

Malone, James. "McCracken Parents' Boycott Made Point—But at What Price?" *Louisville Courier-Journal* 9/30/94:7A.

Marshall, Thomas. *Public Opinion and the Supreme Court.* Boston: Unwin Hyman, 1989.

Mattern, Hal. "Attorney Vows Suit Over Funds to Schools," *Arizona Republic* 6/23/99:B1.

McCann, Michael W. "Reform Litigation on Trial," 17 *Law and Social Inquiry* 715 (1992).

———. *Rights at Work: Pay Equity Reform and the Politics of Legal Mobilization.* Chicago: University of Chicago Press, 1994.

———. "Causal versus Constitutive Explanations (or, On the Difficulty of Being so Positive)," 21 *Law and Social Inquiry* 457 (1996).

McKenzie, William. "Bob Bullock: The New LBJ," *Dallas Morning News* 6/15/93:15A.

McMillan, Kevin Randall. "The Turning Tide: The Fourth Wave of School Finance Reform Litigation and the Courts' Lingering Institutional Concerns," 58 *Ohio St. L.J.* 1867 (1998).

McUsic, Molly. "The Use of Education Clauses in School Finance Reform," 28 *Harv. J.on Leg.* 307 (1991).

Mensing, Phyllis. "School Row a Long Way from Over," *Bismarck Tribune* 2/5/93:3B.

Miller, Calvin. "Panel Ponders Local Impact of Court Ruling on Schools," *Louisville Courier-Journal* 7/11/89:1B.

Miller, Penny. *Kentucky Politics and Government: Do We Stand United?* Lincoln, NE: University of Nebraska Press, 1994.

Minorini, Paul A. and Stephen D. Sugarman. "School Finance Litigation in the Name of Educational Equity: Its Evolution, Impact, and Future" (1999a) in National Research Council, *Equity and Adequacy in Education Finance: Issues and Perspectives*, Helen F. Ladd, Rosemary

Chalk, and Janet S. Hansen, eds. Washington, D.C.: National Academy Press, 1999.

———. "Educational Adequacy and the Courts: The Promise and Problems of Moving to a New Paradigm" (1999b) in National Research Council, *Equity and Adequacy in Education Finance: Issues and Perspectives*, Helen F. Ladd, Rosemary Chalk, and Janet S. Hansen, eds. Washington, D.C.: National Academy Press, 1999.

Mintrom, Michael. "Why Efforts to Equalize School Funding Have Failed: Towards a Positive Theory," 46 *Political Research Quarterly* 847 (1993).

Muir, William K. *Prayer in the Public Schools: Law and Attitude Change*. Chicago: University of Chicago Press, 1967.

Murchison, William. "Court Should Get Out of Public Policy," *Texas Lawyer* 3/21/94:24.

National Commission on Excellence in Education. *A Nation at Risk: The Imperative for Educational Reform: A Report to the Nation and the Secretary of Education, U.S. Department of Education*. Washington, D.C.: The Commission [Supt. of Docs., U.S. G.P.O. distributor], 1983.

National Research Council. *Equity and Adequacy in Education Finance: Issues and Perspectives*. Helen F. Ladd, Rosemary Chalk, and Janet S. Hansen, eds. Washington, D.C.: National Academy Press, 1999.

Neuborne, Burt. "The Myth of Parity," 90 *Harvard Law Review* 1105 (1977).

Neustadt, Richard. *Presidential Power and the Modern Presidents*. New York: Free Press, 1990.

Nichols, Bruce. "Gonzalez Tops Haas in Runoff for High Court: Battle Called Costly, Bitter," *Dallas Morning News* 4/13/94:21A.

New York Times. "Court Overturns Texas School Tax: But Justices Give Lawmakers to June 1993 to Replace 'Robin Hood' System." *New York Times* 2/2/92:A14.

North Dakota Legislative Council. "Education Finance—Background Memorandum." Prepared every two years for the Education Finance Committee.

North Dakota State Census Data Center. *Population Bulletin*. Monthly periodical published by the NDSCDC, North Dakota State University, Fargo, North Dakota 58105.

North Dakota State Legislature. Education Equity Review Committee. 1993 House Standing Committee Minutes, 3/8/93:3 (1993a).

North Dakota State Legislature. Education Equity Review Committee, 1993 House Standing Committee Minutes, 3/19/93:4 (1993b).

North Dakota State Legislature. Education Equity Review Committee, 1993 House Standing Committee Minutes, 3/22/93:3 (1993c).

North Dakota Senate Education Committee. 1993 Senate Standing Committee Minutes, Hearings on House Bill 1512, 4/12/93:1 (1993d).

North Dakota State Legislature. 1993 House Appropriations Committee. Education and Environment Subcommittee. Hearings on Senate Bill 2519, 3/28/95.

Note, "A Statistical Analysis of the School Finance Decisions: On Winning Battles and Losing Wars", 81 *Yale L.J.* 1303 (1972).

Note, "Unfulfilled Promises: School Finance Remedies and State Courts," 104 *Harv. L.R.* 1072 (1991.)

O'Connor, Anne. "Minneapolis NAACP Members OK Lawsuit Settlement," *Star Tribune* (Minneapolis) 4/25/2000:2B

Odden, Allan R. and William H. Clune. "School Finance Systems: Aging Structures in Need of Renovation," 20 *Educational Evaluation and Policy Analysis* no.3 (fall 1998): 157.

Office of Education Accountability. Capitol Plaza, Frankfort, KY 40601; phone (502) 564-4394; 1995 report on the impact of KERA at 263.

Omdahl, Lloyd. "You Can Come Out, The Lawmakers Have Left," *Bismarck Tribune* 4/9/95:3C.

Parrish, Thomas. "The Prichard Committee for Academic Excellence: The First Decade 1980–1990," a publication of the Prichard Committee, P.O. Box 1658, Lexington, KY 40592-1658.

Peltason, Jack W. *Fifty-Eight Lonely Men: Southern Federal Judges and School Desegregation*. New York: Harcourt, Brace, 1961.

Perry, Michael J. *The Constitution, The Courts, and Human Rights*. New Haven: Yale University Press, 1982.

Peterson, Mark A. *Legislating Together: The White House and Capitol Hill from Eisenhower to Reagan*. Cambridge, MA: Harvard University Press, 1990.

Picus, Lawrence. "Texas School Finance Equity After *Edgewood*," Center for Research in Education Finance, School of Education, EDPA WPH 901A, University of Southern California, Los Angeles, CA 90089-0031 (August 1995.)

———— and Linda Hertert. "Three Strikes and You're Out: Texas School Finance After *Edgewood III*," 18 *Journal of Education Finance* 366 (1993).

Prichard Committee for Academic Excellence. *The Path to a Larger Life*. P.O. Box 1658, Lexington, KY 40592-1658: Prichard Committee, 1985.

Ragin, Charles. *The Comparative Method*. Berkeley: University of California Press, 1987.

Ramsey, Ross and Cindy Rugeley, "Leaders of the Pack; Bullock, Laney Carry a Big Stick in Legislature," *Houston Chronicle* 6/6/93: State 1.

Rebell, Michael and Arthur R. Block. *Educational Policy Making and the Courts: An Empirical Study of Judicial Activism*. Chicago: University of Chicago Press, 1982.

Reed, Douglas S. "Democracy Versus Equality: Legal and Political Struggles Over School Finance Equalization" -diss. Yale (1995) AAC 9540607.

————. "Twenty-Five Years after *Rodriguez*: School Finance Litigation and the Impact of the New Judicial Federalism," *Law and Society Review*, v.32:1, 175-200 (1997).

Reedy, Cheryl D. "The Supreme Court and Congress on Abortion: An Analysis of Contemporary Institutional Capacity." Paper presented at the

Annual Meeting of the American Political Science Association, Denver, Sept. 2–5, 1982.

Roberts, Suzanne. "Texas House Passes School Finance Bill," UPI 5/28/93.

Robison, Clay. "Court Should Point Way to School Taxes," *Houston Chronicle* 2/2/92: Outlook 2 (1992a).

———. "Legislative Bipartisanship Endangered," *Houston Chronicle* 11/29/92: Outlook 2 (1992b).

———. "Next School-Finance Hurdle High, Too," *Houston Chronicle* 2/14/93: Outlook 2 (1993a).

———. "School Finance Amendment No Sure Bet," *Houston Chronicle* 3/14/93: Outlook 2 (1993b).

———. "State Supreme Court," *Houston Chronicle* 2/27/94: Voter Guide 10.

Rocha, Gregory G. and Robert H. Webking. *Politics and Public Education: Edgewood v. Kirby and the Reform of Public School Financing in Texas*. Los Angeles: West Publishing Company, 1993.

Rosenberg, Gerald N. *The Hollow Hope: Can Courts Bring About Social Change?* Chicago: University of Chicago Press, 1991.

———. "Positivism, Interpretivism, and the Study of Law," 21 *Law and Social Inquiry* 435 (1996).

Rugeley, Cindy. "The Man Who Took the State of Texas to School," *Houston Chronicle* 9/29/91: Texas Magazine 10 (1991a).

———. "School Plan Puts Officials at End of Rope," *Houston Chronicle* 12/6/91:A1 (1991b).

———. "Governor Spells out School Plan; But Tax Proposal Faces Major Court Test Today," *Houston Chronicle* 4/10/92:A33 (1992a).

———. "'Robin Hood' School Financing Plan Finds Support, Poll Shows," *Houston Chronicle* 4/25/92:A26 (1992b).

———. "State's Top Three Leaders Unveil School Finance Plan," *Houston Chronicle* 11/5/92:A1 (1992c).

———. "Senate Passes School Finance Plan to House," *Houston Chronicle* 1/29/93:A21 (1993a).

———. "School-Funds Proposal Has Familiar Look," *Houston Chronicle* 2/3/93:A1 (1993b).

———. "Richards Selling School Finance Plan, Self," *Houston Chronicle* 4/18/93:A1 (1993c).

———. "Back to Chalkboard for School Funding Plan," *Houston Chronicle* 5/15/93:A1 (1993d).

——— and Melanie Markley. "Financing Plan Threat to Schools: Less State Cash to Urban Districts," *Houston Chronicle* 1/20/93:A11 (1993a).

——— and Melanie Markley. "School Finance Foes Wage Low-Budget War," *Houston Chronicle* 4/11/93:A1 (1993b).

Ryan, James E. "The Influence of Race in School Finance Reform," 98 *Mich. L. Rev.* 432 (1999).

Sabato, Larry. *Goodbye to Good-Time Charlie: The American Governorship Transformed.* 2nd ed. Washington, D.C.: *Congressional Quarterly Press*, 1983.

Salmon, Richard G. and M. David Alexander. "State Legislative Responses," in Underwood and Verstegen, eds, *The Impacts of Litigation and Legislation on Public School Finance*. New York: Ballinger, 1990.

Sanstead, Dr. Wayne G. "A Plan Providing Educational Equity for North Dakota Students." Handout issued by the North Dakota Department of Public Instruction, 3/15/93.

Sarat, Austin and Ralph Cavanagh. "Thinking about Courts: Traditional Expectations and Contemporary Challenges." Working Paper 1979-5 of the Disputes Processing Research Program, University of Wisconsin-Madison, 1980.

Sax, Joseph L. *Defending the Environment: A Strategy for Citizen Action.* New York: Knopf, 1970.

Schafer, Governor Edward T. "Governor Defends Record," *Bismarck Tribune* 3/5/96:4A (Opinion).

Schaver, Mark. "KERA Funding Up, But Short of Goals," *Louisville Courier-Journal* 1/26/96:6A (1996a).

———. "Budget Violates Spirit of KERA, Authors Say," *Louisville Courier-Journal* 1/30/96:2B (1996b).

———. "Majority Thinks Ungraded Primary Should Be Optional," *Louisville Courier-Journal* 2/16/96:1A (1996c).

Scheingold, Stuart A. *The Politics of Rights: Lawyers, Public Policy, and Political Change.* New Haven: Yale University Press, 1974.

Selby, Gardner. "GOP Taps Pauken for State Chair; Christian Coalition Dominates Caucus," *Houston Post* 6/12/94:A1.

Serrano v. Priest, 487 P.2nd 1241 (Calif.1971), at 1247 fn.14 citing Report of the National Advisory Commission on Civil Disorders (Bantam ed.1968) pp. 434–36.

Sexton, Robert. "Similarities of Reform," *Louisville Courier-Journal* 6/10/93: 11A (Forum).

Shank, Patsy. *"Pauley v. Kelly*: A Research Investigation of the Effects of School Finance Litigation on Statewide Public Policy." diss.- U. Va. (1995) AAC 9531050.

Siegel, Peggy M. "The Politics of School Finance Reform," in Campbell and Mazzoni, eds., *State Policymaking for the Public Schools*. Berkeley: McCutchan, 1976.

Silva, F. and J. Sonstelie. "Did *Serrano* Cause a Decline in School Spending?" 47 *National Tax Journal* 199–216 (1995).

Sites, Jeanette A. and Richard Salmon, "West Virginia's School Finance: A Look at the Past and Present," 17 *J. of Ed. Fin.* 318 (1992.)

Skolnick, Ilene. "A Historical Review of New Jersey School Finance Initiatives Based on Judicial, Legislative, and Constituent Actions and the Personal Perspectives of those Involved with These Initiatives, Feb. 1990-Dec. 1992." diss- Rutgers DAI-A 54/05, p.1672, Nov.1993.

Smith, Charles E. "No Thicket Too Political: A Cross-State Analysis of State Supreme Court Opinions' Influence on Legislative Policy-Making." diss University of Kentucky (1994) AAC 9426184.

Smith, Frederic. "First School Funding Plan Quickly Dumped," *Bismarck Tribune* 2/16/93:1B (1993a).

———. "Senate Drops House Plan for School Finance," *Bismarck Tribune* 4/13/93:1B (1993b).

———. "Small v. Large in School Fight," *Bismarck Tribune* 4/16/93:1B (1993c).

———. "Rural Schools Attack Equity Proposals," *Bismarck Tribune* 3/2/95:1B.

———. "School Funding Hike Effort Dies," *Bismarck Tribune* 3/24/95:1B (1995b).

Songer, Donald. "Integrated Models of State Supreme Court Decision Making." Paper presented at the 1995 Annual Meeting of the American Political Science Association, Chicago.

Sorauf, Frank J. "*Zorach v. Clauson*: The Impact of a Supreme Court Decision," 53 *American Political Science Review* 777 (1959).

Stumbo, Greg. "From Last to First," *Louisville Courier-Journal* 4/1/90:3D (Forum).

Stutz, Terrence. "Texas House Approves School Finance Plan," *Dallas Morning News* 2/12/93:1A (1993a).

———. "School Finance Proposal Crushed," *Dallas Morning News* 5/2/93: 1A (1993b).

———. "Richards Tells Texans to Push Lawmakers on School Finance," *Dallas Morning News* 5/14/93:1A (1993c).

———. "House Panel Warily Views School Plan," *Dallas Morning News* 5/15/93:1A (1993d).

———. "Panel OKs New Bill for Schools," *Dallas Morning News* 5/18/93:1A (1993e).

Tallman, Mark. "The 1992 Kansas School Finance Act: A Political and Legislative History," field report submitted in partial fulfillment of the MPA degree, University of Kansas, November 1993.

Tarr, G. Alan and Mary Cornelia Aldis Porter. *State Supreme Courts in State and Nation*. New Haven, CT: Yale University Press, 1988.

Theobald, Neil D. and Faith Hanna. "Ample Provision For Whom?: The Evolution of State Control over School Finance in Washington," 17 *J. of Ed. Fin.* 7 (1991).

Thompson, Kimberly. "Blandford Attacks Schools' Tax Rates," *Louisville Courier-Journal* 10/19/89:3B.

Thro, William. "To Render Them Safe: The Analysis of State Constitutional Provisions in Public School Finance Reform Litigation," 75 *Va. L.R.* 1639 (1989).

———. "The Third Wave: The Impact of the Montana, Kentucky, and Texas Decisions On the Future of Public School Reform Litigation," 19 *Journal of Law & Education* 219 (1990).

Tushnet, Mark V. *Making Civil Rights Law: Thurgood Marshall and the Supreme Court, 1936-1961*. New York: Oxford University Press, 1994.

Ulmer, Sidney and Bradley Canon. Letter, 70 *American Political Science Review* 1215 (1976).

Underwood, Julie and Sparkman. "School Finance Litigation: A New Wave of Reform," 14 *Harv. J. of L. & Pub. Pol.* 517 (1991.)

Underwood, Julie and Deborah A. Verstegen, eds. *The Impacts of Litigation and Legislation on Public School Finance.* New York: Ballinger, 1990.

United Press International, "Kentucky News Briefs," UPI 5/25/84.

————. "Clements, Hobby, Lewis all Say: Harley Clark Ruling Could Have Big Impact on State Government," UPI 4/29/87.

————. "Clements Appoints Panel to Examine Public School Funding," UPI 1/27/88 (1988a).

————. "Clements Says Constitutional Amendment Would Free Schools from Courts," UPI 4/26/88 (1988b).

————. "Lawmaker Unveils Constitutional Amendment for School Funding," UPI 4/29/88 (1988c).

————. "Clements Says State Court Should Not Dictate School or Tax Policy," UPI 10/21/88 (1988d).

————. "Regional News," UPI 6/8/89.

————. "Court Hearing, Bill Signing for School Finance Set Monday," UPI 4/14/91 (1991a).

————. "Richards Decries Role of Courts in Legislative Process," UPI 12/5/91 (1991b).

van Geel, Tyll. "The Courts and School Finance Reform: An Expected Utility Model," in Cambron-McCabe and Odden, eds., *The Changing Politics of School Financing.* Cambridge: Ballinger, 1982.

Vergari, Sandra. "School Finance Reform in the State of Michigan," 21 *J. of Ed. Fin.* 254 (1995).

Verstegen, Deborah. "Efficiency and Equity in the Provision and Reform of American Schooling," 20 *J. of Ed. Fin.* 107 (1994).

Voskuhl, John. "Wilkinson and Key Legislators Agree That They Face a Giant Task," *Louisville Courier-Journal* 6/8/89:13A.

Walfoot, Nina. "Election '92; Kentucky House," *Louisville Courier-Journal* 11/4/92:1B.

Walt, Kathy. "Campaign '94; On the Issues: Crime, Education in Texas; Specifics Sparse in Governor's Contest," *Houston Chronicle* 10/30/94: A1.

————. "The 74th Legislature: Upending Education; Ratliff Slashes State Control in School Reform Proposal," *Houston Chronicle* 2/19/95: State 1.

Ward, James Gordon. "Implementation and Monitoring of Judicial Mandates: An Interpretive Analysis," in Julie K. Underwood and Deborah A. Verstegen, eds., *The Impacts of Litigation and Legislation on Public School Finance: Adequacy, Equity, and Excellence.* New York: Ballinger, 1990.

Warren, Susan. "School Superintendent Tells Administrators to Improve Image," UPI 5/24/84.

Wetzel, Dale. "No Repair This Session," *Bismarck Tribune* 2/6/93:8A (1993a).

———. "Hit Or Miss? School Finance Bill Strides to the Plate," *Bismarck Tribune* 3/28/93:9A (1993b).

———. "Schafer's School Payment Formula Explained," *Bismarck Tribune* 12/9/94:6C.

Wilkinson, Wallace. *You Can't Do That, Governor!* Lexington: Wallace's Publishing Company, 1995.

Wilson, Richard. "Agreement Struck on Four-Prong Plan to Revamp Financing of State's Schools," *Louisville Courier-Journal* 2/21/90:1B (1990a).

———. "Incumbents Fear Ax From Anti-Tax Backlash," *Louisville Courier-Journal* 5/28/90:1A.

Wirt, Frederick M. *The Politics of Southern Equality: Law and Social Change in a Mississippi County*. Chicago: Aldine, 1970.

Wise, Arthur E. *Rich Schools, Poor Schools: The Promise of Equal Educational Opportunity*. Chicago: University of Chicago Press, 1967.

Wolfson, Andrew. "Assessments Faulty in Many Counties, Audit Says," *Louisville Courier-Journal* 12/1/89:1A.

———. "Book on Kentucky Chief Justice More Fawning Than Fault-Finding," *Louisville Courier-Journal* 9/22/93:1B.

Wood, Carter. "Legislators Worry that Judge Will Take Over Education Funding," *Grand Forks Herald* 2/14/93.

Youngblood, J. Craig and Parker C. Folse III. "Can Courts Govern? An Inquiry into Capacity and Purpose," pp. 23–65 in *Governing through Courts*. Eds. Richard A.L. Gambitta, Marilyn L. May, and James C. Foster. Beverly Hills: Sage, 1981.

Index